Essential keys to a happy, healthy,
according to the timeless wisd

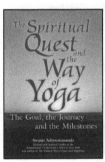

"Vedanta maintains that problems and solution
exist without the other. If nature presents a pro
a solution. In suggesting solutions, Vedanta does not deal with the occult
or the miraculous and does not cater to fads, whims, or pious imaginations.
According to Vedanta, our happiness depends upon peace of mind, peace
of mind on self-control, and self-control on awareness of our true Self."

—from the Introduction

This practical volume examines many of the common barriers to spiritual
fulfillment—such as questions about human suffering, death, doubt of God's
existence, and many others.

Using language that is accessible to people of all faiths and backgrounds, this
book introduces you to the timeless teachings of Vedanta—divinity of the individual soul, unity of all existence, and oneness with the Divine—ancient wisdom
as relevant to human happiness today as it was thousands of years ago.

Also by Swami Adiswarananda

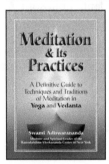

Meditation & Its Practices
*A Definitive Guide to Techniques and Traditions
of Meditation in Yoga and Vedanta*
Drawing on both classic and contemporary sources, this
comprehensive sourcebook outlines the scientific, psychological,
and spiritual elements of Yoga and Vedanta meditation.
6 x 9, 504 pp, Quality PB, 978-1-59473-105-1

The Spiritual Quest and
the Way of Yoga
The Goal, the Journey and the Milestones
Presents a roadmap to self-knowledge, the goal of the spiritual
quest, and shows that reconnecting with the center of your
being, your true Self, is real, tangible, and attainable.
6 x 9, 288 pp, Hardcover, 978-1-59473-113-6

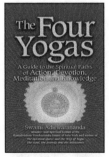

The Four Yogas
*A Guide to the Spiritual Paths of Action,
Devotion, Meditation and Knowledge*
An accessible and comprehensive guide that
introduces the four spiritual paths
of Yoga and what you can expect
as an aspirant on each path.
6 x 9, 320 pp, Quality PB, 978-1-59473-223-2

Vivekananda, World Teacher
His Teachings on the Spiritual Unity of Humankind
Presents a selection of Vivekananda's most inspiring
lectures and an intimate glimpse of his life.
6 x 9, 272 pp, Quality PB Original, 978-1-59473-210-2

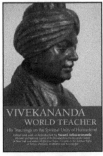

Swami Adiswarananda (1925–2007), former senior monk of the Ramakrishna Order of India, was the Minister and Spiritual Leader of the Ramakrishna-Vivekananda Center of New York, one of several centers of the order in the United States. His works include *Meditation and Its Practices: A Definitive Guide to Techniques and Traditions of Meditation in Yoga and Vedanta* (SkyLight Paths) among many other books.

"Excellent.... Contains usable wisdom and helpful practices from a rich Indian spiritual tradition."
—*Spirituality & Health*

"Reading this book ... gives us a delightful feeling, because he makes the concepts appear so simple and easy to grasp.... Should be read by all aspirants of spirituality who want to understand the correct meaning of ... peace and happiness.... A pleasurable experience."
—*The Vedanta Kesari (The Lion of Vedanta)*

"A most concise and yet comprehensive introduction to Vedanta philosophy for either complete beginners to the subject or those who know something but wish to understand more."
—*Vedanta Magazine*

Also Available

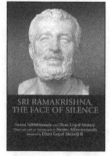

Sri Ramakrishna, the Face of Silence
by Swami Nikhilananda and Dhan Gopal Mukerji
Edited and with an Introduction by Swami Adiswarananda
Foreword by Dhan Gopal Mukerji II
Two classic biographies—published together for the first time—present a portrait of the life of Sri Ramakrishna.
6 x 9, 352 pp, Hardcover, 978-1-59473-115-0

Selections from the Gospel of Sri Ramakrishna
Annotated and Explained
Translated by Swami Nikhilananda
Annotated by Kendra Crossen Burroughs
Foreword by Andrew Harvey
Introduces the fascinating world of the Indian mystic and the universal appeal of his message. Selections from the original text and insightful yet unobtrusive facing-page commentary highlight the most important and inspirational teachings.
5½ x 8½, 240 pp, Quality PB, 978-1-893361-46-1

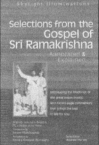

The
Vedanta Way
to Peace
and Happiness

Swami Adiswarananda

Author of *Meditation & Its Practices*
and *The Spiritual Quest & the Way of Yoga*

Walking Together, Finding the Way
SKYLIGHT PATHS® Publishing
Woodstock, Vermont

RAMAKRISHNA-VIVEKANANDA
CENTER OF NEW YORK
"As Many Faiths, So Many Paths"

The Vedanta Way to Peace and Happiness

2016 Quality Paperback Edition, Second Printing

Library of Congress Cataloging-in-Publication Data
Adiswarananda, Swami, 1925–
The Vedanta way to peace and happiness / Swami Adiswarananda.
p. cm.
Includes bibliographical references and index.
ISBN 1-59473-034-2 (hardcover)
1. Spiritual life. 2. Vedanta. I. Title.
BL624.A335 2004
294.5'44 — dc22

004005061

ISBN 978-1-59473-180-8 (quality paperback)
ISBN 978-1-59473-425-0 (eBook)

10   9   8   7   6   5   4   3   2
Manufactured in the United States of America
Cover Design: Sara Dismukes

SkyLight Paths Publishing is creating a place where people of different spiritual traditions come together for challenge and inspiration, a place where we can help each other understand the mystery that lies at the heart of our existence.

SkyLight Paths sees both believers and seekers as a community that increasingly transcends traditional boundaries of religion and denomination—people wanting to learn from each other, *walking together, finding the way.*

SkyLight Paths, "Walking Together, Finding the Way," and colophon are trademarks of LongHill Partners, Inc., registered in the U.S. Patent and Trademark Office.

Walking Together, Finding the Way
Published by SkyLight Paths Publishing
A Division of LongHill Partners, Inc.
Sunset Farm Offices, Route 4, P.O. Box 237
Woodstock, VT 05091
Tel: (802) 457-4000   Fax: (802) 457-4004
www.skylightpaths.com

Contents

Introduction

Vedanta is the wisdom of the Vedic sages. For thousands of years it has inspired people to find solutions to the problems of life and thus reach the highest fulfillment. As a philosophy of living, Vedanta has been tested and verified in the lives of countless seekers, saints, and prophets of India. The Vedanta way is decisive, and its practices are based upon science and reason.

For centuries the Vedanta philosophy was kept carefully guarded by saints and ascetics living in forests and mountains, and never made public. They thought that the teachings would be diluted and misunderstood by the masses, who were prone to believe not in truth but in myths and miracles. In matters of spirituality and religion, truth is often sacrificed to fiction and make-believe. A rational and realistic approach is rare. Religious texts are filled with eulogy, exaggeration, doubtful myths, and loving legends. The average person regards scriptures as infallible, forgetting that the scriptures are in fact remembered words and experiences written down by human beings.

Swami Vivekananda was the first to bring the teachings of Vedanta from the forest to the general public. He thought that because of the developments of science, the time had come to deliver the message of Vedanta to all. According to the swami, the teachings of Vedanta are worth nothing if they are not problem solving. They are useless unless they enrich our lives and lead us to peace and happiness.

Vedanta reminds us that the course of life is mysterious. It is plagued by ceaseless changes and uncertainties. Pain, suffering, illness, old age, and death are harsh realities that cannot be ignored or avoided. Vedanta maintains that problems and solutions go together; one cannot exist without the other. If nature presents a problem, it also points toward a solution. In suggesting solutions, Vedanta does not deal with the occult or the miraculous and does not cater to fads, whims, or pious imaginations. According to Vedanta, our happiness depends upon peace of mind, peace of mind on self-control, and self-control on awareness of our true Self.

This book does not compromise the orthodox views of Vedanta. It deals with such subjects as life and its meaning, mastering the restless mind, the spiritual quest, the practice of meditation, the controversy between faith and reason, and facing the problems of life. Vedanta assures us that we are not living in the final days of our destiny, that every problem has a solution, and that the human soul is not a prisoner of karma or sin. The merciless and inexorable laws of life can be countered and overcome. The book presents both the facts and the fictions of human life and assures us that regardless of background, culture, training, or religious belief, all can follow the Vedanta way to resolve the problems of life and reach the supreme goal.

Competent editors have gone through this book, and I am grateful to them for their valuable contributions. It is my fervent hope that this book will be of help to the readers in their quest for peace, happiness, and spiritual fulfillment.

Swami Adiswarananda
Ramakrishna-Vivekananda Center of New York

1

The Relevance of Vedanta to the World Today

THE CHANGING LANDSCAPE

Science and technology have shaken the very foundation of life's traditional values, beliefs, and thoughts and changed the spiritual landscape of humanity. Economic interest has become the prime concern of life and acquisition of wealth the only measure of success. The sense of duty has been replaced by the rules of doing business. Spiritual values extolled by the prophets have been rejected in favor of material values that are meant to make the world an earthly paradise. Practice of any self-restraint is looked upon as inhibitive and life negating. Holy days have given way to holidays, prayers to psychotherapy, and sacraments to workshops, counseling, and consultations. Contemplation and meditation are practiced not for spiritual enlightenment but for improvement of health, efficiency in action, and management of stress.

The scientific-minded question the infallibility of the scriptures and the belief that creation began at a certain point in time. They find difficulty in accepting anything that cannot be verified by objective evidence. The scientific spirit has led to critical studies of the sacred texts and traditions of different faiths; scholars now point out that many religious beliefs have no sound historical basis.

Frustrated by a sense of crisis, many are seeking solace in new movements, such as fanaticism, atheism, pursuit of art or intellectual reflection, agnosticism, humanism, prophetism, supernaturalism, drug mysticism, occultism, universalism, new-ageism, and nature mysticism.

Fanaticism. Unable to meet the challenges of science, many are taking refuge in fanaticism. They are extremely narrow and dogmatic in their views and intolerant of all honest doubts or intelligent questions. Insecure in their faith, the fanatics seek compensation in dogmatic affirmation of what they want to believe. They often indulge in group hysteria and sentimentalism and reject all rational thinking and scientific inquiry. Out of touch with the world of reality and the march of events, they choose to remain isolated in their religious ghettos. Religious fanatics have even put men and women to death in the name of religion. Fanaticism has been the cause of endless dissension and discord, untold suffering, and bitter hatred, war, and persecution.

Atheism. The atheists reject all notions of spirituality and spiritual quest. For them, this world is all there is. All ideas of God, soul, and spirit are nothing but fanciful imagination. According to them, it is more honest to believe in the visible world than to believe in something unknown, unseen, and unproven. If what the atheists profess is true, then life would have no purpose and no meaning. Atheism is a reaction to traditional religious beliefs and it promotes hopelessness, pessimism, and loss of faith in life.

Pursuit of art or intellectual reflection. The pursuit of art or intellectual reflection as a substitute for spirituality is essentially an escape from the realities of life. Such a pursuit may lead to intellectual enjoyment but not to the peace of soul that comes from within. Followers of this way of life remain satisfied with the symbol of truth and do not seek truth itself.

Agnosticism. Agnosticism neither accepts the mysteries of God nor denies them. It holds the view that what we do not know and cannot know, we need not know. The agnostics are ambivalent and vacillating. They take delight in not being committed to any teaching. Agnosticism is a pseudo-religion of egotistic satisfaction.

Humanism. Humanists advocate doing good and being "human," without telling us what is meant by the word *human.* Humanists forget that the word *human* is a counterpart of the word *divine.* Humanism wants us to remain an animal, but a well-dressed one. But a monkey trained to ride a bicycle, smoke a cigar, drink from a glass, and use sign language is, after all, still a monkey. Hence, humanistic endeavors are often a cover-up for the anguish of the soul. Humanists tend to identify religion with the service of humanity and equate God with the moral ideal. They believe in the self-sufficiency of the material person, and the only values that matter for them are human values. Humanism is secularized religion. It often becomes a rival to the spiritual quest, the essence of which is God-realization, not social reform.

Prophetism. Prophetism believes in the establishment of heaven on earth by a prophet. But the hopes of the prophetists are never fulfilled. While meaningful living calls for acting in the present, prophetists live in dreams of the future.

Supernaturalism. Supernaturalism believes in the existence of other worlds inhabited by supernatural beings who, when propitiated, fulfill our desires and aspirations. Supernaturalists look for miraculous solutions for our earthly problems. But solutions never come.

Drug mysticism. The view of drug mysticism is that drug intoxication frees a person from the worries of worldly life and brings spiritual exaltation. Followers of this doctrine equate psychological void and emotional frenzy with spiritual ecstasy. They believe in drugs that can bring about spiritual exaltation or states of mystic joy. Drug mysticism is false mysticism clothed in spiritual symbolism. This pseudomysticism results only in morbidity and depression, not illumination.

Occultism. Occultism, which dwells on magic and miracles, has become the spiritual preoccupation of many seekers. The followers of occultism hold that through the use of mantras, charms, spells, and the like, they can attain mastery over nature and develop powers usually regarded as superhuman. They talk in terms of clairvoyance, clairaudience, thought reading, and levitation but not about devotion, Self-realization, and longing for the Divine.

Universalism. Universalism is an anthology of teachings of different systems. Although intellectually stimulating, the teachings of universalism lack root and transforming power, both of which come from the life and message of a prophet. For this reason, universalism ends up being nothing more than a loosely knit philosophical system of many heterogeneous thoughts.

New-ageism. An offshoot of universalism, new-ageism is a mixture of occultism, music, art, diet control, health maintenance, astrology, and psychology. It is a revolt against the dogmatic and authoritarian thinking of organized religion. New-ageism advocates unlimited freedom and uncharted spiritual adventure. But freedom is not an easy thing to digest. An adventure without a goal leads nowhere.

Nature mysticism. The nature mystics seek solace in going back to nature. They call it Mother Nature and feel the presence of God manifested in natural beauty and tranquillity. They consider the developments of science and technology unnatural, unfriendly, and harmful and want to follow a lifestyle of the prescientific ages. But to turn the clock backward is impossible.

THE MESSAGE OF VEDANTA

The spiritual crisis of our age has highlighted the importance of the message of Vedanta. Once looked upon as life-negating speculations of the stargazers of the East, Vedanta is now regarded by many thinkers as the teaching that gives us hope for the future.

Vedanta, the final teaching of the Vedas, is based on a set of universal principles. The crown jewel of Hinduism, Vedanta is reflected in the traditions of Buddhism, Jainism, Sikhism, and other Eastern spiritual paths. Vedanta is the message of the Upanishads, the voice of the Bhagavad Gita, and the song of the prophets and Godmen, past and present.

The principles of Vedanta are scientific because they are verifiable and repeatable, democratic because they foster individual freedom, universal because they apply to all people of all time, pragmatic because they focus on human problems and development, and psychological because they relate to human experience. Vedanta maintains the following:

Ultimate Reality. The Ultimate Reality, according to Vedanta, is all-pervading Pure Consciousness, one without a second, beyond all name, form, and epithet. The various names, forms, and epithets used by the different religions to describe the Ultimate Reality are merely attempts to name the nameless and attribute form and epithet to that which defies all names, forms, and epithets. Vedanta asserts that "Truth is one: sages call it by various names" (*Rig Veda* 10.114.5).

The human individual. Human individuals are not civilized animals, as some maintain, but are fallen angels. Their innate nature is divine. Their master urge is freedom of the soul and not sense gratification or pleasure or power, as psychologists would have us believe. Humans are more than libido-driven creatures or a result of the combination of carbon, hydrogen, oxygen, nitrogen, sulfur, and other elements. They are layered beings whose soul remains covered by five material sheaths: physical body, vital air, mind, intellect, and bliss. Consciously or unconsciously, human individuals are in search of their Self.

The creation. Creation is not an act by an extracosmic God or a random process of blind nature but is the evolution and involution of Pure Consciousness. The creation is beginningless.

Good and evil. There is no such thing as absolute good or absolute evil. That which is good for one may be evil for another, and vice versa. Good and evil are a pair of opposites, one of which cannot exist without the other. The view that someday evil will be eliminated and only good will prevail is absurd.

Sufferings of life. The sufferings of life are not due to the retribution of God; to luck, chance, hostile stars or planets; or to any other external agency. According to Vedanta, the causes of the sufferings of life are ignorance that separates us from the center of our being, ego, attachment, aversion, and clinging to life. All the maladies of life have their root in this separation from our true Self.

The validity of spiritual truth. The validity of spiritual truth depends upon direct perception, which is more than belief in scriptures, reasoning, or emotional exaltation. Believing in scriptures is accepting the belief of another person. Reasoning by itself can never give us direct perception of Truth, and emotional exaltation usually is short-lived and deceptive. In contrast, direct perception is perceiving not through the mind but through the soul; it alone can silence doubt and give certainty of faith. Attainment of direct perception calls for purification of the mind, which is the goal of all prayer, meditation, and performance of sacraments and ceremonies. The proof of direct perception is permanent transformation of character.

Human destiny. The soul has no rest and no peace until it realizes through Self-knowledge that it is a focus of the all-pervading, immortal Self. Self-knowledge is the goal of all goals and value of all values. Self-knowledge is not just for the chosen few—it is the destiny of all. It is true immortality; heaven and hell are mere experiences of the mind. Vedanta maintains that immortality through Self-knowledge is to be attained while living, so that it may be verifiable and believable.

The values of life. Vedanta speaks of four human values: righteous conduct, acquisition of wealth, fulfillment of legitimate desires, and freedom of the soul. Righteous conduct emphasizes moral sensitivity and unselfishness, without which a person remains an animal in human form. Acquisition of wealth brings material fulfillment, a step toward spiritual fulfillment.

Fulfillment of legitimate desires is a psychological necessity. Nonfulfillment of legitimate desires creates impediments to spiritual awakening. Freedom of the soul, attained through Self-knowledge, gives meaning and purpose to the other three values.

Existence. All existence is one. There is one life that pulsates in the universe; there is only one Soul that lives in all. Life is interdependent, not independent. Virtue is that which unites us with all, while vice is that which separates us from others. Oneness of existence is the basis of all ethics and morality.

Harmony of faiths. The various faiths are only different ways of reaching the same goal, the direct perception of the Ultimate. Direct perception is the very soul of every faith. Doctrines and dogmas, philosophy and myths, are secondary details. Harmony of faiths is not uniformity but unity in diversity. This harmony is to be discovered and realized by deepening our individual spiritual consciousness. Religious quarrels and hatred begin when the goal is forgotten, ignored, or neglected.

VEDANTA'S CONTRIBUTIONS TO WORLD RELIGIOUS THOUGHT

Vedanta has made three primary contributions to world religious thought:

Spiritual democracy, which ensures freedom of worship. Devoid of democracy, religion becomes authoritative and oppressive. It is the spirit of democracy that repudiates proselytizing, which is psychologically destructive and morally reprehensible.

Spiritual humanism, which calls for serving all, seeing the divine presence in every being. Spiritual humanism is based on one of the cardinal teachings of Vedanta, the oneness of existence. By doing good to others, we only do good to ourselves.

Universal unity, which sees the presence of only one Soul in all. Science has brought about the physical unity of people but not the unity of their minds. Unity based on political considerations, economic interests, cultural ties, or humanitarian principles can never be enduring. Universal unity requires the perception of a Universal Soul that is the soul of all beings. Without this perception, social diversities and cultural pluralities are bound to be explosive and dangerous.

Vedanta's contribution to humanity has been its catholicity of outlook; its spirit of tolerance, even to a fault; and its quest for inner freedom that defies imposition of any limit of race, color, creed, special claims, or economic or political affiliation.

THE CONTENTION OF THE CRITICS

Critics contend that the overall outlook of Vedanta is pessimistic, other-worldly, and self defeating; that Vedanta asks a person to sacrifice material and psychological well-being for the sake of spiritual salvation. Its view of the Ultimate is too abstract, too distant, and too impersonal. It is obsessed with finding a spiritual solution to every human problem, and its social concern is insufficient if not negligible. For Vedanta, knowledge is virtue, not a tool to improve the quality of life. For all these reasons, Vedanta has contributed in no small measure to India's decay and defeat. It has exaggerated human weakness, human unworthiness, and human limitations. Too often, passivity has been its keynote and self-withdrawal its principal virtue. Inertia has passed for tranquillity and hopelessness for dispassion. Vedanta has encouraged self-isolation, selfish individualism, and cowardly retreat from the challenges of life.

The criticisms are not altogether unmerited. At some periods of India's history, Vedanta lost its vision and vigor. The degeneration of the post-Buddhistic era and the subsequent centuries of foreign domination pushed Hindu society into self-withdrawal and isolation. The links between mysticism and humanism and between spiritual values and material values were broken. Vedanta was replaced by a pseudo-Vedanta that encouraged selfish individualism and fatalism. The world was described as a sinister illusion, not as a revelation of the Divine in nature. This is the reason, the critics say, that the Hindus, known for their wisdom of the soul, lag behind the West in developing science and technology.

Vedanta of old emphasized "All this is verily Brahman" (absolute Reality) but ignored its counterpart, "That thou art." In quest of spiritual salvation, Vedanta ignored material salvation. In the worship of God in heaven, it forgot the living God dwelling in every soul. Swami Vivekananda made Vedanta alive and dynamic again, bridging the gulf between heaven and earth, material values and spiritual values, Self-knowledge and service of

God in all. Swami Vivekananda's Vedanta is a call for the soul to rise from slumber, face life, become whole, and manifest its greatness.

Vedanta does subordinate material values to spiritual values and secular humanism to spiritual humanism. This is because Vedanta does not seek to have "the kingdom of the world" (Luke 4:5) or build its "house upon the sand" (Matt. 7:26); Vedanta has discovered that it does not "profit a man if he shall gain the whole world, and lose his own soul" (Mark 8:36). Vedanta knows, as Aldous Huxley said, "We cannot see the moon and stars so long as we choose to remain within the aura of street lamps and whisky advertisements. We cannot even hope to discover what is happening in the East, if we turn our faces and feet towards the West."[1] It also knows only too well that "all who take the sword will perish by the sword" (Matt. 26:53) and that the pursuit of pleasure without peace of soul is suicidal.

Vedanta tells us that the greatness of a person is not measured by what the person does or has, but by what he or she is, and that so-called love of life is a cheap cliché of world intoxication. "Man's right to knowledge and free use thereof" without the wisdom of the soul is a dangerous modern slogan. Vedanta maintains that civilizations perish because of their spiritual bankruptcy and that when a civilization triumphs, it is more by the strength of its spirit than by its physical power. This has been the merciless law of history, and history is bound to repeat itself if we fail to heed its lessons.

2

Life and Its Meaning: The Vedanta View

Vedanta is the teaching of the major Hindu scriptures. It derives its authority primarily from the four Vedas: the *Rig Veda,* the *Yajur Veda,* the *Sama Veda,* and the *Atharva Veda.* Each Veda consists of four parts: the *mantras,* or hymns in praise of Vedic deities; the *brahmanas,* or the section dealing with rituals and ceremonies; the *aranyakas,* or philosophical interpretation of the rituals; and the Upanishads, or the concluding portions of the Vedas (known as Vedanta), which describe the profound spiritual truths.

THE ULTIMATE REALITY

Vedanta describes Ultimate Reality as Brahman. Brahman is nondual Pure Consciousness, indivisible, incorporeal, infinite, and all-pervading, like the sky. Brahman is of the nature of Existence-Knowledge-Bliss Absolute, the ground of all existence, basis of all awareness, and source of all bliss. It is the Reality of all realities, the Soul of all souls, one without a second, the constant witness of the changing phenomena of the universe. From the absolute point of view, Brahman alone exists. Brahman has two aspects: transcendent and immanent. In its transcendent aspect, Brahman is devoid of name and form, sex and attributes. But in its immanent aspect, Brahman is endowed with them. The Upanishads designate the transcendent Brahman by the word *it* and the immanent Brahman by the word *he.* Through its inscrutable power, called maya, the transcendent Brahman appears to be conditioned by

9

time and space and to manifest itself as personal God, the creator, preserver, and destroyer of the universe. The Upanishads describe God as the supreme person:

> His hands and feet are everywhere; His eyes, heads, and faces are everywhere; His ears are everywhere; He exists compassing all.[1]

> The heavens are His head; the sun and moon, His eyes; the quarters, His ears; the revealed Vedas, His speech; the wind is His breath; the universe, His heart. From His feet is produced the earth. He is, indeed, the inner Self of all beings.[2]

The various godheads, such as Shiva, Vishnu, Brahma, Kali, and Durga, are but different facets of Brahman. The Supreme Brahman assumes various forms for the spiritual fulfillment of the individual seekers. All concepts and forms of God, according to Vedanta, are what we think of him and not what he is to himself. Again, various seekers of God, depending upon their advancement, perceive God differently. For example, to the beginner, God appears as an extracosmic creator; to the more advanced seeker as inner controller; and to the perfect knower of God as being everywhere and in everything. Still another manifestation of the conditioned Brahman is the incarnation of God—God's taking human form. According to Vedanta, God incarnates himself to fulfill the needs of the universe, whenever and wherever the need arises. In the Bhagavad Gita Sri Krishna says:

> Whenever there is a decline of *dharma* [righteousness], O Bharata, and a rise of *adharma* [unrighteousness], I incarnate myself. For the protection of the good, for the destruction of the wicked, and for the establishment of *dharma*, I am born in every age.[3]

Thus, according to Vedanta, the supreme Godhead is both formless and endowed with many forms.

THE UNIVERSE

This manifestation of Brahman as the manifold universe is not real but apparent. Through its inscrutable power of maya, Brahman appears as the world of matter and souls and as endowed with the activities of creation, preservation, and dissolution. Maya veils the Ultimate Reality and in its place projects various appearances. Maya is change and relativity. The question that naturally arises when considering the arguments of Vedanta is: If everything is all-pervading Consciousness, why do we see multiplicity? The answer is that it is due to ignorance (*avidya*). *Avidya* is darkness or the absence of the light of the Self. *Avidya* not only veils the Self from us but also projects something in its place, making the unreal appear to us as real. We experience the sky as blue and curved like a vault, but we know that this appearance is an optical illusion. When the two attributes are taken away, what remains is infinite space signified by the name of *sky*. As blueness and curvature rest on the sky, as a mirage rests on the desert, and waves on the ocean, so also the three states of our "becoming" remain grounded on the Self. *Avidya* makes us believe that we are many, even though in reality that which exists is only one—one indivisible Consciousness appearing as multitudes of separate centers of limited consciousness. The belief in separate existences is due to the sense of embodiedness, which is only a habit of thought initiated by ignorance and reinforced by attachment. We take our beliefs very seriously, but in fact there are numberless instances demonstrating that our beliefs are not based on so-called reality: they are merely subjective perceptions. For example, for us the earth has weight, as have all things on its surface, but the universe itself has no weight.

Avidya is essentially that which obstructs the vision of truth. In the language of religion, *avidya* is sin; from the perspective of ethics, it is immorality; from the point of view of aesthetics, it is ugliness; and in the realm of logic, it is fallacy. Vedanta describes *avidya* as neither real nor unreal. *Avidya* does not inhere in us but is at work in our individual minds. The concept of *avidya* and its illusory character presupposes the existence of something that is real. As error implies truth, so illusion implies reality. Another name of *avidya* is *maya*. Maya is made of name and form. Analyzed further, maya is the very mind that attempts to divide the indivisible, to think the unthinkable, to limit the illimitable. According to Vedanta, the sufferings of life are due to the superimposition of maya on Brahman. Maya is the very fabric of life. The philosophy of Vedanta describes maya as inexplicable. If it were real, then the conditions of our life would also be real and could not be changed. In that case, there would be no use embarking on a spiritual quest. Yet it cannot be said that it is unreal, because the sufferings of life are not just imaginary. Maya cannot be fought or escaped; it can be overcome only by the knowledge of Brahman. So long as Truth is not known, maya is delusive; when it is known, maya is Brahman. Knowledge of Brahman is attained only when all superimpositions of maya are seen as illusory notions of the mind.

Maya is comprised of the three *gunas,* or qualities: *sattva, rajas,* and *tamas. Sattva* is balance or calmness; *rajas* is restlessness or imbalance; *tamas* is inertia or darkness. The three *gunas* are present in varying degrees in all objects, gross or subtle, including the body-mind complex of an individual. For example, when *sattva* prevails in an individual, the light of knowledge begins to shine through the body and mind. When *rajas* prevails, the person is stirred by unrest. And when *tamas* prevails, he or she is taken over by inertia. When the universe is in a period of nonmanifestation, the three *gunas* remain in a state of nondifferentiation, or equilibrium. Manifestation begins when the equilibrium of the *gunas* is disturbed.

According to Vedanta, the process of manifestation and nonmanifestation of the universe follows a cyclical pattern. In each cycle there is a recurrence of the same material phenomena, and the same recurrences continue throughout eternity. No material energy can be annihilated; it goes on changing again and again until it returns to the source. Nature presents two movements—from the subtle to the gross and from the gross back to the subtle. Evolution presupposes involution. Only that which was involved before can be evolved afterward. Evolution of the physical universe follows a graduated process. The first element to evolve at the beginning of a cycle is *akasha,* or space, in its subtle form. Then four other elements gradually evolve: air, fire, water, and earth. In the beginning, the five elements remain unmixed. Then, through their various combinations, the elements take their gross forms. From out of the basic gross and subtle elements are produced all objects, gross and subtle, including the body-mind complex of all living creatures.

According to the Puranas, or secondary scriptures of Vedanta, each world period is divided into four ages, or *yugas:* Satya, Treta, Dwapara, and Kali. The Satya Yuga abounds in virtue, with vice being practically nonexistent. But with each succeeding age, virtue gradually diminishes and vice increases, making the age of Kali the reverse of Satya. The approximate duration of each *yuga* has been described as Satya Yuga, 1,728,000 years; Treta, 1,296,000 years; Dwapara, 864,000 years; and Kali, 432,000 years. These four *yugas,* rotating a thousand times, make one day of Brahma, the creator, and an equal number of years make one night. Thirty such days and nights make one month of Brahma, and twelve months make one year. After living for a hundred such years, Brahma dies. Brahma, too, like all other entities of the phenomenal universe, has a limited life span, although this life span seems nearly endless from the viewpoint of human calculations.

THE HUMAN INDIVIDUAL

According to Vedanta, the human individual is essentially a soul that uses its body and mind as instruments to gain experience. What is the nature of the soul? Vedanta maintains that the macrocosm and the microcosm are built on the same plan, and that Brahman is the soul of both. As the soul of every being, Brahman is known as Paramatman. The Upanishads speak of the two souls dwelling, as it were, side by side within each person: the real soul (Paramatman) and the apparent soul (*jivatman*). The real soul is the witness consciousness, serene and detached. The apparent soul is the embodied soul, the experiencer of birth and death, ever in quest of freedom and eternal life. The apparent soul is the ego self—the reflection of the real soul. The real soul has been described as Self and the apparent soul as non-Self.

Vedanta analyzes a person in terms of three bodies, five sheaths, and three states.

THE THREE BODIES

Vedanta says that a human individual has three bodies: physical body, subtle body, and causal body. The physical body is produced out of the gross forms of the five basic elements—earth, air, water, fire, and space (*akasha*)—and is subject to a sixfold change: birth, subsistence, growth, maturity, decay, and death. At death the physical body perishes and its five constituent elements are dissolved. The subtle body is made of the subtle forms of the five basic elements that produced the physical body. It is the receptacle of thoughts and memories and continues to exist after death, serving as the vehicle of transmigration. A human individual enters this world with a bundle of thoughts in the form of the mind, and also exits with a bundle of thoughts, some old and some new. The causal body, characterized by ego sense only, is finer than the subtle body. All three bodies are for the fulfillment of desires, gross and subtle. The soul is different from these three bodies.

THE FIVE *KOSHAS* (SHEATHS)

Vedantic reasoning is an attempt to plumb the depths of human personality to discover the Ultimate Reality that remains embedded within. Vedanta scriptures describe the body-mind complex of a person as consisting of five psychophysical layers, or sheaths, which constitute the personality.

The outermost layer is known as *annamaya-kosha*. This layer is the physical sheath, which consists of flesh, bone, blood, and so forth. It is characterized by weight, color, and form and endures as long as it can assimilate food. It is gross, inert, and subject to change. The physical sheath, according to Vedanta, cannot be the real Self, since it is subject to change and has a beginning and an end.

The second layer is called *pranamaya-kosha,* or the sheath of vital force. It is a channel for the manifestation of cosmic energy. The sheath of vital force is finer than the physical sheath. When joined with the five organs of action, it animates the physical sheath and makes it appear to be a living entity performing the functions of inhalation, exhalation, movement, reproduction, and so forth. This vital force, the modification of cosmic energy, enters the body after its conception and leaves it at the time of its dissolution. Through this sheath the human individual experiences hunger and thirst, engages in various physical activities, and adapts to and struggles against nature. The *pranamaya-kosha* cannot be the real Self, since it too is subject to change and has a beginning and an end. It is merely a vehicle for the inner Self, the Reality dwelling within the sheaths.

The third layer is called *manomaya-kosha,* or the sheath of mind, and it too is made of subtle matter. This third sheath permeates the two outer ones, for through this sheath an individual thinks and reacts, believes and doubts, and feels desires and attachments. The real Self, being identified with the sheath of mind, experiences various pairs of opposites, such as pleasure and pain, light and darkness, birth and death. It is the mind that creates the universe of diversities and forces the soul, as it were, to come under its sway, making it experience repeated births and deaths. The mind is the cause of all bondage, and, again, the same mind is the means to liberation. It cannot, however, be the real Self, because it is unsteady, ever changing, and subject to various modifications.

The fourth layer, the *vijnanamaya-kosha,* is the sheath of intellect, or the discriminating faculty of a human being. It is finer than the mind and also more inward than it. The fabric of the intellect, though subtle like that of the mind, is also material and inert. It appears conscious because it reflects the intelligence of the Self. The focus of this reflection is the ego, or I-consciousness. Identified with the sheath of intellect, the inmost Self distinguishes the desirable from the undesirable; makes decisions, choices, and moral judgments; and experiences the happiness and misery of the different states of life, but with a certain sense of detachment. Also it serves as a storehouse for the memories of past experiences, technically known as *samskaras.* That is, it is the seedbed of all thoughts and desires. The sheath of intellect also cannot be the real Self, since it too is subject to both the fluctuations and the rigidities of ideas. Taken together, the sheaths of intellect, mind, and vital force make up the subtle body of an individual. It is really the subtle body made of thoughts that acts through the instrumentality of the physical body. Our thoughts are our actions in rehearsal.

The fifth layer is the sheath of bliss, *anandamaya-kosha,* through which the human individual experiences varying degrees of happiness. The sheath of bliss, being most proximate to the Self, reflects its light. Like the other sheaths, it too is a product of matter and is subject to change, and therefore this sheath also cannot be the real Self, which is self-existent, changeless, and free from all pairs of opposites.

All five sheaths, according to Vedanta, are modifications of matter, gross or subtle, and thus have no permanent reality. They appear to be endowed with consciousness because they reflect the consciousness of the Atman, or Self, their ground. The five sheaths stand, so to speak, like five lamp shades, one inside the other, around the real Self, whose radiance illumines all of them. While the Atman is one without a second, omniscient and all-pervading, it appears as many because of the varieties and textures of the sheaths. All relative phenomena of the universe are, therefore, reflections of the Ultimate Reality, but these reflections often become distorted because of the imperfections in the mediums of reflection. The so-called personality of a human individual is thus a shadow self, his or her real Self being the Atman (Pure Consciousness), which is the common Self of all beings. In the same way, the entire microcosm is the shadow of the macrocosm. A shadow is always unknowable until one is able to discover the reality that is projecting the shadow. Similarly, the diversities of the universe are always a puzzle until their ground, the real Self, or Atman, is realized. Thus the direct experience of the Atman is possible only when one is able to completely dissociate oneself from all five sheaths.

THE THREE STATES OF CONSCIOUSNESS

Vedantic reasoning takes into account the entire spectrum of human experience and discriminates the Real from the unreal. According to Vedanta, an individual normally experiences three states—waking, dream, and dreamless sleep—which represent three different aspects of our becoming. The conclusions of science about what is real are based on evidence gathered only during the waking state. Vedanta considers these conclusions not incorrect but incomplete, because reality is not exhausted by the external waking universe. Therefore science, or the philosophies of realism, cannot reveal the whole truth.

The dream state—in which the physical body and the gross sense organs generally remain inactive, and the waking world is replaced by a dream world with a dream subject, objects, and instruments of knowledge—provides data for the conclusions of the subjective idealist, and these are also incomplete.

Dreamless sleep is a unique experience, different from that of dreaming or waking. To only consider knowledge gathered from the analysis of dreamless sleep may lead to either nihilism or false mysticism. The state of dreamless sleep is characterized by the absence of any subject/object relationship. The ego sense, though appearing to be nonexistent, continues to function as a monitoring consciousness, since upon waking from dreamless sleep we recollect that we slept soundly. Thus, it cannot be said that the ego remains unconscious during this state, because it is monitoring the absence of all phenomenal experiences and, upon returning to the waking condition, also remembers that it did not dream. The state of dreamless sleep reveals a different dimension of existence, in which a saint is not aware of being a saint, a scholar of being a scholar, or a king of being a king. Vedantic reasoning analyzes the respective experiences of the three states and concludes that Reality transcends all three.

According to general consensus, waking experiences are real and dream experiences are unreal, but in the view of Vedanta, there is really no valid basis for this distinction. The dream state is the waking state for the dreamer. The dream state has its own standards of illusion and reality, which cannot be judged by the criteria of the waking state. The contention that dream objects are created by the dreamer's mind, whereas objects perceived in the waking state exist outside of, and are independent of, the perceiver, is not supported by reason, for neither the dreamer nor the person in the waking state questions the "reality" of his or her own sense perceptions. The objects of the dream world seem to exist outside the dreamer, but they do not. The dream world, like the waking one, has its diverse categories and its living beings, and therefore dream experience is as public as waking experience until the dream breaks.

It is often contended that experiences of the waking state endure for a longer period of time than those of the dream state, which seem to be fleeting and intangible when measured by the standards of the waking state. Therefore, it is concluded, the waking state is more real than the dream state. But this contention does not stand the test of reason, because experiences in dream are also felt to be enduring. The standards of measurement in the two states of waking and dream are not the same. Each state is independent of the other, and it is not valid to measure them with the same yardstick. Therefore, one cannot be said to be more real than the other.

The vast majority of people look upon a dream as nothing but a dream—that is to say, a mere fantasy of mind. Wealth possessed by a person in dream, they point out, cannot be used in the waking state. But it can also be argued that what is wealth to a person in the waking state is of no use in the state of dream. It is generally thought that dream objects are queer and grotesque (when judged by the criteria of the waking state) and are to be considered illusory per se; but from the viewpoint of Vedanta, the dream has its own "waking" conception of reality and unreality, which is proved by the fact that the dreamer perceives dream objects as normal and substantial. Objective realists contend that dream experiences are refuted by those of the waking state but experiences of the waking state are not found to be unreal in dreams. In answer, it may be said that to the dreamer the dream *is* the waking state, and therefore real, and whatever the person experiences in dream is also real to him or her. For example, a man may take a piece of rope to be a snake and feel horrified. The imaginary snake is a terrible reality for him until he discovers that it is really a rope.

TURIYA, THE FOURTH STATE

According to Vedanta, the Self of an individual is distinct from all three states of existence: waking, dream, dreamless sleep. This Self is indwelling and is the experiencer of the three states, yet it remains unaffected by them. The Self has been described as Turiya, or the fourth, the unchanging substratum of all three relative states of existence. Turiya is "being," whereas the three states indicate diverse levels of "becoming." That which did not exist in the past and will not exist in the future but is perceived to exist in the present because of a particular condition of the mind is to be considered unreal. As a desert pervades a mirage, so also Turiya, the omnipresent Consciousness, pervades all three states of existence. Turiya is the watchful witness of the changing phenomena of the three states. It is beyond time, space, and causality, yet without its presence no perception or experience in any of the three states is possible. The concept of a personal God is the highest possible reading of Turiya by the human mind. Turiya is neither subjective nor objective; it is infinite and, therefore, incomprehensible to the finite mind. It is realized as the inmost Self of all beings when the phenomena of the three changing states are overcome through discriminative reasoning. Shankaracharya wrote the following in praise of Turiya:

> I bow to the supreme, immortal, and birthless Brahman, designated in terms of maya as Turiya, the Fourth.
>
> May that Turiya, which, as the World Soul, experiences in the waking state gross objects, good and evil; which, again, experiences in the dream state other and subtle objects produced by Its own mind and illumined by Its own light; and which, lastly, in dreamless sleep withdraws all objects and remains devoid of distinctions—may that attributeless Turiya protect us![4]

Turiya, or the fourth dimension of our personality, is the very ground of our being. It is like an illumined stage on which the three states, like actors, enter and exit in succession. Turiya is like the screen that remains unmoving and unresponsive to the motion pictures projected onto it but gives continuity and meaning to those very pictures. The ignorant identify themselves with the body, thinking it to be the Self, and become overwhelmed by its sixfold change. There are others who look upon the sense organs as the Self and thus despair to think that the Self can become blind or deaf. Others in their attachment regard the mind as the Self and believe that it can be assailed by doubts and desires. On the other hand, atheists say the Self is nonexistent and argue that the concept of a higher Self is baseless. To the Vedantist, the body, mind, and sense organs belong to the category of non-Self; they appear conscious only because they reflect the light of Consciousness or the Self. The presence of the Self, as the very ground of our existence, is not affected by our denial or acceptance of it. People may deny everything, but they cannot deny their own existence.

Turiya is the Absolute, while the three states of existence are relative. A relative phenomenon becomes meaningful only in the context of the Absolute. Conversely, when the Absolute is overlooked, a relative phenomenon becomes easily mistaken for the Real. When duality becomes the only reality, the trivial is taken to be vital and the ephemeral to be eternal. Knowledge is power because knowledge is seeing the Real as it truly is, not as it appears to be. When not illumined by the knowledge of Turiya, life is bound by the experiences of waking, dream, and dreamless sleep. Devoid of the light of Turiya, that which is unreal and impermanent is taken to be real and permanent, creating continual crises. The goal of Vedanta is to resolve these crises by spiritually integrating the three states in the light of Turiya, or Self, which is their ground. The Self is the very essence of our being, while the three states comprise our existence. Knowledge of the Self alone can bridge the gulf that exists between essence and existence.

THE PROBLEM OF GOOD AND EVIL

Questions that are often asked are: Why do we suffer? If suffering is evil, why is there evil? What is the source of evil? If the creator God is all-loving, why does God allow this evil to take its toll?

According to Vedanta, reality is neither good nor evil. There is nothing in the universe that is absolutely good or absolutely evil, that is to say, good or evil for all time. Good and evil are value judgments made by the individual mind in keeping with its inner disposition caused by past karma. If one asks, Why does God permit evil, then the question will come, Why does God permit good?

Good is that which takes us near to our real Self, and evil is that which creates a distance between us and our real Self. The law of karma is the law of automatic justice. It tells us that no action goes without producing its result. The circumstances of our present life, our pains and pleasures, are all the results of our past actions in this existence and in countless previous existences. As one sows, so shall one reap. This is the inexorable law of karma.

Karma produces three kinds of results: results of past actions that have produced the present body, mind, and circumstances; results that have accumulated but are yet to fructify; and results that are being accumulated now. Over the first category of results no one has any control; these are to be overcome by patiently bearing with them. The second and third kinds, which are still in the stage of thoughts and tendencies, can be countered by education and self-control. Essentially, the law of karma says that though our will is free, we are conditioned to act in certain set ways. We suffer or enjoy because of this conditioning of our mind. And conditioning of mind, accumulated through self-indulgence, cannot be overcome vicariously. The effect of karma can be annulled only by other karma. The way out is either to accept both good and bad karma or to give up both.

Vedantists are called upon to act in the living present, to change their fate by changing their way of life, their thoughts, and their actions. Our past determines our present, and our present will determine our future. We are taught that no change will ever be effected by brooding over past mistakes or failures or by cursing others and blaming the world or by hoping for the future. To the contention that the law of karma does not leave any scope for the operation of divine grace, Vedanta's answer is that the grace of God is ever flowing equally toward all. It is not felt until one feels the need for it. The joy and suffering of a human individual are of his or her own making. Good and evil are mind made and not God created. The law of karma exhorts a Vedantist to right actions, giving the assurance that just as a saint had a past, so also a sinner has a future. Through the doctrine of rebirth and the law of karma, Vedanta seeks an ethical interpretation of life. The theory of the evolution of species describes the process of how life evolves. But the purpose of this evolution can be explained only by the doctrine of rebirth and the law of karma. The destiny of the soul is immortality through Self-realization. Existence-Knowledge-Bliss Absolute being its real nature, nothing limited can give it abiding satisfaction. Through its repeated births and deaths, it is seeking that supreme fulfillment of life.

THE VALUES OF LIFE

Vedanta speaks of four values of life, of which *moksha,* or liberation through Self-knowledge, is the fourth. The other three are *dharma,* or practice of right-eousness; *artha,* or attainment of worldly prosperity; and *kama,* or enjoyment of legitimate pleasures. Practice of *dharma* calls for an individual to perform the duties of life in accordance with the laws of morality, ethics, and right-eousness. *Artha* implies acquisition of wealth, necessary for the preservation of life and the promotion of the welfare of others. *Kama* is the enjoyment of legitimate pleasures, without which life becomes joyless and dry. The first three values must find their fulfillment in the fourth, Self-knowledge. Moral perfection when not for the sake of Self-knowledge becomes nothing but enlightened egoism. Wealth and prosperity when not used for the sake of Self-knowledge breed delusion and attachment. Art and aesthetics that do not reflect the light of the Self degenerate into promiscuity. Science and technology when not directed to the attainment of Self-knowledge prove to be dangerous weapons of self-destruction. Therefore, the acquisition of wealth and the enjoyment of pleasures must be guided by *dharma,* or righteousness, and governed by the goal of *moksha,* or Self-knowledge.

SELF-KNOWLEDGE: FREEDOM OF THE SOUL

The supreme goal of life, according to Vedanta, is *moksha,* or liberation. Liberation is the realization of the soul's identity with Brahman, the absolute Reality. It is not merely the cessation of suffering; it is the positive experience of intense bliss. Vedanta scriptures designate this realization as Self-knowledge. Vedanta holds that Self-knowledge alone can conquer death. The *Katha Upanishad* says:

> Having realized Atman, which is soundless, intangible, formless, undecaying, and likewise tasteless, eternal, and odorless; having realized That which is without beginning and end, beyond the Great, and unchanging—one is freed from the jaws of death.[5]

Self-knowledge and immortality are synonymous, says the *Brihadaranyaka Upanishad:*

Whosoever in this world, O Gargi, without knowing this Imperishable, offers oblations, performs sacrifices, and practices austerities, even for many thousands of years, finds all such acts but perishable. Whosoever, O Gargi, departs from this world without knowing this Imperishable is miserable. But he, O Gargi, who departs from this world after knowing the Imperishable is a knower of Brahman.[6]

Immortality is not the result of any spiritual discipline. It is a revelation. Spiritual disciplines purify the heart, and in the mirror of the pure heart the immortal Self is reflected.

Self-knowledge is a burning realization that totally transforms the person. The knower of Brahman becomes Brahman. Self-knowledge, the Upanishads point out, must be attained in this very life. One who dies in bondage will remain bound after death. Immortality, in order to be real, must be experienced before death. The *Katha Upanishad* says: "If a man is able to realize Brahman here, before the falling asunder of his body, then he is liberated; if not, he is embodied again in the created worlds."[7]

Self-knowledge is the consummation of all desires. According to the Vedanta scriptures, one should give up individual self-interest for the sake of the family, the family for the sake of the country, the country for the sake of the world, and everything for the sake of Self-knowledge.

The liberated soul is the free soul, whose life and actions demonstrate the reality of God. Free from all desires and egotism, and ever established in the knowledge of the immortal nature of the soul, the free soul regards the pain and pleasure of all others as his or her own pain and pleasure. Though living in the world of diversity, the free soul is never deluded by it, never makes a false step or sets a bad example. Virtues such as humility, unselfishness, purity, and kindness become natural for a free soul. A free soul wears no outward mark of holiness. As a fish swimming in water leaves no mark behind, as a bird flying in the sky leaves no footprint, so a free soul moves about in this world and departs it leaving no outward mark. While living in the body, the free soul may experience disease, old age, and decay, but having recognized them as belonging to the body, remains undisturbed and even-minded. For the free soul, the world is a stage and life a play. The free soul enjoys the play and the stage, knowing them to be so.

THE PATHS TO THE GOAL

Vedanta advocates freedom in the practice of religion. It maintains that the path to God-realization cannot be the same for all. Spiritual disciplines can never be standardized, because not all persons have the same inborn tendencies and temperament, and each must follow his or her own path. According to Vedanta, there are four basic types of mind: emotional, active, mystical, and philosophical. And in keeping with the four types of mind, Vedanta prescribes the practice of four different paths known as *yogas: bhakti-yoga, karma-yoga, raja-yoga,* and *jnana-yoga.*

Bhakti-yoga is the path for the emotional type. Following this path, seekers worship a specific aspect of a personal God or a divine incarnation. Or they may worship the Ultimate Reality as a deity who is without form but with divine attributes. They establish a human relationship with God, regarding him as father, mother, master, friend, or beloved, according to their temperament. They direct all their emotions to God and worship God through the performance of various rituals and ceremonies. The watchword of *bhakti-yoga* is "Thy will be done," which indicates absolute self-surrender to God. Through self-surrender and ecstatic love, the seeker ultimately attains to God-vision.

The path prescribed for the active type is *karma-yoga,* or the yoga of selfless activity. The watchword of this path is "Work is worship." Seekers following this path perform all actions regarding themselves as the instrument of God and surrender the results of the actions to God. The seeker may be a worshiper of a personal God or look upon the Ultimate Reality as the impersonal Absolute dwelling within him or her as the soul. *Karma-yoga* is nonattachment in action. The practice of nonattachment purifies the heart, and purity of heart leads directly to God-vision or Self-knowledge.

For those who are mystical by nature, Vedanta prescribes *raja-yoga,* the yoga of concentration and meditation. The seeker following this path looks upon Ultimate Reality as the inmost Self. The Self remains unperceived because of the mind's restlessness, which is overcome by ceaseless concentration and meditation on the Self. The watchword of this path is "Know thyself." Through uninterrupted concentration and meditation, the seeker ultimately realizes the true nature of the Self—pure, perfect, and immortal.

The path of *jnana-yoga* is for those who are philosophical and rational in temperament. It is the path of relentless self-analysis, discrimination, and complete renunciation. The watchword of this path is "The Self is Brahman." The seeker practices discrimination, renunciation, and self-control and develops intense longing for liberation. He or she hears about the Self, reflects on it, and meditates upon it. Through ceaseless meditation on the Self, the seeker attains union with it.

However, a seeker may follow any one of these yogas or a combination of two or more of them for the realization of Self-knowledge.

3

The Human Condition

Sufferings of Life

Life is not what it appears to be. It is ever haunted by the inexorable pairs of opposites—pain and pleasure, birth and death, good and evil, light and darkness, and so forth. All that glitters is not gold. Everything is uncertain; nothing is sure. "Man proposes, God disposes" seems to be the law. A human individual is born crying, lives complaining, and dies disappointed. As a rule the young are optimists, while the old only chew the cud of memories, bitter and sweet. Suffering is a universal phenomenon—no one escapes its cruel jaws. Happiness is followed by suffering, joy by sorrow, serenity by restlessness, courage by fear, hope by despair, exaltation by depression. Asked by a king about the meaning of life, a sage once replied, "A man is born, he suffers, and he dies."[1]

Suffering, indeed, is the price of our life on earth. Glimpses of happiness are fugitive and deceptive. Yet we forget this truth in the pursuit of momentary and illusory pleasures of life on earth. The optimist in Longfellow sings the note of hope:

> Tell me not in mournful numbers,
>   Life is but an empty dream!
> For the soul is dead that slumbers,
>   And things are not what they seem.[2]

But the philosopher in Shakespeare sings a different note:

> Life's but a walking shadow, a poor player
> That struts and frets his hour upon the stage
> And then is heard no more: it is a tale
> Told by an idiot, full of sound and fury,
> Signifying nothing.[3]

An average person's pessimistic attitude toward life is reflected in a humorous saying: "He feels bad when things are good, lest he should feel worse when things become better." Life is perplexing. Everyone is in search of happiness; no one knows how to get it, yet like a losing gambler everyone strives for it. It is said that once a young man, unable to decide whether or not to marry, asked Socrates for advice, and Socrates reportedly said to him: "Well, young man, marry if you like. If your wife turns out to be a good woman, you will be happy in life; and if she proves to be otherwise, you will be a philosopher like me!"

An ancient story vividly depicts a human individual in suffering. Once a man, being afflicted by troubles at home, was wandering in a deep forest. At one point he was confronted by a mad elephant with raised trunk ready to attack him. He turned around and began to run, but to his dismay he saw an ugly demoness with raised sword rushing toward him. He now ran sideways and came to a huge tree, which he repeatedly attempted to climb but failed. Frantically trying to escape, he caught hold of two clumps of reeds growing at the top of a dry well near the tree and hung clinging to them. As he was about to drop down into the well, he heard the hissing of a hundred cobras coming from the bottom of the well. Meanwhile, as if things were not precarious enough, two big rats, one white and the other black, appeared from nowhere and began to gnaw at the clumps of reeds. Just then the mad elephant came and began to shake the tree, in which there was a big honeycomb. Some honey began to drip on the head of the man. As he looked up, a few drops fell in his mouth, and forgetting everything he exclaimed, "How sweet is the honey!"

The man in the story stands for the afflicted soul, scorched by the sufferings of life. The forest is the world of delusion, the elephant old age, and the demoness death. The tree is the tree of virtue, which no unrighteous man can climb. The dry well is the pit of illusory enjoyment, and the hundred cobras are a hundred desires. The clumps of reeds represent the lease of life, the two rats the bright and dark fortnights, and the drops of honey fleeting sense pleasures. The moral of the story is that despite the fact that life is plagued by suffering at every moment, a human individual somehow continues to weave dreams of everlasting happiness. The foregoing may sound morbid and pessimistic, but then fact is fact.

SUFFERING: THE MESSAGE OF THE PROPHETS, SAINTS, AND SACRED TEXTS

Of the four noble truths of Buddha, "There is suffering" is the first. The other three are: There is a cause of suffering; there is a solution to the suffering; and the solution is the eightfold way of Buddha. Buddha describes sufferings as *skandas,* or events. First is the trauma of birth; perhaps that is why a baby's first response to the world is a cry. Second is the dread of sickness; third, the decay of old age; fourth, the darkness of death; fifth, separation from loved ones; and sixth, helplessness in situations and circumstances, such as a permanent physical disability or an irreversible illness. Twenty-five hundred years ago the Enlightened One declared that if all the tears that had flowed from human eyes since the beginning of creation were gathered together, they would exceed the waters of the ocean.

In the Bhagavad Gita, Sri Krishna describes earthly life as the "abode of sorrow and suffering," haunted by cycles of birth, disappointment, despair, old age, and death. The *Mahabharata* in bold terms describes true knowledge as perceiving suffering as the "news of all news." In the story of the enchanted pool, when the thirsty king, Yudhishthira, went to drink water at the pool, a voice without form asked him four instructive questions, one of which was "What is the news?" The king replied: "The news for all time is suffering. This world full of ignorance is like a pan. The sun is fire, the days and nights are fuel. The months and the seasons constitute the wooden ladle. Time is the cook that is cooking all creatures in that pan; this is the news."[4] The Upanishads designate suffering as a scorching fire that consumes body, mind, and soul. Its causes are three: other beings, such as animals and fellow men; forces beyond one's control—commonly known as acts of God; and one's own body and mind, which produce ailments both somatic and mental. Christ says: "Come unto me, all ye that labor and are heavy laden, and I will give you rest" (Matt. 11:28).

Shankaracharya gives the following vivid description of the universe we live in:

> The universe is endowed with the unending and manifold miseries of birth, old age, death, and grief; it changes its nature every moment. Like magic, a mirage, or a castle in the air, the universe is perceived, only to vanish ultimately. It is non-eternal, like a tree. Again, like a plantain tree, it has no inner substance.... The Tree of the Universe is constantly reverberating with the tumultuous noise arising from dancing, singing, instrumental music, sport, arrogant uproar, laughter, jostling, lamentations, and such exclamations as "Alas! I am done for!" and "Leave me alone!" induced by hilarity and weeping, which are the results of the happiness and unhappiness of living beings.[5]

Sri Ramakrishna saw that "the world is like an overcast sky that steadily pours down rain: the face of the sun is seldom seen. There is mostly suffering in the world."[6] Swami Vivekananda in his poem "To a Friend" says:

> Where darkness is beheld as light,
> And sorrow understood as joy;
> Where sickness masquerades as health,
> And but the new-born infant's cry
> Tells one it lives—O wise one, say,
> Seekest thou satisfaction here?[7]

In essence, suffering is evil that brings only pain and disintegration. It is real and cannot be explained away or escaped by any means. As ceaseless changes, proverbial uncertainties, deep disappointments, reverses of fortune, separation, disease, and death, suffering robs life of all its enchantment and promise.

WHY DO WE SUFFER?

Why is a soul born on earth, and why does it suffer? There are several views regarding the source of suffering.

The first view maintains that suffering comes from external sources and that it is primarily physical. We suffer because of our blind submission to the forces of nature. All human progress has been achieved by adhering to the "no surrender" principle—nothing has been accomplished by resignation, by willingly putting up with everything, and by letting things happen. The upholders of this view advocate a material solution to the problem of suffering. They aim at eliminating all evil by controlling and conquering external nature and circumstances: by improving the standard of living and the quality of life, by medicine, and by science and technology. As W. Macneile Dixon says: "Give to the pessimist youth and health, a spring morning and a lover, and his mood will change. He will consent to postpone extinction, he will cling to the excruciating wheel of existence a little longer."[8] This view seeks the fulfillment of desires as the answer to the problem of suffering. The material remedy, however, has limitations. First, there is no universal ideal for peace and happiness. Again, the solution to the problem of suffering may call for a change of social or political conditions, and here too there is no solution that is acceptable to all. Then there is the problem of the diversity of human nature. Human greed and selfishness are endemic and make the creation of an ideal society impossible. Human desires are endless. They are never satiated.

The second view looks upon the evil of suffering as a decree of fate. That which is fated cannot be blotted out. What cannot be cured must be endured. It is no use talking about our free will and our freedom of choice. Things do not happen according to our plan: we are not consulted about our birth and death. Everything is preordained and predestined. This view, if taken to be true, leaves no scope for self-improvement and human endeavor and progress. It makes our life meaningless. If suffering gives finality to our existence, "there is, then, nothing to be hoped for," says Dixon, "nothing to be expected and nothing to be done save to await our turn to mount the scaffold and bid farewell to the colossal blunder, the much-ado-about-nothing world." [9]

The third view is that suffering is a chance and random happening. It knows no law, no rule. There is no knowing who will suffer and who will escape suffering. All we can do is take our chances. But this view goes against the very grain of reason and common sense and makes the human individual a victim of statistics. Science tells us that nothing in this universe happens by chance. Everything follows a law and is guided by a purpose. Our universe is a cosmos, not a chaos.

The fourth view maintains that all suffering is mental, caused by delusion, depression, and neurosis—all resulting from heredity and the environment and the lack of self-understanding and self-acceptance. But heredity and environment, although they play an important part in our lives, do not explain adequately the cause of suffering and the cause of inequality between one person and another. This view encourages the victims of suffering to look for scapegoats, blaming something or somebody for their suffering. But a resentful attitude doesn't solve the problem. We cannot solve life's problems except by solving them ourselves. Self-analysis and psychotherapy seek to plumb the depths of our psyche in order to unravel the cause of our suffering and eliminate it by self-understanding and self-acceptance, but they fail to tell us what is the exact nature of our self and precisely how we can eliminate the cause. The view that all sufferings have their roots in the mental level lacks a rational basis. Physical suffering is not always the outcome of mental ailments, nor do mental ailments always have their roots in the physical level. Again, mental sufferings, such as fear, grief, depression, and anxiety, cannot be cured by drug therapy, electric shock treatment, or other physical means, nor can physical sufferings, such as diseases and disabilities, be cured by psychotherapy. This view denies the moral and spiritual dimensions of a person and seeks an intellectual solution to the problem of suffering. But a person's mere intellectual understanding of a problem cannot free the person from that problem. The roots of neurosis and psychosis are not destroyed simply by intellectual understanding and analysis. A human individual is more than a body, emotions and impulses, a mind and intelligence; he or she is more than a product of heredity and environment. The core of the individual's true identity is his or her ever-pure spiritual self, a focus of the all-pervading Cosmic Self. No real solution is ever possible so long as this core is not taken into account and realized.

The fifth view is that suffering is good in disguise. Whatever happens, happens for our good. This view makes both good and evil apparent and not real. To see evil and suffer from it is an error of the human mind, because of its wrong attitude. Evil vanishes when seen with a right attitude. This view is a naive rationalization that looks upon the evil of suffering with a blind eye. We may try to deny or forget suffering and believe that we are fine, no matter how much we are suffering. It would be cruel and inhuman to tell a person who is suffering from mortal illness, permanent deformity, or chronic depression to accept such a condition as good in the guise of evil.

There is a sixth view, which says that no doubt the world we live in is plagued by evil and suffering in all their vicious forms, but this is the only world we have. The world is like an orange and we must squeeze the maximum amount of pleasure out of it. To give up present pleasure in the hope of future gain is unrealistic. The maxims of this view are: "Rather a pigeon today than a peacock tomorrow," "A sure piece of shell is better than a doubtful coin of gold," and "A bird in the hand is worth two in the bush." Those who hold to this view ultimately discover that there is nothing for them to hold on to. They are forced to swallow the bitter pill of suffering that they tried to avoid.

The seventh view attributes suffering either to the will, judgment, or retribution of God or to some external agency that challenges the authority of God, the embodiment of good. In Zoroastrianism, the principles of good and evil are constantly at war with each other. Evil, personified as Ahriman, is ultimately destroyed by the power of good and virtue, represented by Ahura Mazda. Some traditions regard evil as the vengeance of God. We hear of the covenant between God and Moses, and we understand from it that disobedience to God is the source of all evil. Christians believe that our suffering is due to the original sin of the first man, Adam. Only God's grace can absolve man from all sins and assure him eternal heaven, and the descent of grace calls for total self-surrender to God. In Hinduism there are various strata of beliefs regarding the causes of suffering—as God's will, delusion, karma, and desire. The essence of all these beliefs is the soul's fall from its divine nature. Buddhism personifies the cause of suffering as Mara, who tempts the soul with desire, and desire brings delusion. Life is a vale of tears, and the end of sorrow and suffering can come only in nirvana, which calls for waking up from dreaming dreams and desiring desires.

The seventh view seeks a transcendental solution to the problem of suffering, but there cannot be any transcendental solution to our earthly problems. No earthly pain and suffering can be compensated by readjustment after death.

The conventional views of different faiths leave many questions unanswered. Assuming that the world is the creation of an omnipotent, omniscient, and benevolent personal God, either he created evil or evil is due to our misuse of the free will given to us by him. If God is the creator of evil, then he is the most diabolical deity, the greatest criminal that ever existed. If he did not create evil, yet evil exists, then God is not omnipotent. Again, if it is a fact that God gave us free will, not knowing beforehand what use would be made of it, then God is not omniscient. Reason fails to explain what prompted the first man, created in the image of God, to disobey him. If suffering is the lot of a person for a few mistakes on earth in a brief span of life, does this not make a mockery of God's impartial love and justice for his created beings? If creation is God's *lila,* or sport, then God becomes most cruel, callous, insensitive, and malignant. One has to presume then that God created dictators who massacred millions, and filled the earth with disease and destruction. If it is karma that decides our destiny, then it makes God and his grace unnecessary. If our true nature is divine, how could we lose it? If the world of suffering is illusory, how can illusion come from Reality, unless Reality itself is an illusion? In vain philosophers search for appropriate answers to these questions. To quote the words of S. Radhakrishnan:

> Unable to believe that a good God could be responsible for the horrors of nature, Plato held that the goodness of God was made somewhat ineffective by the intractableness of nature which he tried in vain to control. The Gnostics strove to express the idea that God was trying to redeem a world created by the devil. Augustine from this worked out his view of "total depravity" and the scheme of salvation. Some still clung to the idea of the omnipotence of God by paying him the doubtful compliment, as J. S. Mill says, of making him the creator of the devil. Leibniz argues that even if this world is in many ways defective, it is the best of all possible worlds; but this implies an uncomplimentary reflection on the power of God. Hegelian absolutism is unable to account for the lapse of the perfect into the imperfect. Bergson emphasizes the conflict of matter and life in the world and believes that the two are the negative and positive phases of one primal consciousness, but he is not able to account for the rise of the two tendencies from the first principle. Croce arrives at the different forms of spirit, theoretical and practical, but he does not give us any metaphysical deduction of these forms from the one spirit. If the forms are all, then there is no Absolute, and if there is an Absolute, it seems to be a sort of dissolute Absolute.[10]

THE VEDANTA VIEW OF SUFFERING

Suffering, according to Vedanta, is not all physical. It has two other components—mental and spiritual. Physical suffering tears us apart with disease and disintegration. Mental suffering, in the forms of grief, anxiety, depression, and despair, breaks our mind apart. Spiritual suffering surrounds us with the menacing dark night of the soul, when we are tormented by doubt, hopelessness, and loss of faith. Spiritual suffering consumes the very soul.

No material compensation, comforts, and possessions can eradicate suffering. People in modern, affluent societies, despite all their amenities, are victims of depression, violence, and hopelessness. As we increase our capacity to enjoy, so also we increase our capacity to suffer. Yet everyone longs for enjoyment. Suffering, Vedanta asserts, is due neither to the will of God nor to the stars, chance, or luck. If suffering is evil, then evil is inextricably associated with its counterpart "good." If we accept the good, we must also accept the evil. Good and evil, light and darkness, pain and pleasure, birth and death, are pairs of opposites that move together. None of them is everlasting. To think of one without the other is absurdity. Good without evil, or pain without pleasure, or happiness without misery, or even income without income tax, is possible only in a fairy tale.

Both pain and pleasure contribute to our inner growth. The value of light can never be appreciated without the experience of darkness. Unmixed pleasure is neither possible nor desirable. It is not desirable because it could induce us to squander life. It is not possible because pain and pleasure go together. Pain is the price we pay for the most valued experiences of life, known as wisdom and maturity. Through experiences of pain and suffering we learn and grow. It is said that the crown of glory is made with thorns.

A person who has not suffered cannot understand the sufferings of others. One who has never gone through the sorrows and sufferings of life cannot understand the meaning of life. According to Vedanta, no suffering is entirely undeserved. We suffer because we are weak. We are weak because we are out of touch with Reality; when out of touch with Reality, we become lost in the world of dreams and delusions and make ourselves vulnerable to suffering. If the external world contributes fifty percent to our suffering, we contribute the other fifty percent. So Swami Vivekananda says:

> Weakness leads to all kinds of misery, physical and mental.
> Weakness is death. There are hundreds of thousands of microbes
> surrounding us, but they cannot harm us unless we become weak,
> until the body is ready and predisposed to receive them. There
> may be a million microbes of misery floating about us. Never

mind! They dare not approach us; they have no power to get a hold on us until the mind is weakened. This is the great fact.[11]

Again:

> From our childhood, all the time we have been trying to lay the blame upon something outside ourselves. We are always standing up to set right other people, and not ourselves. If we are miserable, we say, "Oh, the world is a devil's world." We curse others and say, "What ungrateful fools!" But why should we be in such a world if we really are so good?... We get only what we deserve. It is a lie to say that the world is bad and we are good. It can never be so. It is a terrible lie we tell ourselves.[12]

THE FIVE CAUSES OF SUFFERING

The causes of suffering, according to Vedanta, are our loss of contact with Reality, our inflated ego, deep attachment to the things we like, chronic aversion to the things we dislike, and stubborn clinging to life that does not let us move forward. Reality, according to Vedanta, has two faces—the absolute and the relative. The Absolute is that which is real for all time, while the relative is that which is real for a few days, a few months, or a few years. The relative appears real because it reflects the light of the Absolute.

Loss of contact with the Absolute gives rise to the ego and its world of fantasies, imaginations, and exaggerated self-concern. The role of ego is to soften the glare of the Absolute and create in its stead a world of dream, imagination, fancy, variety, and novelty, which make enjoyment possible.

Ego creates dreams, overstructuring, overdetermination, and endless fixations, drawing our psychic energy into fixed and rigid channels. Long ago Heraclitus wrote: "Those awake have one ordered universe in common, but in sleep every man turns away to one of his own."[13] So the Upanishads exhort: "Arise! Awake! Approach the great and learn."[14] Each person lives in his or her world of ego. Prompted by the gorging ego, we strive for the impossible—seeking unlimited self-gratification and unbridled self-assertion. In an imperfect world we look for perfection; within the bounds of mortal life we seek immortality; in the midst of uncertainties we seek certainty. Small wonder then that fatigue, frustration, and failure are the bitter fruits of egocentric living. The ignorant live in the world of ego that disclaims the rights of others, distorts the perception of Reality, and disturbs the harmony of life. The world of ego is highly polarized between good and evil, desirable and undesirable. Such divisions are value judgments of the deluded ego, guided by its calculus of "me and mine." The pairs of opposites, such as birth and death, pain and pleasure, belong to the ego and not to the soul. Ego is the connecting link between the past and the present, between one cycle of existence and another.

The ego's world is subject to the law of karma. Vedanta rejects the concept of fatalism and replaces it with the law of karma. Thoughts entertained, words spoken, and deeds done create karma, and our ego is the result of our karma. We suffer from or enjoy the results of our past karma. In his book *Self-Knowledge,* Swami Nikhilananda says:

> Through the law of karma the Vedic seers tried to explain the moral foundation of the universe according to which the righteous are rewarded and the wicked punished, in this life or hereafter, not by the whim of God but by their own action. The theory of rebirth is the necessary counterpart of the law of karma and the immortality of the soul. The soul, being eternal, cannot be annihilated with the death of the body. The idea of eternal reward or eternal punishment after death did not appeal to the minds of the gentle Hindus. It is disproportionate to the law of cause and effect to imagine that the actions of a short span of life, liable to error, should bear fruit that will last for eternity. The idea that the erring soul should not be given another chance to rectify its mistake seemed both unjust and unmerciful to the seers of the Vedas.[15]

Vedanta maintains that our physical and mental sufferings are mere symptoms of a deep-rooted spiritual malady—loss of contact with the Real—and so calls for a spiritual solution to the problem of suffering. A spiritual solution requires reestablishing our contact with the Ultimate Reality. When we are cut off from the Ultimate, the relative world becomes the ultimate. We become identified with our body. The body is material, merely a covering of the soul, subject to the relentless law of the sixfold change. Being identified with the body, we suffer the destiny of the body. We refuse to accept the changes that are universal, the laws of life that are natural and inevitable. We are like bad workmen who quarrel with their tools. The harsh realities of life are not tailored to our fanciful thoughts, aspirations, and goals. We ignore the fact that our real nature is divine, that our soul is a focus of the infinite Pure Consciousness, that the goal of life is to realize this, and that such realization alone can put an end to all our suffering. So Swami Vivekananda says:

> This feeling of "I and mine" causes the whole misery. With the sense of possession comes selfishness, and selfishness brings on misery. Every act of selfishness or thought of selfishness makes us attached to something, and immediately we are made slaves. Each wave in the *chitta* [mind-stuff] that says "I and mine" immediately puts a chain round us and makes us slaves; and the more we say "I and mine," the more the slavery grows, the more the misery increases.... Whenever we say a thing is ours, misery immediately comes. Do not say "my child" even in your mind. If you do, then will come misery. Do not say "my house," do not say "my body." The whole difficulty is there. The body is neither yours, nor mine, nor anybody's. These bodies are coming and going by the laws of nature, but the Soul is free, standing as the witness. This body is no more free than a picture or a wall. Why should we be attached so much to a body? Suppose somebody paints a picture; why should he be attached to it? He will have to part with it at death. Do not project that tentacle of selfishness, "I must possess it." As soon as that is done, misery will begin.[16]

According to Vedanta, the ego is of three kinds: infantile (*tamasika*), adolescent (*rajasika*), and mature (*sattvika*). The infantile ego is too weak to accept the burden of life. It is defensive, self-incriminating, and pessimistic. It has no self-identity or self-image and is always swayed by mass opinion. It tries to run away from the arena of life when the going gets tough, and it looks for hired help or vicarious solutions.

The adolescent ego is aggressive, unsteady, overly optimistic, self-aggrandizing, and domineering. Its credo is: "I am the center; the world is my circumference." The adolescent ego is temperamental and does not always know what it wants or does not want. All our gripes and woes are due to our immature ego. Both the *tamasika* and *rajasika* ego are cut off from Reality and therefore from clear vision. Both are obsessed with self-love. Both try to build elaborate fantasies in which to live, often to the total exclusion of Reality, and unconsciously court neurosis, in order to avoid the harsh facts of life. The more clearly we see Reality, the better equipped we are to deal with problems. Lack of clarity is certain to bring in its wake illusions, misconceptions, and wrong actions. Our view of Reality is like a map that helps us to negotiate the terrain of life. If the map is true and accurate, we will know where we are, what our goal is, and how to get there. If the map is false and inaccurate, we will certainly become lost.

The mature ego is integrated, purposeful, self-controlled, neither aggressive nor defensive, realistic as opposed to pessimistic or optimistic, temperate in everything, and free from dependency. It is endowed with a sense of identity, a sense of reality, a sense of responsibility, a sense of adjustment to changes, and a sense of duty. Vedanta asks us to make the ego strong and mature so that the burden of life will be light. Only a strong ego can bear the normal stresses and strains of life. A strong ego—a measured and mature ego—is less ego.

However, the path to maturity is a graduated one. The infantile ego must pass through the stage of adolescence in order to reach maturity. The ego's boundaries must first be defined and then hardened before they can be softened. Renunciation of ego must be preceded by development of ego. Maturity of ego cannot be achieved vicariously or miraculously. No amount of theoretical knowledge can help us in this regard. Ego maturity calls for mature living, for taking risks and making mistakes and following the guidelines of mature values and actions, leading to a mature goal.

All the sufferings of life are created by the adolescent ego and the infantile ego. The adolescent ego is immature, immoderate, restless, and intoxicated with ambition, attachment, and desire. The infantile ego is weak, blinded by delusion, and driven by impulse and indiscrimination. In his message to Uddhava, Sri Krishna describes the traits of an adolescent ego: "desire, activity, pride, covetousness, haughtiness, praying for comforts, seeing of difference, sense-pleasure, a militant disposition due to pride, love of fame, making fun, display of powers, and aggressive enterprise."[17] The characteristics of an infantile ego, Sri Krishna says, are "anger, greed, falsehood, cruelty, begging, simulation of piety, fatigue, quarrel, grief, infatuation, dejection, a miserable feeling, sleep, expectation, and inertia."[18]

Swami Vivekananda pointedly describes how our immature ego brings all the miseries of life:

That is the one cause of misery: we are attached, we are being caught. Therefore says the Gita: Work constantly; work but be not attached, be not caught. Reserve unto yourself the power of detaching yourself from everything, however beloved, however much the soul might yearn for it; no matter how great the pangs of misery you would feel if you were going to leave it, still reserve the power of leaving it whenever you want. The weak have no place here, in this life or in any other life. Weakness leads to slavery.... Strength is life; weakness is death. Strength is felicity, life eternal, immortal; weakness is constant strain and misery; weakness is death.

Attachment is the source of all our pleasures now. We are attached to our friends, to our relatives; we are attached to our intellectual and spiritual work; we are attached to external objects; and so we get pleasure from them. What, again, brings misery but this very attachment? We have to detach ourselves to earn joy. If only we had the power to detach ourselves at will, there would not be any misery. That man alone will be able to get the best of nature who, having the power to attach himself to a thing with all his energy, has also the power to detach himself when he should do so. But it is difficult to cultivate an equal power of attachment and detachment. There are men who are never attracted by anything: they can never love; they are hard-hearted and apathetic; and they escape most of the miseries of life. But a wall never feels misery; a wall never loves, is never hurt; yet it is a wall, after all. Surely it is better to be attached and caught than to be a wall. Therefore the man who never loves, who is hard and stony, escaping most of the miseries of life, escapes also its joys. We do not want that. That is weakness; that is death. That soul has not been awakened that never feels attachment, never feels misery; that is a callous state. We do not want that.[19]

We must learn that nothing can happen to us unless we make ourselves susceptible to it.... No disease can come to me until the body is ready; it does not depend alone on the germs, but upon a certain predisposition which is already in the body. We get only that for which we are fitted. Let us give up our pride and understand this: that misery never is undeserved. There never has been a blow undeserved; there never has been an evil for which I did not pave the way with my own hands. We ought to know that. Analyse yourselves and you will find that every blow you have received came to you because you prepared yourselves for it. You did half and the external world did the other half: that is how the blow came. That will sober us down. At the same time, from this very analysis will come a note of hope, and the note of hope is this: "I have no control over the external world; but that which is in me and nearer unto me, my own world, is under my control. If the two together are required to make a failure, if the two together are necessary to give me a blow, I will not contribute the one which is in my control—and how then can the blow come? If I get real control of myself, the blow will never come."[20]

The *Panchadasi* gives graphic examples of how attachment masquerades as love:

A child when kissed by its father may cry with pain caused by the pricking of his stubbly beard. The father continues kissing the child, not for the child's sake but for his own.... Against its own will, a bullock is compelled to carry a heavy load by a merchant. He loads it for his own sake and not for that of the bullock.[21]

Sri Shankaracharya says in his *Vivekachudamani:*

Know that it is egoism which, identifying itself with the body, becomes the doer or experiencer, and in conjunction with the gunas such as *sattva*, assumes the three different states [waking, dream, dreamless sleep]. When sense-objects are favourable it becomes happy and it becomes miserable when the case is contrary. So happiness and misery are characteristics of egoism, and not of the ever-blissful Atman.[22]

In the words of Sri Ramakrishna:

This egotism has covered everything like a veil. "All troubles come to an end when the ego dies." If by the grace of God a man but once realizes that he is not the doer, then he at once becomes a *jivanmukta*. Though living in the body he is liberated. He has nothing else to fear.[23]

The attachment of the infantile ego is toward indolence, inadvertence, and delusion, and that of the adolescent ego toward greed, indiscriminate activity, enterprise, unrest, and endless longing. The immature ego is beset with innumerable cares, unbridled hankering for self-gratification, and a hundred ties of hope and is bewildered by many fancies. The characteristics of the mature ego are balance, enlightenment, and freedom from anxiety and dependence, attachment and aversion. Vedanta asks for maturing our ego to face the sufferings of life.

PRINCIPLES OF MATURE LIVING

Mature living calls for achieving perfection in the four aspects of our self-development—physical, mental, moral, and spiritual. They represent the four kinds of fitness needed by a human individual to overcome unavoidable ills and succeed in any walk of life. The first aspect of self-development is physical fitness. It is said that a strong body obeys and a weak body commands. Mastery over the body is the first step toward mastery over the mind.

The second aspect is the control of the mind. Mind, when controlled, is our best friend and, when left uncontrolled, becomes our worst enemy. One who has no control over his or her mind has neither peace nor happiness. A weak mind engenders low self-esteem, lack of judgment, morbid sentimentalism, and confused thinking. Fitness of the mind is achieved by exercising control over our urges and impulses, with the help of reason and discrimination. Mental fitness teaches us not to be bullied by the sway of passions and the pressures of circumstances. It prevents us from wallowing in self-pity and self-indulgence and from giving in to blind, raw impulses. It urges us to hear the bell of reason and moderation. Through mental maturity, passion evolves into compassion and selfish attachment into unselfish love.

The third aspect of self-development is moral perfection. By cultivation of moral consciousness, an individual expands his personality and becomes truly human. Moral consciousness dictates concern for all things in all actions. It inspires the individual to feel for others and share their joys and sorrows. Morality is the backbone of spirituality. It teaches us that what is pleasant is not necessarily good.

Moral consciousness reaches its highest fulfillment in the spiritual, which is the fourth aspect of self-development. Morality without spirituality is incomplete. Why should a person be moral and do good to others? The answer "duty for duty's sake" is barren and unconvincing. The true answer is that the Self that dwells in all of us is the same. By doing good to others, we do good to ourselves. Finally, human individuals are essentially spirit; that is our true identity. Through spiritual education we find a connection with the cosmos and realize our rootedness in the eternal. We discover that all existence is one. Rising above self-love and self-concern, we realize our unity with all, and in this unity we find our ultimate fulfillment.

Mature living of Vedanta asks us to master problems and not weep and wail in despondency, waiting for a miracle to happen or a millennium to come. It asks us to face the law of karma with the karma of self-discipline and self-control. It teaches us to accept the fact that life and its problem of suffering go together. In the spirit of Vedanta, Swami Vivekananda says:

> Cry to all the gods in the universe. I cried for years, and in the end I received help. But the help came from within myself; and I had to undo what I had done by mistake. That is the only way. I had to cut the net which I had thrown round myself; and the power to do this is within. Of this I am certain: that not one aspiration in my life, well guided or ill guided, has been in vain, but I am the resultant of all my past, both good and evil. I have committed many mistakes in my life, but mark you, I am sure that without every one of those mistakes, I should not be what I am today; and so I am quite satisfied to have made them. I do not mean that you are to go home and willfully commit mistakes; do not misunderstand me in that way. But do not mope because of the mistakes you have committed, but know that in the end all will come out straight. It cannot be otherwise, because goodness is our nature, purity is our nature, and that nature can never be destroyed. Our essential nature always remains the same.

What we must understand is that what we call mistakes, or evil, we commit because we are weak, and we are weak because we are ignorant. I prefer to call them mistakes. The word *sin*, although originally a very good word, has a certain flavor about it that frightens me. Who makes us ignorant? We ourselves. We put our hands over our eyes and weep because it is dark. Take the hands away and there is light; the light exists always for us, the self-effulgent nature of the human soul. Do you not hear what your modern scientific men say? What is the cause of evolution? Desire. The animal wants to do something, but does not find the environment favourable and therefore develops a new body. Who develops it? The animal itself—its will. You have developed from the lowest amoeba. Continue to exercise your will and it will take you higher still. The will is almighty. If it is almighty, you may say, why can I not do everything I like? But you are thinking only of your little self. Look back on yourselves from the state of the amoeba to the human being. Who made all that? Your own will. Can you deny, then, that will is almighty? That which has made you come up so high can make you go higher still. What you want is character, strengthening of the will.[24]

Vedanta describes life as a vast ocean, one shore of which is known and the other shore unknown. The ocean has swift currents, countless whirlpools, high winds, and bottomless depth. The individual's life is like a boat on that ocean. To live is to cross this ocean of life. Some feel frightened at the prospect of having to cross the ocean, and become hopeless; they never succeed in crossing. Others look for a hired hand to take them across; they never find such a person and thus miss the opportunity of crossing. Yet others wait for the winds, whirlpools, and currents to subside so that they may cross the ocean easily; they are disappointed to discover that the ocean does not, and will not, change its nature. Still others rush to cross without any preparation; they are carried away by the currents and get drowned. So Vedanta advises us to learn about the nature of the ocean and master the methods of crossing it. We must learn the rules of navigation, because there is no alternative to it.

Mature living asks us to face the changes of life by falling back upon that which is changeless in us. Vedanta maintains that each moment we live, each moment we die: living is dying. The death wish (Thanatos) is rooted in the life wish (Eros). Fear of death is the originator of all fear. To try to ignore death is to live in false optimism, to avoid it is not possible, and to try to escape it is to be haunted by it. To Vedanta, death is merely one of the changes of life; it makes life possible. Every day we die in a measured way in sleep, and we learn to die temporarily in our meditation.

Immortality does not mean going to a far-off heaven or gaining something new; it is the knowledge of our true Self. The Bhagavad Gita tells us that one who has no contact with this Self has no peace, and one without peace has no happiness (2.66). This Self cannot be ignored or bypassed. Those who try to do so only confront the Self as birth and death, fear and frustration, suffering and anxiety. Only Self-knowledge can rob death of its terrifying reality.

So Vedanta says, why cry over the impossible; why try to reach out for the unnatural; why strive for absolute freedom when, as a finite being, one's freedom is limited? Why assume absolute responsibility for events and circumstances, such as birth and death, over which you have no control; why shed tears over limitations and changes that are natural, universal, and inescapable?

Self-knowledge is the affirmation of our Self, the focus of the all-pervading Self of the universe. Self-knowledge is seeing all beings and things in our own Self and perceiving our Self in all. The real solution to the problem of suffering is to be found at the spiritual core of our existence. Socrates defines man as a "philosophical animal"; Plato, as a "political animal"; and Aristotle, as a "rational animal"; but Vedanta defines the human as a "spiritual being." To ignore this core is the shortest and surest way to doom and destruction. Those who deny this Self confront it as sorrow, pain, and suffering at every point of their life. Mature living is marked by self-control, self-regulation, and self-assertion. It is controlling the lower self, which is the mind, by asserting our higher Self, which is our spiritual identity. Delusions and attachments of mind are the causes of all our suffering, and the mind never becomes controlled unless we control it.

Mature living is tempered by dispassion. Dispassion is the opposite of infantilism. A sick mind is too much in love with itself. Dispassion is not a pathological lack of interest in life. Dispassion sets the tone of our response to the continuous challenges of attractions and repulsions, helping us to remain neutral by rising above polarity. It is the only way of dealing successfully with our inner urges. Our body grows in strength by bearing with the physical intensities; our mind too grows in health by exercising control over the emotional intensities. Dispassion is distancing our true Self from the hormonal changes in our glands and remaining calm. A dose of dispassion is necessary to effect a balance in our personality, now tilted toward overly desiring and now toward despairing. Attachment so often takes a severe emotional toll on our vitality, depletes our mental strength, and drains our psychic energy. Dispassion as a therapy preserves our mental strength. It teaches us not to accumulate that which we cannot take with us and not to be possessive about things.

The word *dispassion* often sounds passive, callous, and unfeeling; yet it is just the opposite. Seen through the color of attachment, the words "I love you" mean "I need you." Seen through the spirit of dispassion, the words "I need you" mean "I love you." Dispassion is an endeavor to pierce the barriers of emotional and social conditioning and then to examine the very ground-conceptions of our life and our worldview—their absoluteness, sacrosanctness, and infallibility. We learn by practicing dispassion that our will is not absolutely free, that we cannot have everything we want, and that our self-effort alone is helpless to achieve anything without the intervention of what the Bhagavad Gita calls destiny.

Mature living follows the middle of the road in everything. Too much of anything is bad. Excessive emotional involvement causes distorted vision of the realities of life, makes us prisoners of our passions and delusions, and causes wear and tear of life beyond the normal limit. Driven by passion and emotion, we do not act but react. We try to do *the* best instead of *our* best. But our mind cannot be brought under control all of a sudden. Human nature cannot be hurried. So, in the context of yoga, or our contact with the Real, the Bhagavad Gita advises moderation in all matters:

> Yoga is not for him who eats too much nor for him who eats too little. It is not for him, O Arjuna, who sleeps too much nor for him who sleeps too little. For him who is temperate in his food and recreation, temperate in his exertion at work, temperate in sleep and waking, yoga puts an end to all sorrows.... Renouncing entirely all the desires born of the will, drawing back the senses from every direction by strength of mind, let a man little by little attain tranquillity with the help of the *buddhi* [discriminating faculty] armed with fortitude.[25]

Mature living is free from dependencies. Most of the time we suffer from our dependencies—physical, mental, and spiritual. We become sick when we become weak in our physical immunity. We suffer from agony, despair, and sorrow because of our mental weakness and lack of mental immunity. We feel lost in moments of spiritual doubt when we lose our spiritual immunity. A Sanskrit verse says that nondependence is happiness and dependence is misery. Mature living asks us to develop all three kinds of immunity: physical immunity against physical suffering, mental immunity against mental suffering, and spiritual immunity against spiritual suffering.

In brief, mature living is free and full living. It is living in all our dimensions —physical, emotional, intellectual, moral, and spiritual. It is not the pleasure-fearing slogan of otherworldly asceticism. Neither is it the inertia-loving credo of the escapists nor the chaotic living of the compulsive self-indulgent. Mature living is grounded on self-perception, nurtured by self-control and self-discipline, and expressed as self-dedication, love, and compassion. It is living in the world of reality—not in the dreams and fantasies of our ego. It is living in a big way for a big goal and moving in big steps. A practitioner of mature living first deserves, then desires, and neither broods over the past nor dreams about the future, and acts only on the living present.

VEDANTA'S CALL FOR A SPIRITUAL SOLUTION

Approaches such as the material, psychological, and humanistic no doubt alleviate suffering to some extent, but they are not lasting solutions. The sick and hungry will again be sick and hungry. These approaches act more as Band-Aids than as cures for the wounds caused by suffering. Fulfillment of desires does not ensure health and happiness. Desires are ever multiplying, and life is short. Suffering is individual. Individually we are born and we die, and individually we suffer. No amount of material improvement, psychological adjustment, or social change can put an end to the suffering of an individual until and unless his or her life is transformed. Material life is never secure without a moral basis, and moral life is unsteady without a spiritual basis. Secular morality without spiritual sanction does not inspire us to pursue higher values in the face of opposition. True humanism is more than altruism. It is always spiritual and is based on the realization of the fundamental oneness of reality.

As a real solution to the problem of suffering, Vedanta points to the spiritual. A spiritual solution does not mean blind submission to or acceptance of some earthly or extracosmic heavenly authority; it endows us with the greatest strength, not the greatest powerlessness. Those who regard a spiritual solution as useless should remember the words of Jesus: "The Kingdom of God is within you" (Luke 17:21). This Self-realization is the very goal of all ethical and moral codes of life. No facet of human life is divorced from the goal of Self-realization. Matter serves only as a medium for attaining Self-knowledge, but the materialist who claims that the Self is nothing more than physical and cerebral changes is wrong. If progress involves an ideal to be realized, it is Self-knowledge. Only through Self-knowledge can one overcome the limitations of materialism, humanism, rigid dualism, and abstract monism. The urge for Self-realization is the strongest of all urges. This spiritual urge is neither accidental nor adventitious. Vedanta maintains that our addiction to illusory enjoyments is due to our loss of contact with the reality of the Self within us. Vedanta rejects the view that the human brain is an appendage of the genital gland.

The sufferings of life, such as fear, bereavement, humiliation, disease, despondency, and so forth, are only symptoms of a deep-rooted malady that is spiritual—loss of contact with the Real. Human beings suffer more from the abuse of power and the misuse of freedom than from the lack of them. Material fulfillment, being devoid of spiritual insight, can only create insatiable sense desire, unending delusion, and endless suffering. The solution to suffering cannot come simply by the readjustment of the conditions of material and psychological life. According to science, a human individual is a risen animal, but according to Vedanta, the human being is a fallen spirit. We have no rest, no peace, no certainty, no end of sorrow, until we know our real nature, our luminous self, the focus of the all-pervading Self, the Self that connects us with the vast cosmos and its myriad beings and things. Self-knowledge is the rich harvest of spiritual living. An incident from the life of Buddha illustrates this point:

> Bharadvaja, a wealthy Brahman [Brahmin], was celebrating his harvest-thanksgiving when the Blessed One came with his alms-bowl, begging for food.
>
> Some of the people paid him reverence, but the Brahman was angry and said: "O shramana, it would suit you better to go to

work than to go begging. I plough and sow, and having ploughed and sown, I eat. If you did likewise, you, too, would eat."

And the Tathagata answered him and said: "O Brahman, I, too, plough and sow, and having ploughed and sown, I eat."

"Do you profess to be a husbandsman?" replied the Brahman. "Where, then, are your bullocks? Where is the seed and the plough?"

The Blessed One said: "Faith is the seed I sow: good works are the rain that fertilizes it; wisdom and modesty are the plough; my mind is the guiding-rein; I lay hold of the handle of the law; earnestness is the goad I use, and exertion is my draught-ox. This ploughing is ploughed to destroy the weeds of illusion. The harvest it yields is the immortal fruit of Nirvana, and thus all sorrow ends."[26]

Only a knower of Self goes beyond all pain and pleasure. As the *Katha Upanishad* says: "The wise man, having realized Atman as dwelling within impermanent bodies but Itself bodiless, vast, and all-pervading, does not grieve."[27] Such souls are called free souls. They live in a world of diversity, yet they are unruffled by the pairs of opposites. They regard all beings and things with an eye of equality. Physical birth and death have no meaning for them, the change of body being for them like a change of garments or like going from one room to another. Their compassion for living beings is without bounds. Free from attachment and delusion, they enjoy material objects but never forget their divine Self. They truly demonstrate the virtue of sharing the pain and suffering of others. They truly feel and therefore they can truly heal. The burden of suffering is very heavy, but when free souls completely identify with the suffering person and are able to feel that suffering as their own, the burden of the sufferer becomes lighter. This sharing of the pain and suffering of others, and the self-sacrifice required for that purpose, make the knowers of Self great exemplars of truth.

So Vedanta's exhortations are: If you want happiness, reduce your dependencies. If you want joy, reduce your desires. If you want peace, reduce your ego. If you want security, keep the instincts of sex and palate under control. If you hope for the best, be prepared for the worst. Face the fact that there is no life without suffering. Face the problems by overcoming them. Face the changes of life by falling back on the changeless. Face death by knowing the deathless in yourself; face the uncertainties of life by making them a part of your life. Face the past by acting on the living present. Face the nightmares by waking up. Face the sufferings by developing immunity against them.

Fear of Old Age

The saint-poet Bhartrihari describes old age in the following words:

> Pleasure has no longer any attraction for us; the world no longer respects us: our contemporaries have died away one by one; the friends whom we love as we love ourselves will shortly follow: we hobble along leaning on a stick, and our eyes gradually become dim. Alas! these are signs that our body has been subdued, and that it is trembling at the approach of death.... My face is wrinkled and my hair turning grey; my limbs are weak, and only desire is strong within me.[28]

The description is no exaggeration of a pessimist or a life-denying ascetic. The harsh reality of old age cannot be rationalized or ignored in any way. Old age follows the law of biology: that which is born will one day decline and die. None can escape this inexorable law. The weakening of the body, failing memory, slow withdrawal of life, a sense of restriction, and a form of diminution of personality make old age unbearable. People who have always been too socially oriented and outgoing suddenly wake up one day in old age to discover their diminished social usefulness. Their children do not need them so much any more. The younger generations do not covet their company. Every now and then they are reminded that they are old-fashioned and out of touch with the times. They begin to feel fear: fear of being unwanted and unloved, fear of being ill and dependent, and fear of being a burden and a botheration to others.

It may be that there are elderly achievers who continue to be brilliant, active, and innovative and who move with confident strides. But they are exceptions to the general rule. For the vast majority, old age is a downward slope marked by steady physical and mental decline. As old age sets in, people begin to lose ambition and enthusiasm. They begin losing friends to death, distance, or neglect. People in old age tend to look backward and remember "the good old days," as if all things in the past were good. They often invoke their age to claim their so-called wisdom about things. Because of the weakening of the control mechanisms of the mind, their faults, well disguised in earlier years, become increasingly evident. Unfulfilled desires make them jealous of young people who are still in the prime of their life, striving and fighting for recognition, success, and pleasure. To them, the young are busy indulging in wild dreams and are too immature to understand the meaning of life. They look upon anything new with suspicion. Living in the world of their old memories, the present and fast-changing world appears foreign to them.

We all know that old age is inescapable, yet we refuse to accept it. We do not want to think of it. We try to forget it or ignore it. Our present-day society has created and promoted a youth culture that denies old age. Jokes are made at the expense of old people. The elderly never call themselves old, preferring euphemisms such as "senior citizens" or "citizens of longer living." But old age refuses to reverse its course. To say that it is the greatest time to be old, or old age is the best time of life—the golden years—does not make things much better.

We are constantly searching for a magic cure for the malady of old age. Haunted by the specter of old age, millions are taking recourse to drug therapy, diet therapy, gene therapy, various physical exercises, stress management, hair coloring, hair implantation, and a hundred other ways to maintain their youthful appearance. Billions of dollars are being spent by the cosmetics industry in search of products and ways to hide at least the outward signs of aging. The vast dependence on plastic surgery in the United States to hide the signs of aging is the sharpest index of our anxiety. Jere Daniel, author of "Society Fears Aging" in *An Aging Population*, points out: "In just two decades, from the 1960s to the 1980s, the number of wrinkle-removing face-lifts rose from 60,000 to an estimated 2 million a year at an annual cost of $10 billion."[29] But all our efforts to stop the advance of old age by material and psychological means prove futile. Eventually the lifted face falls again, implanted hair refuses to grow, physical exercises become too difficult, and stress becomes unmanageable. Drug therapy fails, and makeup can no longer hide the advancing signs of old age. At last we succumb and grudgingly accept the inevitable, moaning, crying, and cursing our fate.

Many people get extremely panicky when they begin to see the signs of old age. In their earlier years, they never stopped to think of this inevitability, and now they are emotionally unprepared to accept the fact. They become fearful and depressed. The prospect of loneliness often accompanies the process of aging. Unable to bear this loneliness, some commit suicide, and many others clamor for the right to die rather than be forced to live with the indignities and hopelessness of old age.

Old age has become a widespread social problem in our time. Improvement in diet, technology, and medicine has increased the longevity of people. The U.S. Census Bureau anticipates that sixty-two million people, or almost one in five Americans, will be age sixty-five or older by 2025,[30] and that number will continue to rise as the years go by. Leaders and thinkers are struggling to find a solution for the "problem of old age." There is a growing sentiment that perhaps old people can be dispensed with. Abandoning an old grandfather with Alzheimer's disease in a park has already become news. Caring for the elderly is increasingly becoming seen as a threat to the younger generation and a challenge for the society. Where money is the measure of everything, the elderly are looked upon as an economic liability and a social burden. There are some in the United States who advocate the idea that it is the duty of the elderly to die. They say: "It is a moral responsibility to make room for the young. As leaves fall from the trees in the fall, so old people have a duty to die…. To have reached the age of, say, 75 or 80 years without being ready to die is itself a moral failing, the sign of a life out of touch with life's basic realities."[31] As the aging population continues to expand and more dollars are spent on health care costs that are disproportionately utilized by older persons, the need for budget cutting, health care rationing, and redistribution of health and other resources becomes more pressing. When older adults are viewed as an emotional and financial burden to be borne by the younger members of society, cries for the right to die and legalized assisted suicide grow louder.

THE GUIDELINES OF VEDANTA

Vedanta maintains that sorrowing over old age does not make it any better. To deny it is artificial, and attempts to escape it are futile. Vedanta asks us to wake up to this reality and face it and presents the following guidelines:

Make old age a part of life. Old age is one of the natural phases of life. Those who would attempt to avoid old age must be ready to die young. Those who try to forget it will be taken by surprise when it comes. Acceptance of the fact and preparing for it beforehand is the wisest counsel. There is no need to imitate the ways of younger people. As Carl Jung pointed out, "For the most part our old people try to compete with the young. In the United States it is almost an ideal for the father to be the brother of his sons, and for the mother if possible to be the younger sister of her daughter."[32] The realities of life are not tailored to our wishful thinking and imagination. We may aspire to boundless promise and glory yet must accept life with all its inherent problems and anxieties.

Anxiety is part of life, and it cannot be eliminated altogether. The reasons for anxiety are our attachments, feelings of possessiveness, and fear of the uncertainties of life. We make plans for the future and hope for the best, even when we know that our plans may not work and our hopes may not materialize. We strive for the impossible and want to attain the unattainable. We refuse to accept the changing conditions that are natural and inevitable and pay dearly through our pain, anxiety, and suffering. Youth and old age, like pleasure and pain, birth and death, light and darkness, are inseparable companions. To think of having one without the other is infantile and absurd. Yet people have wanted the one without the other for thousands of years and have invariably been disappointed. It is said that Cleopatra bathed in asses' milk to stay young and beautiful but did not live long enough to find out if it worked. The Spanish explorer Juan Ponce de León searched for the fountain of youth but never found the legendary spring and finally died from a poisoned arrow.

Know that old age is no less meaningful than youth. Youth is generally admired for its beauty, optimism, enthusiasm, spirit of adventure, and forward-looking imagination, but it often suffers from indiscretion, restlessness, instability, anxiety, and depression. Old age may bring many physical problems and limitations to a person, but it endows him or her with the mature wisdom that comes from the experiences of life. This voice of wisdom tells us that optimism without realism brings disappointment; enthusiasm without control is prone to blunders; and an unbridled adventurous spirit can lead us into endless difficulties. External beauty is skin-deep and short-lived; it is of little value without the internal beauty that comes with maturity and wisdom. In old age a person becomes a truth teller, liberated from the haunting desire and dream of being a superman or superwoman. The person becomes more integrated, whole and self-satisfied. All the earlier stages of life find their fulfillment in this wisdom of old age.

Those who think that they can acquire this wisdom ready-made by reading books, or by finding someone who can give it to them, are only courting disappointment. Wisdom must be earned by living life through all its stages, and there is no such thing as vicarious living. By locking ourselves into an obsession with youth, we can only develop fear, anger, and frustration. There are only two ways to face the reality of old age: one is to deny old age and indulge in fantasy and make-believe and in so doing grow old unhappily; the other is to accept advancing age as the fitting transformation of youth and thereby to grow in wisdom, serenity, and authenticity.

Practice nonattachment. Attachment is a form of mental fixation. When a person dwells on anything repeatedly, he or she develops a liking for that thing, and eventually the desire to possess the thing. Any obstacle that gets in the way results in anger. From anger comes delusion, and from delusion loss of discrimination and right judgment. Failure of discrimination and right judgment brings about moral decline and destruction. Thus the Bhagavad Gita asks us not to get attached to things that are fleeting and changeable and that will not accompany us after death. Attachment prevents us from seeing things as they really are. With every attachment there arises a corresponding fear—the fear of losing what we cling to. This fear in turn intensifies the anxiety of the ego, which then seeks to sustain itself by another attachment, and thus our entanglement never ends.

As discussed in the context of suffering, Vedanta tells us that all miseries stem from five causes: loss of contact with Reality, ego and its possessiveness, attachment, aversion, and clinging to life. Reality has two faces: the Absolute and the relative. Absolute Reality is that which is real for all time, while relative reality is that which is real for a limited period of time. When we ignore the Absolute, the world of relative reality becomes delusive and destructive. By reestablishing our contact with the Absolute, we eventually overcome all fear, anxiety, despair, and disappointment, all of which result from attachment. Nonattachment is not being cold, insensitive, and indifferent toward others. It is transferring our attachment to some higher ideal or cause. Practice of nonattachment becomes easy for seekers of God. Such people make God the center of their life, divert all their love and attachment to him, and shower their love on all equally, seeing the reflection of God in them. Those who are not able to do this are advised to practice love and compassion for all beings as the moral duty of a humanist.

Practice nondependence. As people get old, they begin to become dependent on others for support and care, and this causes them to have fear and anxiety for their future. "Who will look after me when I become old and cannot function or work?" is a universal concern of the elderly. Consciously or unconsciously, they live in fear of being neglected, forgotten, and abandoned by their family members and friends.

Vedanta asks us to practice nondependence in all matters. The wisdom of Vedanta says that all dependence breeds misery, while nondependence alone is happiness. Practice of nondependence from an early age makes one less vulnerable to fear and anxiety in the final stage of life. Nondependence has two aspects: physical and mental. Physical nondependence calls for maintaining good health by following the laws of health: diet, exercise, conservation, relaxation, and moderation. Our body, when neglected, abused, or defiled, becomes a burden and a cause of worry in old age. Another component of physical nondependence is material nondependence, without which a person is forced to live on the charity of others. It is the duty of parents to make material provision for their family and for themselves so that in old age they will not be at the mercy of others or even dependent on them for favors.

The other aspect of nondependence is mental. Mental dependence takes the form of emotional dependence on friends, relatives, people, and things. Humans perceive the world through the eye of emotions. Their actions and reactions are guided by emotions. They are bound together by the tie of emotions. Emotion is the vehicle of self-expression, one of the basic urges of human life. When people cannot express their feelings of love, affection, and sympathy, they feel suffocated and live a miserable life. They are heavily dependent on receiving emotional satisfaction from others. Emotional dependence becomes acute when they get old. As in the case of the practice of nonattachment, practice of emotional nondependence calls for transferring our dependence to God, knowing that God alone loves us and cares for us. Prophets and saints tell us that it is a mistake to expect any support from the human world. Human love is mostly guided by selfish motives, and dependence on such love brings nothing but disappointment. The more we are able to depend on God, the less will be our dependence on others. Dependence on God, however, does not come by itself. This requires deepening our God-consciousness by practicing prayer, meditation, and dispassion. Those who are not inclined to follow these practices are advised to develop nondependence through the practice of reading, writing, painting, playing music, or any other emotionally satisfying occupation.

Even world-renouncing monks and ascetics are advised to practice non-dependence. The laws of physical decay and disintegration are universal, and they do not exempt anyone. When the body gets old and begins to break down, it drags the mind down to the physical level. A weak or sick body demands more attention of the mind. Practice of prayer and meditation becomes difficult even for a monk when his body is taken over by the inevitable ailments of old age. Small wonder then that in old age even a monk may begin to feel the chill of dependence. Unless his self-surrender to God is unshakable and his faith in God's caring hands is unwavering, he becomes fearful in old age. Instructing a monk, Swami Saradananda, a direct disciple of Sri Ramakrishna, said:

> It is good to be active, but it depends on several factors. Your health must be good and you must be able to get along with fellow-workers. But suppose you have injured one of your limbs; then it would be difficult for you to work. Therefore I request you to cultivate the habit of reading. Even that is not enough. Suppose you become blind. Therefore it is good that you also practice meditation so that if you cannot read or work, at least you can meditate.[33]

Activity should not be the sole spiritual preoccupation of a monk. He should keep up the habit of intense study of holy texts and the practice of meditation, so that when he is no longer able to be in the field of action, he can be totally nondependent and spend his old age in study and in contemplation of the Divine. The goal of a monk is to be a monk, not to become an administrator, a preacher, a lecturer, or a scholar, but to be a man of God, and in his journey to that goal he is alone with his absolute dependence on God. For a monk who forgets these facts, old age brings not enlightenment but disappointment, frustration, and fear.

Do your duties and do your best. Vedanta says that life is interdependent, not independent. Our individual life is sustained by receiving support from others. Our body is reproduced from the parental cells. Our food is gathered from the vegetable and animal worlds. Our individual mind-stuff is derived from the cosmic source. Many have to suffer and many have to die to keep us alive. The human, superhuman, and subhuman worlds are bound together by a tie of spiritual unity. Therefore we have duties to others: duties to God the Creator and the sages, to fellow human beings, to the vegetable and animal worlds, to parents, and to departed ancestors. By doing our duties, we recognize that bond of spiritual unity and overcome our selfishness and greed and attain to peace and tranquillity. Receiving and giving are the two aspects of living. When we were born, we received help from others for our growth, support, and development. When we grow up, we are expected to repay our indebtedness to others by doing our duties to the best of our ability. Those who do not or cannot repay are forced to live a miserable and demeaning life, and their old age is haunted by feelings of self-defeat and unworthiness.

Contribute to the welfare of others. One of the cardinal teachings of Vedanta is that all existence is one: there is one Self that lives in all; there is one life that pulsates in the whole universe. Each individual is like a leaf of a huge tree. Leaves grow and fall, but the tree continues to exist. When we ignore the fact of oneness, our individual existence becomes separative and delusive. Because of the oneness of existence, our individual welfare depends upon the welfare of the totality. Thus by doing good to others, we really do good to ourselves. We experience the joy of self-expansion. Swami Vivekananda says: "They alone live who live for others, the rest are more dead than alive."[34] Self-sacrifice for the good of others is the highest virtue. The Bhagavad Gita designates this virtue as the greatest *dharma:* "In this [selfless action] no effort is ever lost and no harm is ever done. Even very little of this dharma saves a man from the Great Fear."[35] There is an ancient wisdom that says: "Since death is certain for the body, let this body be used for the good of others." According to the Bhagavad Gita, the doer of good is the best among the yogis: "Him I hold to be the supreme yogi, O Arjuna, who looks upon the pleasure and pain of all beings as he looks on them in himself."[36] Further, the Bhagavad Gita says: "O Partha, there is no destruction for him either in this world or the next: no evil, My son, befalls a man who does good."[37] Our selfless actions for the good of others help us break down the walls of our separative existence, and bring us in contact with our ageless true Self. This contact with our true Self puts an end to all our sorrows and sufferings.

Develop self-awareness. Vedanta reminds us again and again that our true identity is our ageless spiritual Self, the essence of our being and the consciousness of consciousness. This Self uses the body for gathering experiences. While the body, being material, undergoes change, the Self remains unchanged. Science has proved that human organs are interchangeable and replaceable. The physical body is produced by the combination of gross elements. Dependent upon food for its existence, the body endures as long as it can assimilate nourishment. Nonexistent before birth and after death, it lasts only for a short interval between birth and death. One continues to live even after particular parts of the body have been destroyed. The body is no more to us than what an automobile is to its owner. The ignorant identify themselves with the body; the book-learned consider themselves a combination of body, mind, and Self; but the enlightened see the Self as distinct from body and mind. By our identification with the body, we suffer its destiny. Vedanta urges us to overcome our identification with the body by heightening our self-awareness through regulated practice of meditation on the Self.

Keep the goal in view and move forward. Practice of self-awareness endows us with self-knowledge. Vedic sages tell us that life is a journey toward Self-knowledge that alone can guarantee freedom from all fear. Self-knowledge is not our choice but our very destiny. There is no rest and no peace until we reach this goal. Through our pain and suffering, sorrow and disappointment, birth and death, we are journeying toward that knowledge of our Self. When our journey toward that Self is conscious and willing, we call it spiritual quest, and when unconscious, forced by circumstances, we call it evolution. When we deny this Self, we confront it as endless pain, suffering, old age, and death. Self-knowledge may be chimerical to those who are entranced by the glitter of the world; but for the seekers of Truth, Self-knowledge is of supreme value, the greatest achievement of life.

Fear of Death

Death is a terrible reality. The fear of death is the root of all fears. Life is being, but death is nonbeing. In the words of Thomas Gray's elegy:

> The boast of heraldry, the pomp of power,
>> And all that beauty, all that wealth e'er gave
> Awaits alike th' inevitable hour:
>> The paths of glory lead but to the grave.[38]

Saints and sinners, rich and poor, high and low, old and young, learned and ignorant, righteous and unrighteous, all die. Conquest of death has always been the major preoccupation of the human mind. Science, technology, and medicine are all busy finding ways to make life deathless. The shelves of bookstores are filled with literature promising techniques to stop the aging process or ways to conquer death, or at least postpone it. Millions of dollars are spent on efforts to overcome these harsh realities of life. Yet death continues to take its toll.

USUAL RESPONSES TO THE FEAR OF DEATH

In centuries past, death was regarded as a *fitting finale* to life. In art and literature death was celebrated as *ars moriendi,* the art of dying. Death marked the moment of the soul's salvation. According to Plato, true philosophers are always occupied in the practice of dying. Christian monks in the Middle Ages greeted one another with the words *memento mori,* "remember that you must die."

Responses to the fear of death have been various. The response that is most common is "Don't think of death." In the *Mahabharata,* King Yudhishthira was asked by a mysterious being, "What is the greatest wonder in the world?" The king replied, "Every day men see creatures depart to Yama's [i.e., Death's] abode, and yet those who remain seek to live for ever. This verily is the greatest wonder."[39]

The second response to the fear of death is "Accept the inevitable, because death is the universal destiny and there is nothing we can do about it." The third response is "Enjoy life while you are alive, because this is the only life that we have." The fourth response comes from the followers of faith. They say, "Death is the law of earthly life, which is inherently sinful and corrupt. Bear with death as part of purification and education, and hope for eternal life hereafter." The fifth response is "Fight death with material means." There are many who believe that the developments of science and medicine will one day reverse the process of aging and eventually eradicate death altogether. But as we develop smart technology and strong medicine, death also gets smarter and stronger.

However we may want to forget death, death does not forget us. But to accept death as the end of everything makes life meaningless. The notion of enjoying life while ignoring the question of death works well when we are young, but as we grow older we begin to hear the drumbeats of death getting louder and louder. Our optimism turns into pessimism. To enjoy life by being oblivious of the reality of death is infantile and absurd. Our attempt to see only the bright side of life is futile.

Those who accept death as inevitable but still try to get compensation hereafter do not really face the question of death. Everlasting life in terms of time is irrational. That which begins in time will also end in time. Even the longest life will come to an end. The idea of physical immortality is a fanciful dream.

RESPONSE OF VEDANTA

Death is disintegration of the physical body and is never the end of the story. When the physical body becomes broken from illness, old age, or accident, the soul, along with the causal and subtle body, leaves the gross body and looks for another gross body to inhabit. The consciousness of the three bodies is consciousness borrowed from the soul. Deep identification with the body is the cause of the fear of death. The body, being material, is time-bound and subject to the six changes of birth, subsistence, growth, maturity, decline, and death that are common to all material entities. Being identified with the body, a person follows the destiny of the body. When the body dies, the person thinks he or she is dying. But this is not so. The deathless soul only appears to die when the body dies.

The Vedic seers speak of the soul's rebirth. This rebirth is governed by the law of karma that says that our thoughts, actions, and desires determine our destiny. The Bhagavad Gita describes death as one of the series of changes: "Even as the embodied Self passes, in this body, through the stages of childhood, youth, and old age, so does It pass into another body. Calm souls are not bewildered by this."[40] Rebirth gives the soul an opportunity to make things better in the next life. The very fact that life is ever changing indicates that there is some entity within us that is changeless. This changeless entity is our true Self, the constant witness to the changing phenomena of life. There is no escape from the cycles of birth and death until the Self is discovered.

WHERE DO THE DEAD GO?

Vedanta speaks of the four courses that people may follow after death:

First, the yogis who lead an extremely righteous life, meditate on Brahman, and follow the various disciplines of yoga, repair, after death, to Brahmaloka (roughly corresponding to the heaven of the Christians) and from there, in due course, attain salvation, known as kramamukti, or gradual emancipation. Second, the ritualists and the philanthropists, who cherish a desire for the fruit of their devotion and charity, repair, after death, to Chandraloka, or the lunar sphere. After enjoying immense happiness there as the fruit of their meritorious action, they come back to earth, since they still cherish desires for worldly happiness. These are called gods or deities in Hinduism. Third, those who perform actions forbidden by religion assume, after death, subhuman bodies and dwell in what is generally known as hell. After expiating their evil actions, they are reborn on earth. Fourth, the persons who perform extremely vile actions spend many births as such insignificant beings as mosquitos and fleas. The relative value of a created being depends on the degree of consciousness manifested by it. The consciousness manifested by the dweller in Brahmaloka is very high, and the consciousness manifested by the insects is very low. The man endowed with Self-knowledge attains liberation in this very life. His soul does not go to any sphere, for he has realized its identity with the all-pervading Consciousness.[41]

In regard to the universe and its various planes or spheres, Vedanta presents the following theory:

All these spheres are products of matter and energy, or what Samkhya philosophy calls *akasa* and *prana,* in varying degrees. The lowest or most condensed is the solar sphere, consisting of the visible universe, in which prana appears as physical force and akasa as sense-perceived matter. The next is the lunar sphere, which surrounds the solar sphere. This is not the moon at all, but the habitation of the gods. In this sphere prana appears as the psychic forces and akasa as the tanmatras, or fine, rudimentary elements. Beyond this is the electric sphere, that is to say, a condition in which prana is almost inseparable from akasa; there one can hardly tell whether electricity is force or matter. Next is Brahmaloka, where prana and akasa do not exist as separate entities; both are merged in the mind-stuff, the primal energy. In the absence of prana and akasa, the jiva, or individual soul, contemplates the whole universe as the sum total of the cosmic mind. This appears as a purusha, an abstract universal soul, yet not the Absolute, for still there is multiplicity. From this sphere the jiva subsequently finds his way to Unity, which is the end and goal of his earthly evolution.

According to the Non-dualistic Vedanta these spheres are only visions that arise in succession before the soul, which itself neither comes nor goes. The sense-perceived world in which a man lives is a similar vision. At the time of dissolution, these visions gradually disappear, the gross merging in the fine. The purpose of the Hindu philosophers in treating of cosmology is to awaken in man's heart a spirit of detachment from the relative universe.

The experience of happiness in different planes or spheres after death is transitory. The dwellers in these planes come back to earth and commence again their life of pain and suffering. Even the most fortunate dwellers in Brahmaloka must wait a long time before they attain complete liberation. On the other hand, Self-knowledge, which can be attained by every human being, confers upon its possessor liberation in this very life. He does not have to wait for a future time to taste the bliss of immortality. This attainment of liberation through Self-knowledge, while living in a physical body, is the goal of human life. The Hindu scriptures treat of the various cycles and planes and spheres, and also of the various courses open to the soul after death, in order to spur men to strive for Self-knowledge and the attainment of liberation here on earth.[42]

All living beings, without any exception whatsoever, will attain Self-knowledge and liberation.[43]

WHAT HAPPENS AT THE POINT OF DEATH?

Vedanta gives a vivid description of what happens at the point of death:

When the soul departs from the body, the life-breath follows: when the life breath departs, all the organs follow. Then the soul becomes endowed with particularized consciousness and goes to the body that is related to that consciousness. It is followed by its knowledge, works, and past experience. Just as a leech supported on a straw goes to the end of it, takes hold of another support, and contracts itself, so does the self throw this body away and make it unconscious, take hold of another support, and contract itself. Just as a goldsmith takes a small quantity of gold and fashions another—a newer and better—form, so does the soul throw this body away, or make it unconscious, and make another—a newer and better—form suited to the Manes, or the celestial minstrels, or the gods, or Virat, or Hiranyagarbha, or other beings.... As it does and acts, so it becomes; by doing good it becomes good, and by doing evil it becomes evil—it becomes virtuous through good acts and vicious through evil acts.[44]

The thought at the time of death determines the future life of the soul: "For whatever object a man thinks of at the final moment, when he leaves his body—that alone does he attain, O son of Kunti, being ever absorbed in the thought thereof."[45] Vedanta lays great stress on the thought and the state of mind at the time of death as determining the future of the soul. Thought is endowed with a self-creative power. Our inner being changes into that of which we constantly think with faith and devotion. We become that on which we keep our minds fixed and to which we fervently aspire. The ever-recurring thought of a lifetime, whether good or bad, presents itself vividly at the time of death. We cannot get rid of it, as the sleeping man cannot get rid of his dream. Since the character of the body next to be attained is determined by what we think intensely at the time of death, we should always think of God if we want to attain him after leaving the body. The absolution and last unction of the priest does not make death edifying and spiritual after an unedifying and profane life. Even while the priest performs his rites, a dying man may be cherishing in his mind the thought in which he has indulged all through life.

The embodiment of the soul is apparent and not real. Therefore its birth and death are also only apparent. A knower of Self realizes that repeated cycles of birth and death are like nightmares and not real. A knower of Self is truly awakened. Though experiencing disease, old age, and death, such a person remains unruffled by them, knowing that they are characteristic of the body and not of the Self, and is therefore free from desire, which arises when one is identified with the body. For if one has realized oneself to be Brahman, infinite and all-pervading, seeing oneself in the universe and the universe in oneself, one cannot desire anything. Self-knowledge liberates the individual soul from its bondage and delusion. Only Self-knowledge can overcome death.

This is the Vedantic conception of immortality, an immortality to be attained not in heaven but here on earth in this very body through the knowledge of the immortal nature of the Self. About the enlightened person the Upanishads say: "Dwelling in this very body, we have somehow realized Brahman; otherwise we should have remained ignorant and great destruction would have overtaken us. Those who know Brahman become immortal, while others only suffer misery."[46]

According to the Upanishads, unillumined souls go to heaven or return to earth for the satisfaction of their unfulfilled desires. Those who desire are reborn. But those who do not desire are not reborn. There is the verse: "When all the desires that dwell in his heart are got rid of, then does the mortal [man] become immortal and attain Brahman in this very body."[47] The knower of Atman is like someone who is awakened from sleep and dreams no more of empty things.

THE SOUL'S JOURNEY TO FREEDOM

The soul's three basic desires—immortality, unrestricted awareness, and unbounded joy—are attained only when it discovers its true identity, the all-embracing Self. In search of its identity, the soul changes bodies and places, and finally, knowing the limitations of all pleasures and realizing that everything finite is shadowed by death, it practices detachment and desirelessness and realizes its immortal Self. Immortality is the return of the reflection of the sun to the sun. It is the river of individual consciousness meeting the infinite ocean of Pure Consciousness. It is the realization that we are like leaves of a tree and that our true identity is the tree. It is our separative existence joining the infinite existence of absolute freedom.

The journey to this final freedom is a solitary one; a person is born alone, suffers alone, and dies alone. By realizing the true Self, one becomes united with all beings and things and attains to final freedom. Only then comes the end of all sorrow, all fear, all anxiety.

The doctrine of rebirth is the most plausible theory to help us understand the meaning of life and the diversities of existence. Each person is born with a blueprint of his or her mind that carries the impressions of past lives. Death seems fearful because we died many, many times before. Although we do not remember the incidents, the effects of those experiences remain stored in the conscious mind in a minute form. In the Bhagavad Gita, Sri Krishna tells Arjuna: "Many a birth have I passed through, O Arjuna, and so have you. I know them all, but you know them not, O scorcher of foes."[48] In the Bible, Jesus identifies John the Baptist as the prophet Elias reborn. "If ye will receive it, this is Elias, which was for to come" (Matt. 11:14).

THE EXHORTATIONS OF VEDANTA

Death is an inescapable and inevitable reality. To ignore it is utter foolishness. To avoid it is impossible. To hope for physical immortality is absurd. The exhortations of Vedanta in this regard are the following:

Make death a part of life by understanding that life without death is incomplete. As soon as we are born, we begin to die. Life is sacred and so we cannot afford to squander it in daydreams, fantasies, and false hopes. Life without death, pleasure without pain, light without darkness, and good without evil are never possible. We must either accept both or rise above both, by overcoming embodiment through the knowledge of the Self. Death is certain for all who are born. As the Bhagavad Gita says: "For to that which is born, death is certain, and to that which is dead, birth is certain. Therefore you should not grieve over the unavoidable."[49]

Develop immunity against death by practicing meditation and dispassion. In meditation we try to reach our true identity, the deathless Self, by crossing over the three states of consciousness and becoming *videha,* or bereft of body-consciousness. In this practice, we partially and temporarily die in our physical and mental existence. Along with meditation, practice dispassion, which is knowing that nothing material will accompany us when we leave this earth and that nothing in this world can be of any help to us to overcome death.

Build your own raft. Vedanta compares this world to an ocean, the near shore of which we know, while the far shore remains a mystery to us. The ocean has bottomless depth, high winds, fearful currents, and countless whirlpools. Life is a journey, an attempt to cross this ocean of the world and reach the other shore, which is immortality. No one can take us across this ocean. Vedanta urges us to build our own raft by practicing meditation on our true Self. No practice of this self-awareness is ever lost. As we go on with our practice, all of our experiences of self-awareness join together and form a raft of consciousness, which the Upanishads call the "raft of Brahman." Sitting on this raft of Brahman, a mortal crosses the ocean of mortality: "The wise man should hold his body steady, with the three [upper] parts erect, turn his senses, with the help of the mind, toward the heart, and by means of the raft of Brahman cross the fearful torrents of the world."[50] The word *Brahman* in the verse signifies Om. Repetition of Om and meditation on its meaning are prescribed for this practice. Vedanta asserts that Self-knowledge, or knowledge of Brahman, alone can rob death of its paralyzing fear. So long as this Self is not cognized and realized, life will be shadowed by death and the world we live in will be the world of sorrow and suffering.

Free yourself from all attachments. Our attachments and desires keep us tied to our physical existence. We often hope for the impossible and want to achieve the unachievable. To free ourselves from these attachments and desires, we need to cleanse ourselves. Just as we cleanse our body with soap and water, so do we cleanse our mind with self-awareness. The *Mahabharata* advises us to bathe in the river of Atman: "The river of Atman is filled with the water of self-control; truth is its current, righteous conduct its banks, and compassion its waves. O son of Pandu, bathe in its sacred water; ordinary water does not purify the inmost soul."[51]

Know your true friends. Know that our only true friends are our good deeds—deeds by which we help others in most selfless ways. At death, everything of this world is left behind; only the memories of all the deeds we performed in this life accompany us. The memories of good deeds assure our higher destiny and give us freedom from fear of death, while the memories of bad deeds take our soul downward. Therefore a person must try to accumulate as many memories of good deeds as possible while living.

Perform your duties. Life is interdependent. For our existence and survival, we are indebted to God, to our fellow human beings, and to the animal and vegetable worlds. Many have to suffer to keep us happy, and many have to die for our continued existence. We are indebted to all of them. To recognize this indebtedness and make active efforts to repay them is the sacred duty of life. By doing our duties, we become free from all sense of guilt. Be a blessing to all, not a burden. Remember, when you were born you cried, but everybody else rejoiced. Live your life in such a way that when you die everybody will cry, but you alone will rejoice.

Know for certain that death has no power to annihilate your soul. Our soul, our true identity, is the source of all consciousness. It is separate and different from our body and mind, which are material by nature and are subject to change and dissolution. The consciousness of the soul in each of us is part of the all-pervading Universal Consciousness and is the deathless witness to the changes of the body and mind. The Universal Consciousness is like an infinite ocean, and we are like drops of water. We rise to the sky from the ocean, and again we fall into the ocean as raindrops. All will in the end, sooner or later, come together as part of the ocean.

4

Awakening of Spiritual Consciousness

THE MEANING OF AWAKENING

The awakening of spiritual consciousness is the key to attaining the spiritual experiences described by all religious faiths. It is awakening in the real sense of the term. A person can be physically awake but intellectually asleep, or even intellectually awake but still spiritually asleep. Spiritual awakening opens up a new horizon of spiritual awareness that dramatically changes the dynamics of a seeker's journey to the goal. Like a storm it takes over the mind and soul, lifts seekers up, and makes them restless for the realization of Truth. Christian mystics designate it as a "call" from within. St. John of the Cross describes it as the last rung of the mystical ladder. Plotinus speaks of it as the soul's movement toward the Godhead—the flight of the alone to the alone. Walt Whitman says, "Swift arose and spread around me the peace and knowledge that pass all arguments of the earth." To William James it is the "overcoming of all the usual barriers between the individual and the Absolute."[1] The tradition of Buddhism describes Buddha not as a prophet or saint but as "the awakened one" in a world where all are dreaming dreams of hope and happiness, power and glory.

Among the spiritual seekers, most are content with the assurances of the scriptures and observance of ceremonies. For them, religious life is at best intellectual stimulation, or at worst merely social formality. But there are some who are adventurers. They are not content with adherence to rituals or assurances of the scriptures or intellectual understanding of truth.

66

They want something tangible and enduring, and so they struggle hard for spiritual awakening.

Spiritual awakening, according to Vedanta, is the awakening of the very soul. Such awakening is always preceded by moral and ethical awakening. In spiritual awakening the soul rises from its slumber in the subconscious state and begins to move toward the superconscious by crossing the barrier of the conscious. It is waking up to the Reality of all realities—Truth Absolute.

Direct perception of truth is the very essence of the spiritual quest. It is different from blind belief, intellectual understanding, or emotional thrill. Belief is believing in the beliefs of others. Reason is a very weak instrument to lead us to the truth; often our so-called reason is used in an attempt to justify our preconceived opinions. Emotional thrill comes and goes and is of no lasting value. None of these elements can silence our doubt, give us certainty, and transform us.

In contrast, direct perception is seeing through the soul's, not the mind's, eye. Direct perception of truth always silences doubt, is never negated by any other subsequent experience, is conducive to the welfare of all beings, is not opposed to reason and common sense, and, finally, brings permanent transformation of character. Such perception never comes forth of itself. It is never given to us by anybody, nor can it be attained vicariously. It calls for awakening of spiritual consciousness. As Sri Ramakrishna says:

> You may indulge in reasoning or discussion, but if you feel no longing or love, it is all futile. Second, the awakening of the Kundalini [spiritual consciousness]. As long as the Kundalini remains asleep, you have not attained knowledge of God. You may be spending hours poring over books or discussing philosophy, but if you have no inner restlessness for God, you have no knowledge of Him.[2]

THE CENTERS OF SPIRITUAL CONSCIOUSNESS

In symbolic language, Tantra speaks of the kundalini—the coiled-up spiritual power dormant in all living beings. When awakened through the practice of spiritual disciplines, it rises and passes through six centers of consciousness located in the spinal column, where there are three principal nerve channels for the passage of energy. The latter are known as the *ida, pingala,* and *sushumna.* The *sushumna,* the central and most important nerve channel, is inside the spinal cord; the *ida* is at the left of the *sushumna,* while the *pingala* is at its right. Through the *ida* all sense perceptions are received and sent into the brain, while through the *pingala* all motor responses are transmitted from the brain to the body. All three have their meeting point at the base of the spine.

The spinal column resembles a number of figure eights placed horizontally and piled one on top of another. The *sushumna* channel begins at the lower extremity of the spine, runs up through the spine itself, and extends to the top of the head. Contained within the *sushumna* channel are six centers of consciousness, which have been described by Tantra as lotuses. For ordinary persons, the channel of *sushumna* remains closed at the bottom, and the head of each lotus is hanging down. According to Tantra, these six centers range from the lowest plane of gross impulses to the highest plane of pure bliss.

The first center is called *muladhara* (root support). Located at the base of the spine, it has four petals and is crimson in color. It manifests the earth aspect of matter, governs gross physical urges, and controls the sense of smell. Dwelling on this level of existence, a human individual is guided by gross, subconscious desires. The second center is called *svadhisthana* (own abode). It is located at the base of the organ of generation, is of vermilion color, and has six petals. This center manifests the water aspect of matter, governs the sense of taste, and controls the sense organ of the palate. Existence at this center is constantly swayed by gross impulses and imaginations and by various animal propensities. The third center is known as *manipura* (city of jewels). It is situated in the region of the navel, has ten petals, and is the color of heavy dark rain clouds. This center manifests the fire aspect of matter and controls the impulses of perception, especially sight. As clouds obstruct the vision of the sun, so do the clouds of emotions and impulses obstruct the clear vision of truth.

The fourth center, known as *anahata* (unobstructed), is located in the spine at the level of the heart. It has twelve petals and is the color of scarlet flame. This center manifests the air aspect of matter, governs the perception of touch, and controls the emotional being of our personality, and especially the organ of touch. Existence at this center is characterized by experiences that are subtle and spiritual, as opposed to gross and material. One distinctive feature of this lotus is that its filaments are tinged with the rays of the sun. This fourth center is distinguished from the "lotus of the heart," which is eight-petaled and located below it. The lotus of the heart is not a center of consciousness but an inner recess resembling a lotus with its petals turning upward. This inner recess has been compared to a lotus because many nerve channels (*nadis*) proceed from the heart and spread throughout the body like the rays of the sun. The lotus of the heart is also known as *anandakanda* (root of bliss), in which concentration upon one's Chosen Ideal is usually practiced.

The fifth center is called *visuddha* (pure), located in the region corresponding to the throat. The lotus of this center has sixteen petals and is a smoky purple color. The fifth center manifests the ethereal aspect of matter and influences our perception of sound and, therefore, the organs of hearing and speech and the power of perception. Existence at this center is marked by complete purity. The sixth center is known as *ajna* (command, where the command of the Divine from above is received). The lotus of this center is situated in the region between the eyebrows, has two petals, and is white in color. The sixth center is the actual seat of the mind and controls all our thoughts and visions and the dynamic movements of our will. By reaching this center of consciousness, one attains a vision of truth that is almost absolute in nature. Beyond the six centers there is a plane called *sahasrara*. It is located at the crown of the head and has a thousand petals; it is as white as the silvery full moon and as bright as lightning and contains all colors. The *sahasrara* is the summit where individual consciousness meets with the all-pervading Universal Consciousness.

Through the practice of prayer and meditation, the inner consciousness slowly becomes awakened and travels upward, following the channel of *sushumna* from the lowest center (*muladhara*), passing through the next five centers, and finally reaching the highest point (*sahasrara*) at the crown of the head. The awakening of the first center activates the roots of the memories of the past; the second, gross impulses; the third, awareness of the sense of individuality. The awakening of the fourth center brings spiritual experiences and visions; the fifth, partial spiritual absorption; the sixth, deep spiritual absorption but still with faint I-consciousness (*savikalpa samadhi*). At the *sahasrara,* one attains total spiritual absorption (*nirvikalpa samadhi*).

For most persons, the mind is forced to go back and forth between the three lower centers, at the organs of evacuation (base of the spine) and generation and at the navel. At these stages, a person's mind remains immersed in worldliness. It constantly broods over the cravings of lust and greed; eating, sleeping, and procreation become its dominant preoccupations. All perception and cognition of the mind at these three centers are influenced by animal propensities.

But when the mind reaches the fourth center, seekers first experience spiritual awakening. New vistas open up before such seekers—they see the same world but in its fine and spiritual form; they see light all around and visualize the individual soul as a flame. When their minds reach the fifth center, they want to talk and hear only about God and do not enjoy anything else. Conversations on worldly subjects cause them great pain, and they immediately leave a place where people are talking of these matters. Reaching the sixth center, their minds are taken over by a deep spiritual absorption that is not only spontaneous but also continuous. They see the living form of God like a light inside a lantern; they want to touch the form but are unable to do so. Finally, when their minds reach the crown of the head, they attain total absorption. Overcome by the intense inebriation of pure bliss, they lose all outer consciousness. The mind no longer wants to come back to the level of body-consciousness. Only extraordinary souls can come down from that exalted state, and then with great effort.

There is nothing mystical, miraculous, or esoteric particular to Tantra about the awakening and rising of kundalini power. Kundalini in the form of cosmic energy is present in everything, even in a particle of matter. Only a fraction of it is operating, while the rest is left "coiled up" and untapped at the "base-root." While Vedanta describes the Absolute as Pure Consciousness, Tantra calls it Shiva-Shakti: Shiva as the Absolute and Shakti as its creative power. Any conception of Pure Consciousness that denies Shakti is only half the truth. The goal is to realize the truth as one by bringing Shiva and Shakti together.

As Swami Nikhilananda describes:

> The coiled-up Kundalini is the central pivot upon which the whole complex apparatus of the body and mind moves and turns. A specific ratio between the active and total energies of the Kundalini determines the present condition and behavior of the bodily apparatus. A change in the ratio is necessary to effect a change in its present working efficiency by transforming the grosser bodily ele-

ments into finer. A transformation, dynamization, and sublimation of the physical, mental, and vital apparatus is only possible through what is called the rousing of the Kundalini and its reorientation from "downward-facing" to "upward-facing." By the former the physical body has been made a "coiled curve," limited in character, restricted in functions and possibilities. By the force of the latter it breaks its fetters and transcends its limitations.[3]

SIGNS OF AWAKENING

FALSE AWAKENING

Awakening can be temporary, false, partial, sudden, or stumbled upon. A seeker can have temporary awakening as a result of grief or other spiritually stimulating external circumstances, or the nearness of a great spiritual personality. But such awakening does not last long, and consciousness again falls. A person can experience false awakening caused by heightened imagination. In partial awakening, spiritual consciousness rises to the upper region to a certain extent, because of the practice of control of breath and other spiritual disciplines, but it soon comes down. Momentary excitement of emotions often causes the consciousness to rise suddenly, but it invariably falls when the excitement abates. The stumbled-upon state is one in which the seeker achieves awakening unexpectedly and is unable to handle its impact. Regarding this state, Swami Vivekananda observes:

> In a good many cases there is the danger of the brain's being deranged; and as a rule you will find that all those men, however great they were, who stumbled upon this superconscious state without understanding it groped in the dark and generally had, along with their knowledge, some quaint superstitions.[4]

Awakening falsely or partially or temporarily is always dangerous, because there is the fear of fall—and when the consciousness falls, it falls violently. The risk of falling remains until the consciousness passes the sixth center. So once awakened, the consciousness must be kept moving upward. Any awakening achieved without the support of moral and ethical purity is always fraught with danger. A steel-frame moral foundation serves as a strong platform to stop the falling consciousness from rolling downward violently. An illustration of sudden awakening may be drawn from the book *Sri Ramakrishna, the Great Master,* by Swami Saradananda, a direct disciple of the Master:

> One day a few Vaishnava devotees came with an absent-minded young man. We had never seen them before. The reason why they came was that they wanted to show the young man to the Master and know the Master's opinion about the strange spiritual state that had suddenly come upon him. Word was sent to the Master and he saw the young man. The face and chest of the young man were red; and he was seen taking the dust of the feet of all with humility. As he was repeating God's names he was having frequent tremors and horripilation, and both his eyes were reddish and a little swollen owing to an incessant flow of tears. He was of dark-blue complexion, was neither fat nor thin, and had a tuft of hair on his head. His face and limbs were graceful and well-built. He was wearing a white cloth without borders that was not very clean and had, we remember, neither wrapper nor shoes. He seemed quite indifferent to the cleanliness or preservation of his body. We were told that the high-strung state had come on him suddenly when one day he was singing the praises of Lord Hari. Since then he had been taking virtually no food and having no sleep; he would weep day and night and roll on the ground because God had not been realized. He had been in that state for the last few days.... The moment the Master saw the young man he said, "Ah! It is, I find, the commencement of the madhura-bhava [spiritual mood of regarding oneself as the sweetheart of God]. But this state will not last; he cannot retain it. As soon as a woman is touched lustfully this spiritual mood will vanish." Be that as it may, the Vaishnava devotees accompanying the young man returned home with him. They felt a little consoled at the Master's words that at least the young man's brain was not deranged. However, a little afterwards news reached us that the Master's prediction was perfectly fulfilled; the young man had been overcome by the fateful calamity. He had ascended fortunately to a very high plane indeed owing to the momentary excitement of sankirtan [congregational religious singing and

dancing], but alas he came down to a very low plane owing to his mind's reaction to the experience.[5]

Swami Vivekananda warns seekers about the danger of awakening the kundalini in an untimely or sudden manner owing to indulgence in emotionalism:

> During meditation suppress the emotional side altogether. That is a great source of danger. Those who are very emotional no doubt have their Kundalini rushing quickly upwards, but it is as quick to come down as to go up. And when it comes down, it leaves the devotee in a state of utter ruin. It is for this reason that kirtanas [congregational religious singing and dancing] and other auxiliaries to emotional development have a great drawback. It is true that by dancing and jumping, etc. through a momentary impulse, that power is made to course upwards, but it is never enduring. On the contrary, when it traces back its course, it rouses violent lust in the individual.[6]

TRUE AWAKENING

True awakening is preceded by certain signs, generally four in number. First is the growing discrimination between the Real and the unreal. The seeker begins to wonder, "Where is my real home, who is my real friend, what is my real wealth?" The second is intense dispassion. Imbued with intense dispassion, the seeker, as Sri Ramakrishna says, sees the world as a deep well and regards relatives as venomous cobras. Every enjoyment is marred by fear:

> The rich are afraid of thieves, the beautiful of deformity, the healthy of disease, the learned of rivals, the aristocrats of dishonor, the virtuous of slander. Yet man somehow forgets this truth in the rhapsody of his fear-haunted and momentary happiness.[7]

The third sign is the struggle for self-control, which causes the seeker to make an all-out effort to subdue the outgoing sense organs. The fourth sign is great spiritual longing, an intense restlessness day and night for the knowledge of truth.

True awakening begins to appear when consciousness reaches the fourth center, at the heart. Seekers experience spiritual emotions such as the shedding of tears, a continuous thrill in the body, horripilation, and so forth. They see light and other visions and hear voices. Often they hear within the uninterrupted sound of the spheres or the ringing of a distant bell. Succeeding signs without the background of the preceding ones are regarded as suspect, and preceding signs without the succeeding ones are meaningless. As Shankaracharya says in his *Vivekachudamani:*

> The result of dispassion is knowledge, that of knowledge is with-
> drawal from sense-pleasures, which leads to the experience of the
> bliss of the Self, whence follows Peace. If there is an absence of
> the succeeding stages, the preceding ones are futile. (When the
> series is perfect) the cessation of the objective world, extreme sat-
> isfaction, and matchless bliss follow as a matter of course.[8]

The surest sign of authentic awakening is the permanent transformation of character. The outward symptoms of deep spiritual fervor without renunciation, self-control, and devotion do not indicate authentic awakening. So it is said that out of one hundred seekers, eighty may become charlatans, fifteen may go insane, and only the remaining five may be blessed with a vision of real truth. Awakened consciousness brings steady wisdom, and an awakened person of steady wisdom has been aptly described by the Bhagavad Gita: "In that which is night to all beings, the man of self-control is awake; and where all beings are awake, there is night for the muni who sees."[9]

METHODS OF AWAKENING CONSCIOUSNESS

There are five tested methods of awakening spiritual consciousness, according to Vedanta. One is fervent prayer, in which the seeker feels like a helpless baby crying for its mother. The second method is *japa,* or repetition of a sacred name. Faith and love act as a most powerful lever to rouse the coiled-up kundalini. Repetition of a sacred name creates sound vibrations that eventually induce the consciousness to rise. The third method is *vichara,* or discriminating reasoning, by which the seeker tries to persuade the consciousness to wake up from its slumber. The fourth method is meditation. Meditation is keeping the mind focused like a searchlight on the consciousness, so that it will rise. The fifth method is *pranayama,* or control of breath, by which a person rouses the consciousness forcibly to the fourth center. By controlling the breath, the vibrations of thoughts, emotions, and activities of the mind are controlled and an upward movement of consciousness is generated. However, attempts to awaken consciousness through control of breath, without first building a strong moral and ethical foundation of purity, may bring dangerous consequences, such as a breakdown of the nervous system, derangement of the brain, and even incurable disease. So the wisdom of the traditions of Vedanta cautions that recourse to *pranayama* is to be taken only when other risk-free methods have been tried and have failed. The safest way, according to this wisdom, is that of *japa* and meditation. A disciple once asked Sri Ramakrishna's eminent direct disciple, Swami Brahmananda: "Sir, how can the Kundalini be aroused?" The swami replied:

> According to some, there are special exercises, but I believe it can
> best be done through repetition of the Divine Name, and medita-
> tion. Especially suited to our present age is the practice of japa,
> or constant repetition of the Divine Name and meditation upon it.
> There is no spiritual practice easier than this. But meditation must
> accompany the repetition of the mantra.[10]

Success depends upon sincerity and intensity of effort. Only real effort can bring a real result. There is a humorous story about a man who lived alone in an apartment and was faced with an invasion of mice; one day he bought a mousetrap. Before going to bed, while setting it up, he realized he needed a piece of cheese to put in the trap to attract the mice. Upon opening the refrigerator, he found to his dismay that he had no cheese. Desperate, he thought that after all mice were dumb creatures and it wouldn't matter if he put a picture of a piece of cheese in the trap instead of real cheese. So he cut a picture of cheese from a catalog, put it in the trap, and went to bed. Upon waking up the next morning he was anxious to see the result. Lo and behold, he saw that the picture of the cheese was gone and in its place was a picture of a mouse!

Yet when everything has been said, the question remains: Can spiritual awakening be scheduled? The answer is no. No spiritual practice can hurry awakening. Awakening comes by divine grace, and the descent of this grace cannot be programmed. Yet spiritual practices are necessary. They prepare our physical and mental system for the blessed moment. Spiritual awakening comes like a full burst of light, and our body, mind, and nervous system must be made ready for the impact of that burst. Nobody knows when that blessed burst will come, and so we must wait and prepare ourselves. We feel drawn to the Divine only when the Divine draws us. We rise to God-consciousness when God lifts us up. We feel longing for God when God longs for us.

5

Faith or Reason?

The spread of secular education and the increasing influence of science and technology are challenging traditional religious beliefs. Adherence to theological doctrine is giving way to the acceptance of the laws of physical science, and religious myths and legends are being set aside in favor of verifiable data. The concern for "hereafter" has been replaced with a focus on the "here and now." An external God and eternal life in heaven after death are looked upon by many as fairy tales that people choose to believe in order to console themselves. While religious dogma condemns doubt and calls for unquestioning belief, science demands rational justification for any theory or belief.

According to science, that which is true is rational and universally observable; the validity of such a truth rests not on faith but on experimentation, verification, and demonstration. Scientific education has replaced faith with reason as the primary vehicle for obtaining knowledge. Anything that is claimed as special or exclusive is considered arbitrary and suspect. The religious traditions that lean heavily on the infallibility of their dogmas, creeds, or leaders denounce this new perspective. Thus, the ascendance of education and science has stirred up a controversy that divides the spiritually minded into two camps: the upholders of faith and the believers in reason.

IN SUPPORT OF FAITH

Traditionalists look upon faith as the final authority in deciding the validity of spiritual truth. For the faithful, the validity of a spiritual teaching rests solely on faith and never on reason, because the reality of God is self-evident and not dependent upon denial or acceptance by the human mind. The proof of the existence of anything is the faith that it exists. One's faith is followed by one's perceptions and cognitions.

In any walk of life, reason follows faith. We perceive a thing and then reason about it. This is also the process in the realm of religion. That which is envisioned by faith is systematized by reason for the understanding of the average mind. The prophets and Godmen and Godwomen of different religions are guided by faith, not by reason. They perceive Ultimate Reality directly and speak about it with childlike simplicity. Philosophical thoughts develop later to systematize what has been realized through faith. Myths and rituals are then created in an attempt to concretize what had been mystically experienced and philosophically systematized. We reason and argue about a thing as long as we have not developed faith in the existence of that thing or we are doubtful about its existence. Faith is, therefore, the mature form of reason.

REASON RELIES ON APPEARANCE

Reason addresses the appearance of things and not their essential nature. It is dialectic and discursive in its approach and can only give diagrams of Ultimate Reality, not a fully realized portrait of it. Science reduces all things—even living beings—to ideas in order to understand them better. Faith, on the other hand, is concerned primarily with the essence of a thing and not merely with its appearance. Faith is an appeal to the heart and not to the head. The essence of every religion is love of God or love of that which is ultimately real, and love is a function of faith and not of reason. Love is being and not knowing. In order to love a person, one does not need to have knowledge of the physiology and biochemistry of that person. In order to love God, one does not need to reason about God's existence. The ultimate proof of God, or that which is absolutely real, depends on faith and not on reason. Faith brings everything to life. The concept of God becomes a living reality when it is inspired by faith. The power of a saint or a prophet is not his or her philosophy but that person's unwavering faith in the presence of God. Reason begins with doubt and also ends with doubt, and such doubt springs from another kind of faith—faith in the infallibility of reasoning. The cure for doubt is, therefore, not reason but faith. One who continuously doubts and therefore reasons develops a taste for doubting and reasoning, and in the course of time, the habit becomes a means of sophisticated intellectual pleasure.

REASON AS AN IMPEDIMENT TO TRUTH

Reason is not only a hindrance in the practice of religion; it is a positive impediment. It has been said that reason is a lame man's crutch. It is never able to establish beyond doubt the validity of any spiritual truth. The movement of reason is from "general" to "particular." It seeks to make finite representations of the Infinite, an exercise that is frustrating to reason itself. When reason refutes a hypothesis, it implicitly suggests a new one, which in turn can be refuted by another hypothesis. Thus it is like a game of solitaire that is never finished. Where speculation is both the goal and the means to attain the goal, there can never be a satisfactory conclusion. A person who waits for decisive proof about the efficacy of a spiritual path in order to commit to it can never do so, because each doubt resolved reveals a new one requiring another solution.

Reason can never inspire faith. It can never be a perfect instrument of knowledge. The tools of reason are inference, analogy, and assumption, which can never provide a direct glimpse of ultimate Truth. Furthermore, a perverse mind can resort to perverse arguments. What reason often fails to take into account is that the validity of a perception is determined by the perceiver's mind, which has limitations and biases. The goal of religion is not to have an opinion about truth but a vision of it. Religion does not seek knowledge of God but God. Such vision is possible only through faith. At best, reason can give various degrees of probabilities and approximations of Truth but no finality. In order to reason about a thing we have to create a distance between it and ourselves, and the more we try to understand, the more distance we create. Faith, on the other hand, brings us nearer to the object of faith. The thesis of reason about the presence of God is that God is "nowhere," while the thesis of faith is that God is "now here."

REASON VERSUS SPIRITUAL TRUTH

Faith is the very life-breath of religion. It is a superior kind of reasoning that teaches us how the human individual is organically related to God, the totality.

Any reasoning that takes the individual away from the totality is a form of self-love, the root cause of all the sufferings of life. Self-love springs from an egotism that has a childish belief in its own self-sufficiency. Faith is that reason which focuses our attention on the smallness of the individual ego and the folly of self-love and urges us to love God, the center of our inner-most being. Faith is the very essence of one's commitment to a spiritual goal. An aspirant who is devoid of faith meanders aimlessly like a boat filled with a cargo of uncertainties and doubts that floats around but never comes into harbor. The universe of reason is composed of dry concepts and cate-gories. To depend on reason for a vision of Truth is like searching for the living among the dead. Reason is like a judge who attentively listens to all the evidence but disappears when it is time to make a decision. The message of reason is always fragile, vacillating, and uninspiring. It can never inspire faith in God or in spiritual matters. To believe in the infallibility of reason is a form of weakness. Those who believe exclusively in reason will get con-sistency but never Truth. The approach to Truth lies in the twilight of cer-tainty and mystery. Reason is all certainty and no mystery, and it leads to morbid determinism.

According to the upholders of faith, truth that is authentic is universally true, irrespective of time and place. Spiritual truth cannot be verified unless it is experimented upon by living it in one's own life, and to live it one must have faith in it. The spiritual quest, therefore, begins with faith; it is sustained by faith; and it attains its culmination through faith. Faith matures into con-viction, and conviction reaches its fullness in realization.

LIMITATIONS OF THE DOUBTING MIND

The theology of reason is based on doubt. The doubting mind is a victim of cynicism that scoffs at what it does not understand. Such a mind doubts the validity of the scriptures but believes in the infallibility of a newspaper report. It is skeptical about the holiness of a saint but is willing to accept the evil of the sinner. Those guided solely by reason are forced by their own intellectual rigidity to live in a universe filled with dry concepts and cate-gories. Blind reason constantly challenges a person's faith or philosophy of life and makes him or her feel insecure and unhappy. Intellectual rigidity is really a form of fanaticism that evaluates everything in the light of its own creed. Those with a compulsion to reason cannot accept that which is easily acceptable by others and are thus haunted by a passion for knowing. When such people finally arrive at "knowing," they do not have time to enjoy and appreciate what they know.

One who lives by reason is guided by the philosophy of necessity and utility. Such business-minded people are always looking for profit and personal victory. They must have a reason for everything they do or say or think. Their doubting intellect dominates everything. All their feelings and actions, perceptions and volitions, are dictated by reason. Whatever they do, they do as a duty. If they smile, it is because they think they ought to smile. If they are kind, it is because they have a reason to be so. They eat for nourishment, sleep for rest, work for earning, and study for a career. If they are inclined to embark on a spiritual quest, they do so as a practice of spiritual discipline. Such people are like machines, automatic and meticulous in every respect but devoid of any feeling. As a result they become possessed by a sense of determinism that makes even the trivialities of life appear unduly significant. Determinism cripples every movement of their lives, because they are looking for a cause or justification for everything. They are never at peace because they are trying to know the anatomy of a peaceful mind. They never feel happy because they are always in pursuit of happiness. Nowhere do they find Truth, since they are determined to first define it. They are perpetually insecure because they are frantically trying to be secure.

People of reason always live in the future, because their present is made up of uncertainties and probabilities. Always anticipating the future, they make plans and draw up programs that are never carried out. Unable to believe in themselves, they cannot believe in others. Doubts and determinism follow from inner devaluation, and the devalued personality is always pessimistic, projecting its negativity on everything. In the realm of religion, when reason becomes the sole pathfinder, everything turns tasteless and dry. The intellect becomes the victim of its own reasoning, creating problems that it cannot solve and raising questions it cannot answer. That which is infinite cannot be grasped by the finite mind. Our finite perceptions of Truth and Reality are not exhaustive but suggestive. That which is real and true in the ultimate sense can be felt but never defined and measured. It is "seeing" and not "seeking." Seeing is a subjective experience. Seeking separates the subject from the object, while seeing brings them together and finally merges them. Seeing requires total commitment of the whole mind to the object of faith. It is a form of revelation. Truth is self-revealing. We do not invent but only discover it. Revelation does not occur through technology, and it is not validated by majority vote.

The findings of reason are always fragmentary. They are half-truths, and half-truths can create even more confusion than ignorance. The theology of reason teaches: "Have faith in God but keep your powder dry." One who is guided by this theology can neither have faith in God nor keep the powder dry. As long as one seeks Truth, one does not see it. Seeing is feeling, and it is done by the heart; seeking is defining, which is a function of the head. The more we try to seek, the less we are able to see; the more we are able to see and feel, the less we are inclined to seek and know. Feeling brings warmheartedness, and the warmer the heart gets, the cooler the head becomes. Reasoning not only heats the head but also chills the heart and blurs the vision. Small wonder, then, that men and women of reason are often heartless and cruel, insensitive and callous. In fact, faith is more important than reason, not only in the realm of religion but also in the field of scientific research. Scientists often make their discoveries through intuitive faith, usually in moments of relaxation and rest, and the discovery comes in a flash. These are more like inner revelations than data arrived at exclusively through rational and painstaking experiments.

ARGUMENTS IN SUPPORT OF GOD'S EXISTENCE

No amount of reason can inspire faith in God or in any phenomenon that is spiritual. Generally speaking, there are four arguments supporting the existence of God:

1. The law of cause and effect suggests the existence of God as the cause of all causes. In other words, God is postulated as the First Cause.

2. The purposeful order that can be observed in nature and through scientific observation suggests that there is a designer or creator of the universe.

3. Our quest for perfection leads us to postulate the existence of a being who is supremely perfect. God is the embodiment of that perfection.

4. The creative process reveals a moral order in which good produces good, evil produces evil, and nothing happens by chance. Therefore, it is natural to postulate a being who is the controller of the moral order of the universe and the dispenser of justice and happiness. This being is God.

These arguments are based on inference and speculation, and they do not and cannot give any finality to the fact of the existence of God. Unfortunately, a philosophy of life based only on reason reduces everything to nothingness. Reason is too fragile an instrument for navigating in the realm of the spiritual, because, by nature, it is vacillating and self-doubting. Arguments to support the existence of God based solely on reason will always fall short and often lead to a conclusion that nature or the visible universe is merely an arbitrary and mindless creation.

Although reason lauds itself for its progressiveness and criticizes faith for depending on the authority of the scriptures and traditions, it too accepts the experiences of the past in order to move ahead on its path of scientific inquiry. No reasoning is possible without a hypothesis. The present is meaningless and rootless unless it has the past as its ground. If religious traditions call certain acts blasphemous, science also labels certain things as superstitious. Each follows its own methodology and creed. The goal of reason is consistency, while that of faith is wholeness.

Faith in reason is nothing but agnosticism. The agnostic is like a person who is all dressed up but has no place to go. It is not that such persons do not believe in anything; they are actually incapable of belief, or it may be said they believe in not believing. There is an anecdote that beautifully illustrates this predicament: Once there was an agnostic society whose members were constantly exhorted to "hold on" at all costs to their conviction of agnosticism. The words *hold on* became their official dogma. A devout member of the society had an accident and was about to die. In his last moments he unconsciously drew his hands together to offer a final prayer. The head of the society, who was seated at his bedside, became greatly alarmed to see one of his most loyal members abandoning his creed and in an agitated voice said to the dying man: "Brother, *hold on* to our motto to which you have been faithful all your life! Never give in." The dying man opened his eyes and sadly said: "You ask me to hold on, but, brother, there is nothing to hold on to!"

IN SUPPORT OF REASON

What the religious traditions call faith is really unquestioning belief in the authority of the scriptures or the doctrines of religion. Such belief has no foundation. Belief can turn into conviction only through conscious reasoning about what one believes in. One cannot really believe in something for which one does not find a logical rationale.

BELIEF AS IMAGINATION

Belief is a form of imagination—the creation of images and concepts, dogmas and creeds, that are substitutes for ultimate Truth. It is wishful thinking about Truth and not Truth itself. Truth becomes known only when we have risen above all beliefs and imaginings, and this is possible only through reason. That which distinguishes the Real from the imaginary is reason and not belief.

Divorced from reason, religious traditions and beliefs degenerate into millennialism, which encourages a fatalistic attitude toward life. Looking toward a millennium yet to come, followers cease to live in the present. They consider themselves chosen people, waiting for the coming of the kingdom of God. Those who adhere to such dogmas tend to put the responsibility for their lives in the hands of Providence or fate and accept the conditions of their lives as preordained. They live in fear and uncertainty yet often take delight in pessimism and mass hysteria.

THE PROBLEM OF VALIDATING SPIRITUAL EXPERIENCES

To disbelieve in the efficacy of reason is to make the validity of spiritual truth contingent upon so-called mystical experiences, which are always personal and private, possibly even the result of autosuggestion, hallucination, or mental degeneration. An individual may see visions and hear voices that can very well be the products of his or her own mind; indeed, they are often the product of bereavement, worldly disappointment, or disease. When the validity of a spiritual truth becomes dependent solely on the private and personal experience of an individual, there is no end of uncertainty and self-deception. Furthermore, a spiritual experience may be borrowed;

that is, the person has duplicated an experience he or she has read or heard about, or it may be a form of sentimentalism that can never be accepted as authentic testimony.

The truth of an experience becomes suspect when it is not amenable to reason. Spiritual seekers who do not cultivate reason always leave themselves open to attacks from rival creeds, which hold competing beliefs and dogmas. That which is true for one person under certain conditions must prove itself true for all persons under similar conditions, and that which is spiritually true is also universally true, irrespective of time, place, and historical conditions. This truth cannot be challenged. Reason, therefore, liberates spiritual truth from the bonds of dogmatic supernaturalism and false mysticism, self-hypnotism, and occultism. Reason is the most infallible guide for the seeker of Truth in the realm of religion, which too often is rife with make-believe prophecies, irrational beliefs, and conflicting traditions. True spiritual adventure is possible only when the seeker is guided by reason and not by belief or hearsay. The alternative to reason is blind faith, which robs a spiritual individual of his or her human dignity characterized by independent thinking.

FAITH AND DOGMATISM

Blind faith in what has not been proved by reason when combined with the frenzy of emotion eventually leads to fanaticism. A dogmatic person is always a fanatic because of the uncertain foundation of his or her belief. Fanatics are not fully convinced about what they believe, which accounts for the rigidity of their views. Since they are not convinced they are right, they have no tolerance for disagreement. Not fully satisfied with their own views, they exhibit excessive tension and anxiety. They often claim that their religion is best and their method most superior. Claims of superiority over others is a form of defensiveness; the more such people cultivate defensiveness and exclusiveness, the more fanatical they become in their views.

Dogmatists are devoid of spiritual identity and individuality; therefore, they make little effort on their own behalf and overemphasize the doctrine of divine grace. Incapable of taking upon themselves the responsibility of a spiritual quest, they look instead for a means to passively satisfy their need for certainty. They are not searching for real truth, which requires honest effort, but for someone else's solution to the mysteries of life. Psychologically speaking, a dogmatist is an immature person. Mature people never think that they are infallible or perfect. They are always anxious to enrich their store of knowledge by learning from others. Dogmatists, on the other hand, believe they have nothing to learn from others. Their rigid views only indicate inner weakness and insecurity.

A mature person is flexible and supple in his or her thinking. In the realm of religion, a mature person has a distinct and individual spiritual inner disposition, a decisive commitment to the goal, and an implicit conviction that he or she has spiritual potential. There is always a reason for what mature persons believe and a conviction for what they follow. They exhibit honest doubt. They live neither on the memories of the past nor on the expectations of the future but in the reality of the present. One who has not learned to discriminate cannot have faith. One who cannot distinguish between truth and falsehood in ordinary religious matters cannot recognize ultimate Truth. Faith born of reason is the only testimony of Truth. In contrast, the immature person in the realm of religion has a basic mistrust for teachings other than his or her own, suffers from insecurity, is isolated from those with different beliefs, and substitutes moralism, conventionality, and rigidity for spiritual conviction. Often he or she fails to distinguish that which is authentic from that which is imitation, or that which is essential from that which is incidental or accidental. Guided by asceticism, sacramentalism, and emotionalism, the immature person does not use his or her own faculties of reasoning and thinking and is governed by the collective thinking of the group or community.

Dogmatists foster hatred and persecution. Whenever reason is discarded in favor of faith, there arise oppressive traditions and heartless rites. The rewards of religion then become the privilege of a select few. Myths and legends that are meant to provide concrete presentations of abstract truth instead become impenetrable encrustations around that truth. Superstition passes for sacred tradition, emotion for devotion, and imagination for realization. Religious dogma has provoked religious wars, inquisitions, and various forms of persecution. The brutality perpetrated in the name of religion down through the centuries, and even to this day, is unparalleled. The religious hierarchy systematically discourages honest doubt and brands noncompliance with dogma as heresy. Spiritual quest becomes a means not for the attainment of truth but for the fulfillment of worldly desires, for gaining wealth and power, or as an escape from facing the difficult challenges of life.

HARMONIZING FAITH AND REASON

The foregoing arguments in support of faith or reason are equally strong. What, then, should be the way? Must one discard reason altogether in order to have faith? Is the faith that suppresses honest doubt sincere? Should one cultivate skepticism in order to be spiritual? Can a spiritual quest and a scientific outlook go together? Vedanta offers a synthetic view that reconciles faith with reason and answers these questions.

THE REALIZATION OF TRUTH

The contentions of Vedanta are marked by several points of emphasis, the first of which is that the validity of Truth depends neither on faith nor on reason but on the realization of Truth in life. The reality of God is not contingent upon the negation or affirmation of scripture or reason. Religion is realization, from the viewpoint of Vedanta. Realization of Truth is neither scholasticism nor blind faith in any creed or dogma or miraculous event, nor ethics tinged with emotion. Realization is more than believing. Believers in faith run the risk of being deluded by their emotions, and believers in reason by their intellectual preferences. There is a difference between the conception of Truth and its direct perception; between what we believe emotionally, comprehend intellectually, or really know spontaneously. Blind faith depends on theological evidence, while unbridled reason relies on unrestrained skepticism. The extreme form of the first is dogmatism that often claims to know everything about God; and the extreme form of the second is the philosophy of atheism that believes more in denial than in anything else. Such faith or reason can never give us the certainty of inner conviction.

The Upanishadic exhortation is "Do not seek God but see him." It is seeing through the eye of integral vision, in which our entire self participates. Merely believing in the existence of God is neither seeking God nor seeing God. Such belief or faith is neither conviction nor realization but mere opinion, unsubstantiated by personal experience. On the other hand, mere reasoning, because it is intent on seeking, is unable to see that which is self-evident. Realization is seeing the self-revealed. It is revelation and becomes possible when the instruments of perception are cleansed. God, according to Vedanta, has two aspects—macrocosmic and microcosmic. Seeing God in everything (the macrocosm) begins with seeing God as one's indwelling Self (the microcosm). Our perception of the Real depends on what we believe to be the nature of Reality. What we perceive outside is the reflection of what we see within ourselves.

The goal of the spiritual quest is liberation. Liberation does not mean going somewhere that we have not been before or acquiring something new. It is a state of "being," as distinguished from the feverishness of compulsive "becomings." It is unitive vision, by which one sees one's own Self in all things and all things in one's Self. The state of liberation is that of perfect freedom that transcends all varieties of perception—moral, intellectual, and spiritual. A liberated soul is not just a knower of Truth but the very embodiment of Truth. He or she is neither a theologian who believes in a creed nor a philosopher who indulges in speculation. He or she is neither a traditionalist who clings to orthodoxy nor a futurist who lives in the days yet to come. The free soul communes with the Truth and is not content with either describing it or gathering facts about it.

FAITH MATURES INTO REALIZATION

Realization of Truth proceeds from an inner maturity or evolution that begins with the dawning of faith. Faith matures into conviction through reasoning and discrimination; intellectual conviction about Truth inspires the mind toward uninterrupted concentration; and this concentration eventually culminates in the final revelation of Truth. Vedanta accepts both reason and faith as instruments for the realization of the ultimate spiritual goal. There cannot be genuine faith without reasoning and discrimination. On the other hand, one cannot discriminate Truth from untruth unless one has implicit faith in Truth. Neither faith nor reason singly can give any finality about the real nature of Truth. The realization of Truth is possible only through the application of both. The testimony of faith without the foundation of inner conviction is mere conjecture, while the conclusions of reason unsupported by personal experience only indicate that which is not Truth, since the Ultimate Reality, infinite and incorporeal, defies all attempts of the finite human mind to define and know it.

The Upanishads indicate the Ultimate Reality as the imperishable Absolute, "the Ear of the ear, the Mind of the mind, the Speech of speech, the Life of life, and the Eye of the eye,"[1] the very ground of our being, which cannot be grasped by the discursive intellect or described in words. All our attempts to describe the Ultimate end in profound silence. "He by whom Brahman [the Absolute] is not known, knows It; he by whom It is known, knows It not. It is not known by those who know It; It is known by those who do not know It."[2] The vision of the Ultimate varies from individual to individual depending on the spiritual seeker's disposition of mind. Our realizations of the Ultimate indicate how it appears to us and not what it "really is" in itself. These realizations have been described by the various religious systems as communion with God, union with God, *samadhi,* nirvana, and so forth. Vedanta regards them as different photographs of a cathedral or temple taken from different angles of vision. Each is true and unique but never complete.

REALIZATION AS IMMEDIATE PERCEPTION

Another point of emphasis in Vedanta is that realization of Truth must be direct and immediate. Our ordinary perceptions are indirect because they are experienced through the instruments of the senses—eyes, ears, nose, skin, and tongue. These experiences are neither direct nor immediate and are often vitiated by the imperfections of the instruments of perception. For example, imperfection in a person's eyes may lead him or her to see an object doubled or disfigured; or the perversions of the mind make a person see or feel something in a distorted way. Direct perception of the Ultimate Reality is neither unconscious nor conscious. It is superconscious and free from all attachments and aversions. Superconscious realization of Truth is known as intuitive realization.

THREE INSTRUMENTS OF KNOWLEDGE

According to Vedanta, there are three instruments of knowledge: instinct, reason, and intuition. Instinctive experiences are automatic and unconscious, such as breathing. In such activities the I-consciousness remains dormant. Reason is the mature form of instinct. The vision of reason is wider than that of instinct. One's I-consciousness becomes active when one uses reason as an instrument of knowledge. The experiencer in this state is able to separate him- or herself from the act of experiencing as well as from the object experienced. Experience through reason is, however, not direct because it is conditioned by reason. It is an experience that is conscious but not spontaneous. It is not a decisive realization, because it is not supported by the entire self. We reason about a thing until we are convinced about it and are able to see it directly. An experience conditioned by and dependent upon reason is, therefore, not founded on the absolute certainty of realization. Intuitive realization is the mature form of reason and is always amenable to reason. The vision of intuition is the widest. It is superconscious, direct, and immediate. Intuitive realization never conflicts with the experience of relative facts, just as the adulthood of a person does not negate his or her childhood. Intuitive experiences are marked by three characteristics: they are universal; they do not disturb or contradict faith; and they are conducive to the welfare of all beings.

INSPIRATION—THE GIFT OF FAITH

Intuitive realization of Truth is inspiration. It is the direct vision of the tranquil heart negatively corroborated by reason; that is, absolute Truth cannot be realized except through the heart, but its realization is established only when all possible alternatives to it are negated through reasoning. The ideal knower of Truth is a free soul who has transcended all pairs of opposites, such as pleasure and pain, good and evil, and virtue and vice. The proof of the genuineness of intuitive realization is not anything private or mystical; its surest indication is the transformation of character. As a tree is known by the fruits it bears, so too a knower of Truth is recognized by the total transformation of his or her character. Such a knower of Truth becomes the very embodiment of Truth, living and moving under its spell. For that person the experience of Truth is not only spontaneous but also continuous. This realization, according to Vedanta, has two aspects: *jnana,* or subjective experience, which is inner, and *vijnana,* which is objective realization of the same through living. Realization becomes complete when what is intuitively experienced within the heart manifests in the form of spiritually creative, spontaneous actions in everyday life. The depth of an aspirant's spiritual realization is always proportional to the degree of spiritual creativity he or she has achieved. Intuitive realization is possible only when an aspirant has been able to overcome the mind, which by nature is restless, turbulent, obstinate, and not easily subdued by reason.

FOUR DISCIPLINES FOR CORRECT REASONING

Overcoming the mind is never possible without the practice of intense spiritual disciplines. Skeptics often look upon the disciplines to overcome the mind as a form of brainwashing and self-indoctrination. The traditions of Vedanta, however, contend that superconscious realization is never possible unless the mind is pure and free from all attachments and aversions, that is, free from all conditioning. The mind and the senses, already conditioned by various habits and preconceived ideas, must be deconditioned by the practice of spiritual disciplines. Nevertheless, the direct perception of Reality is not something that is produced by the practice of spiritual disciplines. It is a revelation. Truth is revealed in the mirror of the heart when it has been thoroughly cleansed. Prayer and meditation, sacraments and ceremonies, vows and austerities cannot give us the vision of Truth; they only help us to remove the coverings of the mind. They are only means to enable the aspirant to pursue his or her path of reasoning until Truth is realized; for when the Real is experienced directly, all reasoning comes to a stop and all doubts are stilled forever. We no longer reason about that which we directly perceive.

Vedanta emphasizes that reasoning must be supported by the practice of four disciplines: discrimination, dispassion, self-control, and longing for liberation.

The first discipline is the practice of discrimination between the Real and the unreal. This discipline begins with the notion that there is a vast difference between things as they are and their appearance. For example, for the ordinary person the sky is blue, and the earth and sky meet at the horizon, but for the scientist, this reality is merely an appearance. Vedantic reasoning asserts that if this world were real, it would never change, and therefore there would be no use for spiritual inquiry. On the other hand, if it is unreal, then it is not a matter of concern to anyone. But our everyday experiences are otherwise. Yet we are not happy with things as they are and seek something abiding and unchanging. The marks of Reality, according to Vedanta, are its unchanging character, its continuity, and its universality. The nature of Supreme Reality is Satchidananda, or Existence-Knowledge-Bliss Absolute. It is nondual, infinite, incorporeal, and immutable. This is the Reality of both the macrocosm and the microcosm.

Vedanta describes this Reality as Brahman, or the absolute, all-pervading Pure Consciousness. The multifarious names and forms of beings and things are real only in appearance. The world of appearances Vedanta designates as maya. This maya is the world of duality. Our perceptions of the world are not possible without the nondual and unchanging background that the Upanishads indicate as Brahman. Brahman and maya are not two realities but one, inseparable reality. Nor are the two aspects ever in conflict; they complement each other. As the shadow of an object has no meaning without the object to which it belongs, similarly the world of maya is inexplicable without the knowledge of Brahman. Salvation, according to Vedanta, is this very knowledge of Brahman, and we are all moving toward this salvation, consciously or unconsciously. The three basic aspirations of all living beings are to exist eternally, to know the unknown, and to be happy. The fulfillment of these three aspirations is attained only through the knowledge of Brahman, since Brahman is of the nature of Existence-Knowledge-Bliss Absolute. While the ignorant think that it is difficult to attain the knowledge of Brahman, the knowers of Brahman declare that it is not possible to remain eternally ignorant. So long as one has not realized Reality, one confronts it everywhere as the inexorable law of cause and effect. According to Vedanta, Brahman is the Light of all lights, and salvation is inner illumination. By this illumination, one is able to transcend the world of duality and polarity, which includes all our perceptions of relative reality.

The second discipline is the practice of dispassion and the renunciation of that which is intellectually perceived to be unreal. It is the habit of the average mind to cling to something emotionally, even though convinced about its unreality intellectually. Through the practice of dispassion, the aspirant must overcome the habit of emotional clinging.

The third discipline is self-control. Mastery over the mind and the senses involves their control and regulation. No regulation is ever possible without prior control. Achieving control and regulation of the mind and the senses requires devotion to the quest for Truth, along with the practice of fortitude, which is even-mindedness under all conditions; implicit faith in one's spiritual worthiness and in the spiritual hypothesis; the practice of contentment; complete concentration; and the practice of self-settledness.

The fourth discipline is intense longing for Truth. All spiritual practices and all reasoning become futile unless one feels a deep inner longing for the realization of Truth.

THREE TESTS OF REALIZATION

Vedanta further emphasizes that the validity of spiritual realization depends upon three tests: *shruti,* or testimony of the scriptures; *yukti,* or reason; and *anubhuti,* or personal experience. Any of these singly may enable a seeker to attain the probability of Truth but not its final certainty. Such certainty can be attained only when all three tests are applied to certify Truth.

Testimony of the scriptures (shruti). Scriptures, Vedanta asserts, cannot be taken as exhaustive accounts of Truth. They are merely suggestive. They are what Sri Ramakrishna indicates as almanacs, which, although they forecast rain, do not contain the actual rain. Scriptures have value insofar as they are considered testimonies of the experiences of the past knowers of Truth. To believe in such testimonies without verifying them through reason and personal experience is like believing in the beliefs of others, which cannot serve as an inspiration for life. The authority of the scriptures, therefore, must be supported with the testimony of reason and personal experience.

Vedanta contends that scriptures have no value for the ignorant, since they have no interest in them. They are equally of no use to the knowers of Truth, because they have realized Truth directly in their lives and are therefore no longer dependent upon the scriptures. That which is spoken of by the scriptures must be experimented upon, verified through reason, and demonstrated through living. Therefore, an aspirant is advised to dwell on the essence of the scriptures and align his or her life accordingly. Shankaracharya, the great exponent of Vedanta, is said to have remarked that what has been described by numberless scriptures can be put forth in half a verse: "Brahman alone is real; the phenomenal universe is unreal; the living being is none other than Brahman."[3] Sri Ramakrishna compares the scriptures to letters:

> A man lost a letter. He couldn't remember where he had left it. He began to search for it with a lamp. After two or three people had searched, the letter was at last found, The message in the letter was: "Please send us five seers of sandesh [a sweet] and a piece of wearing-cloth." The man read it, and then threw the letter away. There was no further need of it; now all he had to do was to buy the five seers of sandesh and the piece of cloth.[4]

Merely reading scriptures over and over again does not and cannot bring forth the revelation of Truth. It is like reading an old letter over and over again without following its instructions. Sole dependence on reason for the certainty of Truth, however, often leads one to intellectual rationalization. Reasoning works well only when it is directed toward a goal. Without a goal, reason can only construct systems and can yield no conclusions. Unless the mind of an aspirant is free from all attachment and aversion, his or her reasoning is bound to be conditioned by them. Furthermore, reason tries to ascertain the validity of Truth within the context of time, which is ever changing, whereas the validity of ultimate Truth is to be judged by the standard of eternity. Ultimate Truth is eternal and unaffected by the changing phenomena of the universe and, according to Vedanta, remains the same throughout all time—past, present, and future. At the same time, the realization of absolute Truth does not negate the validity of our day-to-day relative experiences and values.

Reason (yukti). The efficacy of reason as an instrument of knowledge depends not merely on its perfection but also on its right use. According to Vedanta, the right use of reason is its rational as opposed to irrational use. Rational use calls for sincerity of purpose and honesty of doubt. The goal of reason is to dispel doubts and help one to discover Truth for oneself; but no reasoning, however perfect, can dispel doubts that have no rational bases. Rational doubts are always sincere, well thought out, plausible, and relevant. Irrational doubts, on the other hand, are irrelevant, unreasonable, obsessive, devoid of any clear perspective, and often rationalized expressions of the doubter's emotional and intellectual fixations. They frustrate and defeat the very purpose of reasoning. Rational use of reason initiates a process of positive and creative thinking and is free from the pressures of any tradition, authority, convention, or emotion. In contrast, irrational use of reason is negative and, therefore, destructive and pessimistic. It is a form of compulsive skepticism that is often prone to raise a doubt merely for the sake of doubting. In a sense, a compulsive doubter is incapable of sincere doubting and, therefore, incapable of reasoning and facing Truth. The watchword for the rational use of reason is *exploration,* while that for its irrational use is *manipulation.*

The traditions of Vedanta mention three types of reasoning: *vada, jalpa,* and *vitanda. Vada* is academic reasoning, the goal of which is to discover Truth without having a bias for or against the hypothesis. This type of reasoning seeks to establish facts by highlighting the merits of a hypothesis. *Jalpa* is reasoning in which the main purpose is to overthrow the arguments of the opponent by any means, rational or irrational. It is reasoning in a dogmatic and negative way. The third type of reasoning, *vitanda,* seeks only to lay bare the defects of, misrepresent, or confuse the opponent's contentions without trying to suggest an alternative hypothesis.

Rational reasoning in Vedanta is not arguing. Neither is it reasoning with any bias for or against the hypothesis. It is *vichara,* or a process of rational discrimination between the Real and the unreal. Absolute Reality is affirmed by negating all that is relative. The contention of Vedanta is that an average mind is subject to irrational doubts, preconceived ideas, and personal sentiments. Unless guarded by reason, it can easily lapse into inertia and delusion. There is no way of dispelling these prejudices of the mind except through reasoning. Vedanta exhorts an aspirant to scrutinize the meaning of Truth and to make a critical estimate of what he or she has realized to be true.

Gaudapada, the author of the *Mandukya-karika,* lays down two principles to reconcile reason with scripture. According to him, scriptural testimony may be taken to be valid only when it is conclusively established that its meaning is beyond doubt and that it is in accordance with human reason.[5] Reason, and not tradition, sets the standard of Truth. Shankaracharya in his *Mandukya-bhashya* commentary elucidates the following progression of Vedantic reasoning: first, Vedantic reasoning seeks to clearly ascertain the meaning of the scriptural statement in the context of its goal; second, it then proves the logical untenability of all contrary concepts; third, it establishes the intelligibility of nondualism; and fourth, Vedantic reasoning exposes the mutually contradictory nature of all dualistic views about Reality. While reasoning by itself is inconclusive, scriptures by themselves cannot dispel doubt nor evoke conviction. The methods of valid knowledge according to nondualistic Vedanta are perception, inference, verbal testimony, comparison, postulation, and nonapprehension. But no one of these singly, nor several together, nor all of them in combination can decisively establish the finality of Truth, which is transcendental.

For example, perception may be defective because of the imperfection of the sense organs. Moreover, the scope of the perceptions of the sense organs is limited, and therefore the knowledge of Reality is always incomplete. Inference is dependent upon sense-perceived facts and can only suggest the probability of Truth and not the certainty of it. Neither can verbal testimony of the sacred texts give us the direct vision of God, since no one can see God or the soul merely by studying sacred texts or hearing them read. Also, the scriptures are not always unanimous and are often self-contradictory. The purported meaning of a scriptural text may be quite different from its literal meaning. Comparison, another method, is possible only when there is a parallel object to compare with. Since there is nothing comparable to the Supreme Reality, its existence cannot be established by comparison. Postulation is another kind of inference, based on previous experience, and therefore the reality of God cannot be postulated. This is also the case with regard to nonapprehension, which indicates the nonperception of an object.

Personal experience (anubhuti). The last resort for an aspirant, therefore, is personal experience. But even personal experience by itself is as incomplete and inconclusive as the foregoing methods, for one's personal experience can be deceptive, temporary, reflected, or false. In view of the insufficiency of the various instruments of knowledge, Vedanta contends that the validity of a transcendental experience of spiritual truth can be assured only when that experience is corroborated by scriptural testimony and affirmed by reason.

Vedantic Reasoning

Vedantic reasoning follows a threefold process: *shravana,* or hearing the sacred texts; *manana,* or reflecting with reason on what has been heard or read; and *nididhyasana,* or meditating on what has been reasoned about.

Shravana, in order to be accepted by the mind, must first be put to the test of reason. The aspirant must grasp the true meaning of the scripture and not just its literal meaning. It is the spirit, and not the words, that is important. An aspirant is asked to apply reason in order to ascertain the purport of a scriptural text; that is, he or she must reason about the following six characteristic points regarding the text: correspondence of the introductory passage with the concluding one, frequency of reference to the central theme, originality, fruitfulness, commendableness, and reasonableness.

The aspirant must reason with an open mind, and he or she must be endowed with *shraddha,* or faith in him- or herself, in the teaching, and in the teacher. An aspirant of Vedantic faith reasons for the purpose of believing. Even in most secular matters one must depend on, and have implicit faith in, the hypothesis. A scientist must have faith in his or her hypothesis to proceed with an experiment. A lawyer must believe in the cause of the client in order to win the case. A medical doctor must have confidence in the diagnosis and prognosis given to the patient, so that the patient can successfully be treated. No reasoning is possible unless there is a hypothesis to begin with. Hence, initial or hypothetical faith in scriptural testimony is essential. The opposite of faith is cynicism, which is always mistrustful and constrictive in its outlook. Reason, when it is not committed to the goal of realization of Truth, is aimless and results in mere drifting logic. Vedanta emphasizes creative reasoning as opposed to speculative reasoning. Reasoning becomes creative when directed toward the realization of Truth. The only way one can shake off the fixations and various preconceived ideas of the mind is through the right use of reason.

Vedantic reasoning does not seek to prove or disprove the reality of the world; its sole purpose is to have the direct apprehension of that which is ultimately Real. *Shravana,* or hearing of the scriptures, is the first step toward this direct apprehension. The knowledge gained through *shravana* is mediate and not immediate. Mediate knowledge becomes immediate only when all doubts have been dispelled and all contrary notions have been refuted. There is, therefore, a vast difference between mere hearing about Truth and direct experience of the same.

Manana, the second step, is reflecting on the meaning of a scriptural text. It is a process of positive reasoning that seeks to grasp Truth intellectually. But intellectual perception is not direct realization. Direct realization is achieved through the practice of *nididhyasana,* or meditation, which is the third step. Repeated meditation transforms the intellectual perception into a direct vision by which the seeker not only perceives Truth intellectually but also feels it spontaneously within him- or herself. Vedanta describes how the three steps work in this way: *shravana* initiates mental activity about the probability of Truth in the scriptural testimony; *manana* raises honest doubts and tries to refute them in order to gain conviction in the hypothesis; and *nididhyasana* leads to concentration of mind on the conviction of Truth so it may become intuitive realization. The knowledge that is gained through hearing of the scriptural text is confirmed through reflection and then transformed into direct experience through meditation. The realization of Truth is possible only when one is able to overcome all pairs of opposites and all unconscious urges, which are the projections of one's ego.

Liberation, according to Vedanta, is freedom from all dictates and superimpositions of ego. It is seeing every relative phenomenon as a reflection of absolute Reality. Expressed in theological language, it is the attainment of an all-pervading God-consciousness by which one sees God in everything, both with eyes open and with eyes closed. Any realization that falls short of this God-consciousness is a halfway house toward the realization of absolute Truth. The atheist does not believe in God. The agnostic is doubtful about God's existence. The theist sees the reality of both God and the world. The natural scientist believes that everything is inert matter. The Vedantist, on the other hand, sees everything as the living God. There is but one ultimate Truth, not two, and God is the embodiment of that ultimate Truth. The process of directly experiencing Truth is a movement from lower truth to higher truth and not from falsehood to truth. Each relative phenomenon of the universe, according to Vedanta, is not false but is a reflection or conditioned expression of ultimate Truth. Thus, there is one God, one Truth, and one salvation for all seekers, irrespective of the diversities of their religious beliefs and philosophies. Diversities are inevitable because of the diversity of mental dispositions, the different levels of spiritual perception of different persons, and the diversity of human languages through which thought and experience are expressed.

CATEGORIES OF ASPIRANTS

All spiritual aspirants come under three broad categories: those who contemplate the essential identity of God, the totality of all souls, and the individual soul; those who recognize the potential unity between God and humans and yet make a distinction between the two; and those who believe God and humans are not similar and can never be so. Vedanta philosophy calls these three categories of aspirants, respectively: *advaitins,* or nondualists; *visishtadvaitins,* or qualified nondualists; and *dvaitins,* or dualists. For the first, Ultimate Reality is experienced as intuitive revelation of Truth; for the second, as a lovable Supreme Being; and for the third, as a sustainer and savior. Salvation, according to Vedanta, is the attainment of nondual God-consciousness that transcends all limitations of space and time, caste and creed, sect and nationality. For the *advaitins,* any concept of salvation that does not have nondual God-consciousness as its goal cannot be complete and final.

The Vedantic concept of salvation as nondual God-consciousness does not conflict with any human thought or aspiration. It is most scientific because it puts an end to all doubts and is verifiable by one's own experiences in this very life. It is most democratic because it is attainable by all. Such salvation alone can bridge the gulf that exists between the so-called sacred and secular and make the diverse relative priorities and goals of human life meaningful in the background of one common and ultimate goal.

TRANSFORMATION OF CHARACTER

Philosophy relies solely on reason, which tends to develop a mechanical outlook on reality. Vedanta, on the other hand, relies neither on scripture, nor on reason, nor on personal experience, nor on the alliance of the three. The transformation of character is the only proof it accepts. The goal of reasoning, according to Vedanta, is to be not only intellectually wise but also to be spiritually illumined. The exhortation of Vedanta is to achieve emancipation from all authority—religious or philosophical, conventional or traditional—and this emancipation is possible only by the direct realization of Truth. Emancipation, however, is not denunciation. It is transcending one's psychophysical limitations. Direct realization is Truth actualized and experienced, which transcends Truth conceptualized. That which is Truth must be conclusive, universal, and also able to solve problems. The following soul-stirring words of Swami Vivekananda, from a letter he wrote to a young man in India, vividly highlight the essence of Vedanta:

> I do not believe in a religion or God which cannot wipe the widow's tears or bring a piece of bread to the orphan's mouth. However sublime be the theories, however well spun may be the philosophy, I do not call it religion so long as it is confined to books and dogmas.[6]

The validity of any knowledge depends upon its usefulness in everyday life, and the means to acquire that knowledge must be effective in attaining the goal. The goal of Vedanta is not to construct systems of thought but to put an end to the sufferings of human life in a decisive way. All these sufferings, in the view of Vedanta, are ultimately due to either nonapprehension or misapprehension of Reality. Ego and egotism do not let one see the Real and live in it. The vast majority of people live not in reality but in the polarized world of their imaginations. In brief, the sufferings of life result from a deep inner crisis that is essentially spiritual. There can be no material or psychological solution to a crisis that is spiritual, because material and psychological sufferings are merely symptoms having a spiritual crisis as their root cause. Another name for this spiritual crisis is the crisis of self-identity. The cause of all crises, according to Vedanta, centers on one question: *Who am I?* or in Sanskrit, *Koham?* The Vedantic answer to this question is *I am he* (the Absolute), or *Soham*. All our sufferings come to an end only when we discover our real identity, our true Self, which Vedanta indicates as Atman—the common Self in all beings of the universe.

TRUTH IS ONE, PATHS ARE MANY

The keynote of Vedanta, and our final point of emphasis, is "Truth is one: sages call it by various names" (*Rig Veda* 10.114.5). That which is ultimate Truth is one without a second. The various concepts of the Ultimate Reality are due to the various angles of vision and also to different levels of experience of the same. These concepts, according to Vedanta, are mere interpretations and not exhaustive descriptions. In the light of the nondual vision of Vedanta, they are not contradictory but complementary. All concepts of Reality can be brought under three broad categories: dualistic, qualified non-dualistic, and nondualistic. So long as we remain identified with our body, the Ultimate Reality appears in the form of a personal God; when we look upon ourselves as a soul encased in a physical frame, we see Reality as the whole and ourselves as a portion of it; and, finally, when we are able to transcend the ideas of both body and mind, we feel that we are one with it. If God made human beings in God's own image, then human beings also make and remake the image of God, the Ultimate Reality, in their own image as they progress on the path of God-realization. According to one of the texts of Vedanta, the Ultimate Reality, undivided Pure Consciousness free from all attributes of name and form, assumes different forms for the fulfillment of the spiritual aspirations of various seekers in keeping with their respective inner dispositions, which are always conditioned by culture, creed, tradition, and history. Limited by the ideas of time, space, and causation, the Ultimate Reality appears to the dualists as a personal God and also as Divine Incarnations; to the qualified nondualists as the indwelling Reality, and to the nondualists as absolute Pure Consciousness.

The dualistic, the qualified nondualistic, and the nondualistic concepts also indicate the three successive stages in the spiritual evolution of one and the same seeker. They represent the milestones of the seeker's spiritual progress. The Ultimate Reality is like the sun toward which the seeker is journeying. The three different concepts of Reality are like three different photographs of the sun taken by the aspirant as he or she journeys toward it. The dualist sees God as the creator of the universe, which is different from and dependent upon God. The dualist's religion is based on faith and bound by the authority of the scriptures. The qualified nondualist takes God to be the cause and the universe to be the effect; that is, God, the cause, has become the universe, the effect. This type of aspirant tries to make a compromise between faith and reason, and he or she often subordinates faith to reason. The nondualist, on the other hand, perceives God in everything. For the nondualist, the cause is the same as its effect, and therefore God is all in all. The nondualist uses both faith and reason as instruments for the attainment of direct experience of the Ultimate Reality; such experience is immediate and intuitive and not based on mere intellectual speculations or dry formulations.

For the dualist, God has created the universe; for the qualified nondu-alist, God has become the universe; and for the nondualist, God appears as the universe. While the first two concepts limit the idea of God, nondualistic Vedanta presents a limitless idea of God that transcends all bounds of creed and culture, name and form, and yet fulfills the spiritual aspirations of all. For the nondualist, God is like a circle whose circumference is nowhere but whose center is everywhere. The Ultimate Reality as nondual Pure Consciousness is all embracing: It includes the personal God of the dualist and the personal/impersonal God of the qualified nondualist, which are like two huge waves in the ocean of infinite God-consciousness. Sri Ramakrishna describes the impersonal absolute Reality as a boundless expanse of water, and the forms of the personal God as blocks of ice formed on the water by the cooling influence of divine emotions. Because of the deep love of the worshiper, the Infinite reduces itself, as it were, to the finite, and appears before the worshiper in a tangible way as God with form. With the rising of the sun, the ice melts away; so also, with the dawning of knowledge, God with form melts into the shoreless ocean of pure spirit.

Types of Worship

The nondualistic vision of Vedanta harmonizes the diverse modes of worship practiced by the different seekers on the path of God-realization. A beginner worships God through symbols and images. For such aspirants, their own individuality is real and the physical universe is tangible, and therefore God is external and personal. They cannot think of God except as a person. Their relationship with God is formal and their worship ritualistic. As seekers progress on the path of God-consciousness, God appears to them as their inner controller. Their mode of worship at this stage is guided more by love than by law, and it is more internal than external. In the course of time, as they reach the third stage of God-consciousness, they see God as their inner being or as indwelling God-consciousness. Their prayer and worship at this stage take the form of contemplation and meditation. The third stage culmi-nates in the fourth, where the worshiper, the object of worship, and the act of worshiping merge into one. The worshiper's indwelling Pure Consciousness becomes one with the absolute Pure Consciousness. To quote the words of Swami Vivekananda:

Thus man, after this vain search for various gods outside himself, completes the circle and comes back to the point from which he started—the human soul; and he finds that the God whom he was searching for over hill and dale, whom he was seeking in every brook, in every temple, in every church, the God whom he was even imagining as sitting in heaven and ruling the world, is his own Self. I am He, and He is I. None but I was God; this little I never existed.[7]

At this stage the worshiper sees God both inside and outside him- or herself, both with eyes open and with eyes closed. The spirit of Vedantic worship has been highlighted by the prayer of the great sage Vyasa:

O Lord, in my worship I have attributed forms to Thee, who art formless. O Thou teacher of the world, by my hymns I have, as it were, contradicted Thy indescribable nature. By going on pilgrimage I have, as it were, denied Thy Omnipresence. O Lord of the universe, pray, forgive me these three transgressions.[8]

According to Vedanta, all spiritual experiences of the Godhead as personal or impersonal, as father or mother, and so forth are equally true because they are experiences of one and the same Ultimate Reality. The diversities of experience only indicate how Reality as nondual Pure Consciousness appears and not what it really is. The nondual realization of Truth is the deepest of all forms of realization attainable by a human being. All dualism ends in nondualism. All our attempts to seek or see, know or define the Ultimate Reality culminate in being it. Sri Ramakrishna compares this nondual realization to a monotone and all other spiritual realizations to diverse melodies. The monotone is the basic note, or keynote, of the melodies and can never be in conflict with them. While the Reality is one, Vedanta advocates diverse paths for the realization of it in the context of the diverse temperaments and dispositions of the human mind. Unity in diversity is the very plan of life, and therefore Vedanta calls for freedom of worship. What is important is not the path but the realization of the goal. The goal of all spiritual quests is the direct experience of Reality, or ultimate Truth. Direct experience is more than emotional fervor or intellectual assent. It is not just hearing or acknowledging Truth; it is becoming one with it. The foundational concept of all religious teachings is that human nature is really divine, and that religion becomes meaningful for us only when this divinity is manifested in our lives.

SPIRITUAL INDIVIDUALITY

Direct experience is an organic growth from within; it cannot be given by any external authority. Philosophies, theologies, creeds and dogmas, rituals and doctrines have value only because they are believed to evoke faith in our inner divinity. But each seeker represents a spiritual individuality with a peculiar spiritual temperament and disposition, and therefore each has to attain direct experience in his or her own way. The path of one cannot, or need not, be the path of another. Another name for salvation, or liberation, is emancipation—emancipation from the pressure of all conventions, traditions, and injunctions. No genuine spiritual quest begins until the aspirant begins to believe in him- or herself. A true aspirant depends on his or her spiritual individuality and is not looking for any windfall or miraculous realization. Therefore Vedanta stresses the growth and development of the spiritual individuality of each seeker so that each is able to manifest a capacity for rational thought and free choice.

The growth and development of spiritual individuality is the first step toward the direct experience of Truth. Emphasizing this need for spiritual individuality, Swami Vivekananda points out:

> I am glad that sects exist, and I only wish they may go on multiplying more and more. Why? Simply because of this: If you and I and all who are present here were to think exactly the same thoughts, there would be no thoughts for us to think. We know that two or more forces must come into collision in order to produce motion. It is the clash of thought, the differentiation of thought, that awakes thought. Now, if we all thought alike, we would be like Egyptian mummies in a museum, looking vacantly at one another's faces—no more than that! Whirls and eddies occur only in a rushing, living stream. There are no whirlpools in stagnant, dead water.
>
> When religions are dead, there will be no more sects; it will be the perfect peace and harmony of the grave. But so long as mankind thinks, there will be sects. Variation is the sign of life,

and it must be there. I pray that sects may multiply so that at last there will be as many sects as human beings and each one will have his own method, his individual method of thought in religion.[9]

FAITH, REASON, AND REALIZATION

The goal of Vedanta is to realize Truth. The concern of Vedanta is not to prove or disprove the reality of the world of phenomena but to establish the sole reality of Brahman through direct experience. The image of the Ultimate Reality from a theological perspective is one of finite creation. But a finite creator is no creator at all. Teleological proof gives only a glimpse of a conscious principle behind the creative process but cannot describe the nature of that principle. So, too, ontological proof can only suggest a probability, not a certainty. The scriptures are also not decisive, and their conclusions are divergent. Inner experience by itself is not enough because a person can be deceived by his or her perceptions. Of faith, reason, and experience, not one singly can serve as the final testimony of Truth. Vedanta seeks to integrate all three harmoniously. Vedanta points out that the finite human mind can never exhaustively define or describe the Infinite. There will always remain an element of mystery about it.

Any reasoning that does not accept the limitations of the mind is perverted reasoning. It seeks to conquer, measure, and possess the Infinite by cutting it down to the mind's finite size. Efforts to obtain God by means of sacraments, penances, disciplines, or rituals have never succeeded. Similarly, all attempts to acquire God-like omnipotence through medicine, psychology, industry, or technology have proved to be futile. Theologians have tried to formulate an image of the Ultimate by separating it from the world. When the Ultimate is separated from the world of relative phenomena, both the Ultimate and the relative become meaningless. Furthermore, the more we know of the Ultimate, the more we discover how little we know about it. The more we push forward the frontier of our knowledge about the universe, the more we realize the vastness of it.

Direct experience, though intuitive and transcendental, is always amenable to reason, and it is based upon facts and verifiable by logic. This verification, however, must include an analysis of all the sense data experienced by an individual. Any realization of ultimate Truth calls for investigation and analysis of the totality of experience, including not only those of the waking state but also those of dream and dreamless sleep.

As mentioned earlier, Vedanta upholds nondualism (*advaita*), as opposed to atheism, agnosticism, theism, monism, dualism, qualified nondualism, or scientific rationalism. Nondualism seeks to spiritualize everything. The atheist denies God, the agnostic doubts God's existence, and the theist looks upon God as a distant being who is different from the world of phenomena. The monist denies any reality of the external universe and pictures God as a metaphysical principle far beyond the reach of the average human mind. The dualist wants to establish the reality of both God and the world at the same time. The qualified nondualist, anxious to prove an organic relation between God and the phenomenal world by declaring the latter an extension of God, overemphasizes the personal aspect of God. The scientist imagines mutation in the immutable. Nondualistic Vedanta presents a concept of God that is not at variance with any of these ideas yet transcends them all. The God of nondualistic Vedanta is the Supreme Brahman. It is immutable Pure Consciousness. It is devoid of all attributes, names, and forms, yet at the same time it can assume different forms for the fulfillment of the spiritual aspirations of all seekers in keeping with their respective diverse dispositions.

A seeker is called upon to harmonize faith with reason and the ideal with the actual. Without this harmony, there would be no links between what we think intellectually, feel emotionally, and realize intuitively. It would reveal neither meaning nor purpose. Harmony is possible only in the context of direct experience of Reality. Direct experience includes all experiences. It is a mode of consciousness that, once attained, is never lost. It continues throughout all the states of consciousness. Various religions and spiritual philosophies use different words to describe this same experience: communion with God, merging in Brahman, nirvana, God-consciousness, and so forth.

Direct Experience of Truth

Vedanta is more than a philosophical system. The Vedantist is not content with speculating on Truth but seeks its direct experience, which is intuitive, and uses philosophy only as a stepping-stone toward that end. There is a world of difference between speculating on Truth philosophically and realizing the same directly through intuition. Intuitional realization is self-certifying because it puts an end to all doubt. Reconciling reason with intuition, Swami Vivekananda says:

> Stick to your reason until you reach something higher; and you will know it to be higher because it will not jar with reason. The state beyond consciousness is inspiration (samadhi); but never mistake hysterical trances for the real thing. It is a terrible thing to claim this inspiration falsely, to mistake instinct for inspiration. There is no external test for inspiration; we know it ourselves. Our guard against mistake is negative: the voice of reason. All religion means going beyond reason; but reason is the only guide to get there. Instinct is like ice, reason is like water, and inspiration is like the subtlest form or vapor; one follows the other. Everywhere is this eternal sequence: unconsciousness, consciousness, intelligence; matter, body, mind; and to us it seems as if the chain begins with the particular link we first lay hold of. According to some, the body creates the mind; according to others, the mind, the body. The arguments on both sides are of equal weight and both are true. We must go beyond both, to where there is neither the one nor the other. These successions are all maya.[10]

Vedanta maintains that direct experience of Truth alone can make all our values and virtues meaningful. The principles of morality ask us to be pure and righteous, and the codes of ethics require us to be honest and sincere. But why should one be moral and ethical and do good to others? What is the spiritual incentive for it? Can morality and ethics themselves serve as the goal of life? In answer to these questions, Vedanta points out that all our values and virtues become meaningful only when they lead us toward the supreme goal—liberation through Self-realization. One cannot do good without first being good. One is asked to do good to others because one comes nearer to Truth by doing good than by not doing it. When one does good to others, one is really doing good to oneself, because the well-being of one (the microcosm) depends upon the well-being of all others (the macrocosm).

According to nondualistic Vedanta, the direct experience of Reality is ineffable, because it has no comparison, no parallel, to describe or objectify.

The Real is like the endless horizon. We may be able to see it, but we can never take hold of it. All philosophy, theology, and cosmology are attempts to describe and define the Infinite, which is indescribable and indefinable. But such descriptions and definitions always fall short because it is possible only to describe and define the appearance of Reality, not Reality itself.

The ineffability of direct experience of the Ultimate rests not in any particular assertion of Vedanta. Other great traditions similarly affirm this view: "He that hath seen Me hath seen the Father" (John 14:9); or, "I Am That I Am" (Exod. 4:14); or, once again, in the Vedanta tradition, "Atman is subtler than the subtlest and not to be known through argument."[11]

Vedanta maintains that there is only one religion behind all the religions and it is the religion of God-consciousness. For the individual, this religion begins when he or she stops seeking God in the outside world, in temples and churches, and is no longer satisfied with merely accepting the beliefs of others. After searching for God outside, the seeker ultimately returns to him- or herself. To quote Swami Vivekananda: "A straight line, infinitely projected, must end in a circle."[12] The goal of Vedantic reasoning is not to define God but to know the limitations of reasoning.

Vedantic nondualism is not in conflict with any of the various philosophical systems of thought. While these systems contradict one another in the exclusiveness of their claims, Vedanta harmonizes and integrates them all. The goal of all philosophical systems is to discover a basis of unity in the midst of diversity. Their conclusions differ because of their diverse angles of vision, which result from their varied beliefs and notions. The basis of unity may be purely material, or a process of ceaseless change, or a dual principle of change and permanence, or a combination of pure substances (God, souls, and atoms), or subtle vibrations. Then again, the unity may be based upon the personality of a supreme Godhead, or on the nature of Pure Consciousness that is endowed with all good and great qualities.

Nondualistic Vedanta declares that the basis of this unity is Nirguna Brahman: indivisible Pure Consciousness devoid of all attributes, names, and forms, and one without a second. Vedanta says: "All that exists is verily Brahman." The manifold universe is not anything different from Brahman but is merely an appearance of it. Vedanta designates this appearance as maya. Brahman (Ultimate Reality) and maya are like an infinite ocean and its countless waves. Both the ocean and the waves are composed of the same stuff, but when one's attention is fixed on the waves, one fails to see the ocean; and when one sees the ocean, one does not see the waves. The waves belong to the ocean, and the ocean cannot be in conflict with the waves, no matter how different the two appear to be from each other.

Direct experience does not come about by a miracle; it is neither an emotional thrill nor an escape into another realm of existence. Real experience, from the point of view of Vedanta, is dwelling in uninterrupted God-consciousness. But God-consciousness is not something that can be given to us: it is a revelation from within. God-consciousness is not for the physically weak or intellectually indolent. Nor is it for escapists or opportunists. Uninterrupted God-consciousness can be attained only by those who sincerely long for it and strive for it. As Shankaracharya says in his *Vivekachudamani*:

> A disease does not leave off if one simply utters the name of the medicine, without taking it; [similarly] without direct realization one cannot be liberated by the mere utterance of the word Brahman.[13]

What is needed, as a first step toward direct realization, is faith in our innate divinity. Spiritual seekers may believe in all the holy scriptures, adore every divine incarnation, and live in the constant company of saints and holy people, but unless they have faith in themselves, that is to say, in their potential divinity, all efforts will prove to be futile. The disciplines of Vedanta seek to arouse faith in our potential divinity and spiritual possibility. "Religion," in the words of Swami Vivekananda, "is the manifestation of the divinity already in man."[14] To be divine, Vedanta asserts, is most natural to us; to be otherwise is a perversion of our basic nature. Spiritual progress, according to Vedanta, is measured not by the increasing amount of time we devote to prayer and meditation but by the greater degree of conviction we gain in our innate divinity. The more we develop faith in our inner divinity, the more we become free from our dependence on external authorities, such as tradition, scriptures, rituals, and philosophical reasoning. A genuine spiritual quest is always spontaneous, and it is never prompted by fear or considerations of gain or loss. While conventional religions describe atheists as those who do not believe in God or adhere to scriptural injunctions, atheists, according to Vedanta, are those who do not believe in their own divinity.

THE FOUR CARDINAL PRINCIPLES OF VEDANTA

Vedanta is not a new or a specific religion. It is the essential spirit behind all the religions of the world. The four main themes or cardinal principles of Vedanta are oneness of existence, divinity of the soul, nonduality of the Godhead, and harmony of religions.

ONENESS OF EXISTENCE

The universe of beings and things, according to Vedanta, is one homogeneous and undivided existence. It exists not just as matter but as undivided Pure Consciousness, which is no other than God. The Bhagavad Gita describes God as a Cosmic Person who eats through a million mouths, walks through a million feet, encompassing everything in the universe. The Upanishads designate the Godhead as Virat, or the Supreme Purusha (Person), whose head is the *akasha,* or infinite space; whose eyes are the sun, moon, and stars; and whose feet are the earth. There is thus only one life, one consciousness, that pulsates throughout the universe. Oneness of existence is the basis of all ethics, morality, love, and fellow feeling. An action is regarded as ethical when it is conducive to the welfare of all. Ethical actions are good because they help us realize the oneness of existence. Evil actions are those that deny this oneness of existence. The Bhagavad Gita points out that an individual's existence and well-being are linked with the existence and well-being of all. The individual is dependent on the cooperation of fellow human beings, on the animals and vegetation from which he or she draws food, and also on the support of many other living beings and organisms. The person who denies this interdependence and seeks selfish enjoyment of life disturbs the very fabric of life and ultimately endangers his or her own existence.

DIVINITY OF THE SOUL

The second cardinal principle of Vedanta is the divinity of the soul. This is a fundamental principle of all religions. But what is the nature of the soul? The soul is that which unifies all our experiences of the physical and mental planes. While some religious systems regard the mind as the soul, Vedanta maintains that the soul is different from the mind and the body. The soul is all-pervading Pure Consciousness individualized in a body-mind complex, and it is immortal and pure. The body and mind are mere instruments of the soul. Divinity being its innate nature, the soul can never be tainted. This divinity is neither created nor derived and cannot be borrowed. The soul is deathless and, therefore, birthless. The doctrine that the soul was created as divine and immortal at a point in time before its birth in a body is contradictory to rational thinking, since whatever is born must eventually die.

Despite the assertions of the idealists, not all persons are created equal. Theism fails to give a rational explanation for why there is such inequality within the creation of a just and merciful God, and its promise of life in the eternal hereafter offers no real solace. Heredity and environment give only a partial explanation for some of the differences in the psychophysical characteristics among individuals. Vedanta seeks an explanation in the theory of rebirth. Neither the materialistic doctrine of the utter annihilation of the soul after death nor the theistic doctrine of an eternal reward in heaven or eternal retribution in hell satisfies the rational mind. Both theories are incompatible with the moral and spiritual laws of the universe. The doctrine of eternal suffering denies the erring individual any chance for regeneration through repentance for sins he or she may have committed. The theory of rebirth is a more probable explanation, and an inevitable corollary of the eternal nature of the divine soul. Why does the immortal, divine soul suffer manifold miseries? And if divinity is our soul's innate nature, why then do we not manifest this divinity in our actions? In answer, Vedanta says that the soul's sufferings are due to its identification with its apparent embodiment as a physical and mental being. Embodiment is the result of previous desires of the body and mind that have not been extinguished. Desires result from our past thoughts and actions, both virtuous and unrighteous. While virtuous thoughts and actions help to manifest divinity in us, unrighteous thoughts and actions create distance in our minds from our innate divinity. All our prayers and worship, our penances and austerities are intended to arouse faith in our own divinity through a process of purification of the body and mind. The soul attains its freedom from the bondage of conditioning when it regains the knowledge of the Self, or soul, which Vedanta describes as liberation. The soul is divine because it is nondifferent from God. Liberation is the realization of our divinity, which remains forever the same no matter what we think about it. No mortal can ever attain immortality; similarly, the mundane can ever be divine. If divinity were accidental to the soul, it could never be our own, for only that which is our real nature can ever belong to us.

NONDUALITY OF THE GODHEAD

The third cardinal principle of Vedanta is the nonduality of the Godhead. Although the Ultimate Reality is always one and undivided, the appearances of it are endless due to the diverse mediums of the individual minds through which it is perceived. God as the Ultimate Reality is always one, and all seekers, regardless of their religious beliefs and traditions, are calling on the same God. The language and dialects of their prayers may differ, but the spirit of worship is always the same. Multifarious images of God are revealed in various ways to limited, individual minds. But Vedanta speaks of four stages of divine revelation:

First, God as absolute, ultimate, transcendental Reality, described by the Upanishads as Brahman, the all-pervading Pure Consciousness. In this aspect, Reality cannot be labeled as knower, thinker, creator, or actor, for it alone exists.

Second, God as immanent in the universe. In this aspect, God appears as the World Soul, the inmost essence of all beings and things.

Third, the personal God: the transcendental Reality endowed with a divine personality, appears to the seeker in keeping with his or her spiritual aspirations.

Fourth, the Divine Incarnation, or God, assuming a human form.

These four stages are not in conflict but are simply different realizations of a seeker at different stages of his or her inner evolution. As long as seekers consider themselves psychophysical beings, they cannot help being dualistic and experiencing the ultimate transcendental Reality as external and endowed with a personality. When those same seekers regard themselves more as souls than bodies, they feel themselves to be a part of the Ultimate. When they are totally oblivious to their physical and psychological individualities, they realize that the same God they had been seeking outside is alone abiding both inside and outside themselves.

HARMONY OF RELIGIONS

The fourth cardinal principle of Vedanta is the harmony of religions. Truth as Ultimate Reality is one without a second, but the paths leading to its realization are many, because of the variety of human temperaments and dispositions. Vedantic harmony has three aspects: unity in diversity, true acceptance of all religions, and harmony based on the goal.

Unity in diversity. First, this harmony is not uniformity but unity in diversity. It is the harmony of the goal that leaves the differences of the paths undisturbed. Every religious system has four parts—ritual, myth, philosophy, and experience. The first three become meaningful only when they are done for the sake of the fourth. While experience is internal and most vital, the other three are nonessential: like the protective husk surrounding the grain, they exist for the preservation and perpetuation of the fourth. Religious strife results from the overemphasis of the first three—ritual, myth and philosophy—which are bound to vary because of the diversities of cultural traditions.

True acceptance of all religions. The second aspect of Vedantic harmony is the true acceptance of all religions, rather than simply tolerance of them. Tolerance is actually looking upon all faiths other than one's own as inferior. The Vedantist views all religions as revelations of God that are not antagonistic but complementary to one another. These different religious systems, like so many photographs of the same building from various angles, give us multiple images of the one Truth from diverse perspectives. The idea of uniformity is alien to Vedanta and is neither desirable nor possible.

Harmony based on the goal. The third aspect of Vedantic harmony is neither partisan nor eclectic but a harmony based on the goal. Partisan harmony is the harmony of uniformity. Even though characterized by depth and intensity, it suffers from narrowness of outlook. It is sectarian in its traditions and rigid in its formulations. Lacking in breadth, it proves to be one-sided and intolerant of others' views and advocates conversion of all to its beliefs. Partisan harmony denies religious freedom and, by so doing, fails to serve as a bond of unity for all religions. Eclectic harmony, on the other hand, is broad and catholic in its view. But its inherent defect is that it seeks to accept and appreciate the teachings of different religions in a selective way, culling the best of the various traditions and making an anthology of them. Eclectic harmony is more intellectual than spiritual and practical. Its bond of unity is not organic. It ignores the diversities of culture, country, and human disposition, and as a result, it is never able to project itself as a living religious teaching capable of being followed in individual lives. In trying to do the impossible of making all teachings equally significant for all seekers, eclectic harmony only succeeds in achieving a superficial and rootless universalism that has no bearing on the everyday life of the individual. To be living and practicable, spiritual teaching must have for its base a set of rituals and traditions of its own. This is absent from eclectic harmony. All paths lead to the same goal and are equally true, but an individual has to make a choice to reach the goal. Another difficulty with eclectic harmony is that in the long run it proves to be a sect of its own. The selected teachings of different religious systems that it tries to bring together eventually take the form of another scripture. But no collection of scriptural gems can take the place of a religious scripture that derives its authority from the spiritual realizations of a saint or prophet or knower of God.

In contrast to eclectic and partisan harmonies, Vedantic harmony is an organic synthesis of conservatism and universalism. It combines the orthodoxy of the partisan with the liberal spirit of the eclectic. While emphasizing the unity of the goal, it also accepts the diversities of the paths leading to that goal and encourages orthodoxy in adherence to one's own path. Vedanta maintains that only one who has been orthodox from the beginning can be truly liberal in the end. Liberalism without orthodoxy is meaningless, for it has nothing to be liberal about. While the goal remains the same for all, the paths have to vary to suit the needs of different seekers. Unity in diversity is the very law of nature. As Sri Ramakrishna points out: "As many faiths, so many paths."[15]

According to Vedanta, the different religious systems are so many paths, and they can be classified in four broad categories: *jnana-yoga,* or the path of knowledge and discrimination; *bhakti-yoga,* or the path of devotion and self-surrender; *raja-yoga,* or the path of concentration and meditation; and *karma-yoga,* or the path of selfless service.

The efficacy of a particular path depends on the need and inclination of a particular seeker. The path of one seeker need not be the path of another.

The practice of the harmony of religions, as advocated by Vedanta, is natural and in keeping with science and reason, which focus our attention on the physical unity of the universe. There has not been and will never be one religion for all, because there cannot be uniformity of philosophy, mythology, and ritual for all of humanity. Any attempt to impose uniformity is bound to fail because it will go against the very laws of life.

The harmony of religions, Vedanta contends, is not something that can be formulated by doctrine, enforced by decree, or promoted by such means as interfaith conferences or the study of comparative religion. Harmony of religions, Vedanta asserts, already exists. We have only to realize it in our individual lives by deepening our spiritual consciousness. Harmony of religions is based not on the Fatherhood or Motherhood of God, nor on the brotherhood of man, but on the oneness of Truth. It is the harmony of principles and not of personalities. It is a revelation rather than a formulation. Even in the realm of science, all inventions and formulations are essentially revelations. Whether it is Newton's law of gravity or Einstein's theory of relativity, scientific discoveries are essentially revelations of natural laws that have been operating since time immemorial. It cannot be said that before Newton's discovery of the law of gravity, apples rose up in the sky instead of falling to the ground, or that before Einstein, everything was fixed and absolute. Similarly, in the realm of religion, a seeker does not *make* God but *discovers* God, and as the seeker discovers God, so does he or she discover harmony. Vedantic harmony is spiritual, yet it does not deny the need of creed, philosophy, ritual, and dogma. It only asks the seeker to outgrow them. A tender plant needs hedging around, but the plant must outgrow the need for the hedge. The consummation of Vedantic realization is seeing God everywhere and in everything.

Vedanta, with its message of universal harmony based on its vision of nondualism as indicated in the Upanishads and the Bhagavad Gita, provides a durable basis for peace and unity. Harmony and peace are the crying needs of our time, when the world is plagued by narrow nationalism, religious fanaticism, and political tension. Science has annihilated distance through improved means of communication and has obliterated the geographical isolation of individual nations and cultures. But physical unity does not make for a meeting of minds. Any unity based on moral, ethical, political, or economic considerations is too fragile to survive the test of time. Universal unity is possible only in the context of a Universal Soul—the Soul that transcends the barriers of all race, culture, and religion. This is where the message of

Vedanta becomes relevant. It focuses our attention on the message of the Upanishad:

> There is one Supreme Ruler, the inmost Self of all beings, who makes His one form manifold. Eternal happiness belongs to the wise, who perceive Him within themselves—not to others.[16]

The Self of Vedanta is the Self of all, irrespective of religious and cultural diversities. It is the Self of all beings and things of the universe. Anything that is not illumined by the light of this Self is fraught with fear and pursued by death. One who does not see the Self lapses into the world of non-Self, which is self-destructive. Hence Vedanta says: It is not enough to acquire knowledge of the diverse categories of nature; one must grow in the wisdom of the inner Self. It is not enough to be charitable and tolerant; one must accept all as part of oneself. The goal of Vedanta is not speculation on the Self but its realization. As stated earlier, according to Sri Shankaracharya, the whole range of Vedanta philosophy can be expressed in half a verse: The Self (Brahman) alone is real, the world is illusory, and the individual Self and the Supreme Self are nondifferent. But how is this Self to be realized? In answer, Vedanta points out the following Upanishadic verse:

> Atman, smaller than the small, greater than the great, is hidden in the hearts of all living creatures. A man who is free from desires beholds the majesty of the Self through tranquillity of the senses and the mind and becomes free from grief.[17]

The conclusions of Vedanta are based neither on scriptures nor on philosophy but on direct perception. The scrutiny of critical reason is no threat to Vedanta. Vedanta welcomes critical reason—not because reason can prove the reality of the Self but because reason dispels the superstitions of the mind.

6

Mastering the
Restless Mind

The mind plays a most crucial role in human life. A human individual's real strength lies not in muscle but in tranquillity of mind. Tranquillity is vital not only for survival but also for success and fulfillment in any walk of life. It is the source of power, creativity, and self-confidence. It is as important for a saint or a mystic as it is for a scientist, an artist, an engineer, or a workman. The Bhagavad Gita (6.5–6) tells us that mind is our best friend when kept under control and our worst enemy when we lose control over it. So the saying goes: "He who is the master of his mind is a sage, while he who is a slave to his mind is a fool." But what is mind? There are thinkers who have tried to explain the mind in such terms as a function of the brain, a product of heredity, a product of the environment, or a byproduct of the bodily processes. These views only describe how the mind acts and reacts but not why. They fail to explain a person's moral commitment, aesthetic sensibility, and spiritual aspiration. They leave out the most essential part of a human individual—the soul—and reduce a human being to either a creature at the mercy of circumstances or a stimulus-response mechanism. Yoga and Vedanta consider these views to be incomplete and inadequate.

The seers of Yoga and Vedanta give a spiritual interpretation of human nature and the mind. Mind, according to them, is a positive entity that stands between the body and senses on the one hand and the knowing Self on the other. While the knowing Self of an individual is the focus of the all-pervading Universal Self, the mind serves as the ego self. The mind is the leader of the sense organs and pervades the entire body. Though closely connected with the body, the mind is independent of it. The functions of the mind are four: deliberation, determination, I-consciousness, and memory. Mind is called our second body, or subtle body. The gross body is an extension of the mind. The relation between the subtle body and the gross body is like that between a seed and a plant. Both mind and body are material by nature. The body is made of five gross elements—earth, air, water, fire, and space (*akasha*)—and the mind is made of the subtle forms of the same five elements. Being material by nature, these elements do not possess consciousness of their own. The body derives its consciousness from the mind, and the mind from the knowing self. The mind is not destroyed with the death of the body. Mind is the receptacle of the memories of past lives, and it transmigrates from one birth to another. We are born with a particular mind that we bring with us from our past, and it is this mind that seeks expression through our thoughts and actions in the present life. We perceive the world through the prism of our own mind. Our mind is our interpreter, guide, and constant companion. It receives sensory perceptions of sight, sound, touch, taste, and smell; interprets them according to its built-in conditionings; and then responds through its motor organs. Thus the world of an individual is in his or her mind. Our birth and death, suffering and enjoyment, virtue and vice, bondage and liberation are all experiences of our mind.

The mind has three levels of consciousness: subconscious, conscious, and superconscious. The conscious is that level from which a person makes decisions, choices, and value judgments. Beneath the conscious lies the subconscious, hidden and unperceived, exerting its influence on the conscious. The conscious is like the steering of an automobile, while the subconscious is like the propulsion. Above the conscious there is a third level, the superconscious, where individual consciousness comes in contact with the universal consciousness. The subconscious is guided by instinct, the conscious by reason, and the superconscious by intuition. I-consciousness, or the ego, operates only in the conscious level. In the subconscious level it is unmanifest, while in the superconscious level it almost vanishes.

The mind is subject to three *gunas,* or the three modifications of matter: inertia (*tamas*), passion (*rajas*), and tranquillity (*sattva*). Preponderance of any one of the three over the other two affects the mood of the mind. *Tamas* overpowers the mind with darkness, and *rajas* with agitation, while *sattva* gives the mind stability. In regard to perception of reality, *tamas* causes nonperception and *rajas* distorted perception, while *sattva* brings clarity of perception. The mind of each individual represents a specific composition of the three *gunas,* and this composition determines the person's disposition, character, likes, and dislikes. The *guna* composition becomes altered as we change our way of living. Mind experiences rise and fall.

Yoga and Vedanta speak of six subtle centers of consciousness located along the spinal column and known as chakras, or lotuses. They are located at the base of the spine, at the level of the organ of generation, at the navel, at the heart, at the throat, and in the space between the eyebrows. The six centers are like six windows through which the mind perceives the outside universe. When the mind dwells in the three lower centers, it broods only on eating, sleeping, and gross sense enjoyments. When it rises to the fourth, it feels spiritual longing and makes spiritual effort. By rising higher, it eventually goes beyond the six centers and merges in the Universal Consciousness. The basic urge of the individual consciousness is toward unity with the Universal Consciousness, and so the natural flow of the mind is cosmocentric. But because of the blocking of ego, the flow of the mind becomes obstructed, falls back upon itself, and breaks into countless waves of negative emotions and urges, such as lust, anger, jealousy, and possessiveness. Unable to be cosmocentric, the mind becomes egocentric.

The mind is known for its proverbial restlessness. The Bhagavad Gita (6.34) describes the mind by four epithets: "restless," "turbulent," "powerful," and "obstinate." A restless mind addicted to sense pleasures has been depicted as a "mad elephant" or a "huge tiger." Swami Vivekananda has compared the restless mind to a monkey that is not only drunk with the wine of desire but also simultaneously stung by the scorpion of jealousy and taken over by the demon of pride. The restless mind is marked by several signs. It is dull, excited, or scattered, and never concentrated. Impulsive and hypersensitive, it has low frustration-bearing tolerance and is often guided by arbitrary whims and passing sentiments. Carried along by the waves of impulses, darkened by imaginations, unstable, fickle, and full of desires, it is constant prey to delusions and fancies. It swings from hyperactivity to depression, from self-pity to self-aggrandizement, from overoptimism to overpessimism. It is secretive and negative, divided and discontented. Harassed by its own anxieties and tensions, it drifts aimlessly and is unable to find rest. A person with a restless mind does not act but only reacts, does not live life but merely copes with it.

Mental restlessness manifests itself in the physical level as emotionally charged speech, restless body movement, sharp mood changes, uneven breath, restless movement of the eyes, and lack of concentration. From the point of view of the *gunas,* the restless mind is dominated either by inertia or by passion, and from the point of view of the centers of consciousness, it dwells in the three lower centers.

The mind is restless because it is weak. It is weak because it is impure, and it is impure because it has become a slave to the body and the senses. The weak mind is at the root of all suffering. The five causes of suffering, according to Yoga and Vedanta, are (1) ignorance that blocks the perception of the reality of oneness; (2) deluded ego that projects its own world of fancies and desires; (3) deep attachment that expresses itself as possessiveness; (4) strong aversion that seeks the pleasurable and shuns the painful; and (5) clinging to life, which is the inability to change and grow. Impurities of mind are the subtle deposits of past indulgent living. They are not simply impure thoughts. Having been repeated over and over again, the impure thoughts have become persistent habits, striking roots into our body chemistry. Habits are always formed little by little. These habits are called *samskaras.* *Samskaras* cannot be overcome by mere intellectual reasoning and analysis. Time cannot erase them; change of place or diet cannot uproot them.

Some try to overcome restlessness by pampering the desires of the mind. But pampering eventually becomes suicidal. It is false psychology that says we can overcome our mind by yielding to its desires. Desires, like flames of fire, are insatiable. The more we add fuel to them, the more they burn, until in the end they destroy their very base, the mind. Unrestrained desires and unbridled gratification of libidinal urges only lead to disintegration and destruction.

Others try to overcome restlessness by punishing the mind. They resort to self-torture and mortification. But punishing only represses the urges and desires, driving them underground. Repression heightens the awareness of the desired object, causing fantasy and personality disorders. Still others try to escape restlessness of mind by change of environment. But soon they discover that they are being pursued by their restlessness. Wherever we go we carry our mind with us. The way to overcome the restless mind, according to the seers of Yoga and Vedanta, is to face it. Facing the mind has four aspects: self-acceptance, self-control, self-regulation, and moderation.

SELF-ACCEPTANCE

Self-acceptance is the first aspect of facing the mind. This acceptance is not fatalistic and helpless passivity. Neither is it looking for scapegoats. Self-acceptance is acknowledging the fact that the problem of restlessness is our own creation and we ourselves will have to overcome it. The solution to the problem will always elude our grasp so long as we deny this responsibility. Lack of self-acceptance is at the root of all despair, self-pity, tension, and cynicism. Self-acceptance teaches us that obstacles and imperfections are not to be avoided but acknowledged and overcome. A limitation or deficiency, when accepted with a positive attitude of mind, becomes a driving force for self-mastery. Benjamin Franklin said: "Those things that hurt, instruct."

SELF-CONTROL

The second aspect of facing the mind is self-control, which is control of mind. According to Yoga and Vedanta, the unruly mind never comes under control unless it is controlled consciously. Such control is never a windfall. It cannot be attained vicariously or miraculously or by mechanical or chemical means. The four paths of yoga outline four ways to achieve control of mind: persuasion, purification, eradication, and subjugation.

The path of knowledge, or *jnana-yoga,* upholds the way of persuasion. It relies heavily on reason. The virtues it prescribes for practicing control are discrimination between the realities and the unrealities of life; detachment, which is freedom from thirst for all sense pleasure; restraining the outgoing propensities of the mind and the senses; withdrawal of the mind; fortitude; self-settledness; faith; and longing for liberation. Intellect, the leader of all the faculties of the mind, is persuaded to reflect seriously on the harmful consequences of sense enjoyments and renounce them voluntarily.

The path of devotion, or *bhakti-yoga,* advocates the way of purification. The virtues prescribed for practicing control are purity of food, including whatever the mind draws in through the senses for enjoyment; freedom from desire; practice of devotion, and keeping holy company; truthfulness; doing good to others; straightforwardness; nonviolence; compassion; charity; and not yielding to despondency or excessive merriment. *Bhakti-yoga* relies not so much on controlling the mind as on directing it toward the Divine. It maintains that the mind cannot give up the lower pleasures of life until it has tasted something higher.

The path of selfless action, or *karma-yoga,* follows the way of eradication of the ego. The virtues prescribed for practicing control of mind are giving up brooding over the results of action, nonattachment, eradication of the ego, and dedication of the results of action to the Divine. According to *karma-yoga,* all mental restlessness is due to the worldly ego and its attachments, involvements, and actions, and the only way to overcome restlessness is eradication of the ego. But ego, hardened by repeated selfish actions, cannot be eradicated by any means other than performance of unselfish actions. Karma alone can rescue a person from the bondage of karma.

The path of meditation, or *raja-yoga,* emphasizes the way of subjugation. It relies not so much on reason or devotion or eradication of ego as on willpower. The virtues that it prescribes for practicing control are nonviolence, truthfulness, noncovetousness, continence, nonreceiving of undesirable gifts and favors, external and internal cleanliness, contentment, austerity, study of sacred texts, self-surrender to the Divine, control of posture and breath, and withdrawal of mind. According to *raja-yoga,* reason is too weak to uproot the ingrained tendencies, devotion requires inborn faith in God, and ego eradication is a slow process. Only strong willpower can bring the wayward mind back to tranquillity. *Raja-yoga* aims at controlling the subconscious with the help of conscious efforts. By control of posture and regulation of breath, along with the practice of the other prescribed virtues, the follower of *raja-yoga* confronts the agitated mind and subdues it.

Self-control is achieved by following any of the four ways or a combination of them. Self-control is neither negative nor inhibitive. It is the technique of dealing with desires. Desires cannot be crushed or repressed. They cannot be fulfilled completely or postponed indefinitely. The only way is to reduce them to a healthy level. Self-control calls for withstanding the intensities of the gross impulses and urges, especially those of lust and greed. Our body grows in health by bearing with the physical intensities; so also our mind gains in strength by bearing with the intensities of its cravings and urges. Mind, like body, needs exercise for its health and fitness. Unfortunately, we neglect this need of the mind. It is rightly said that the only mental exercise most people get is "jumping to conclusions, running down their friends, sidestepping responsibility, and pushing their luck"!

There are those who argue that self-control weakens the impulses of life, making us forget the immediate as we fix our eyes only on the eternal. They say that self-control creates a mood of otherworldliness, pessimism, and depression and encourages escapism. It makes a person unauthentic and fosters neurosis. But the logic for self-control is compelling. If we are all muscle and metabolism, then we can never escape death. If we are nothing more than our wild impulses and emotions, we can never get rest; and if we are all desires and dreams, we will ever remain unfulfilled. Yoga and Vedanta assert that our real nature is the pure Self and that we are not a slave of our body and mind but their master. Life is a rebellion against the laws of material nature and not submission to them.

SELF-REGULATION

The third aspect of facing the mind is self-regulation. Self-regulation involves concentrating the mind on a single object and meditating on that object at a fixed center of consciousness. The object of concentration and meditation is called the Chosen Ideal. The Chosen Ideal may be the knowing Self, which is the focus of the all-pervading Universal Self, beyond all name, form, and attribute, or it may be the same knowing Self with name, form, and attribute superimposed upon it. No lasting serenity is ever possible without practice of concentration on a fixed Chosen Ideal. The reason is that concentration cannot develop roots if the Chosen Ideal is changed frequently. Meditation culminates in absorption in the Chosen Ideal, which is the goal of all regulatory practice. In order to reach this absorption, each path of yoga suggests a number of supporting regulatory practices. *Jnana-yoga* prescribes hearing the great Vedic sayings and reflecting and meditating on their meaning. *Bhakti-yoga* advises prayer, ritualistic worship, *japa* (repetition of a sacred word), and meditation. The follower of *karma-yoga* adopts the supportive practices of either *bhakti-yoga* or *jnana-yoga*. *Raja-yoga* advocates concentration and meditation. The goal of concentration and meditation is to cultivate a single thought-wave. A restless mind is like a lake that is constantly being agitated by the winds of desires. As a result of this constant agitation, our true Self at the bottom of the lake cannot be perceived. When a single thought-wave is consciously cultivated by the repeated and uninterrupted practice of meditation, it develops into a huge wave that swallows up all the diverse thought-waves and makes the mind transparent and calm. The concentrated mind is the mind that has taken this form of one single thought-wave.

Self-control and self-regulation represent respectively dispassion and practice—the two disciplines prescribed by the Bhagavad Gita (6.35) for overcoming restlessness of mind. The two must be followed simultaneously. Unless one practices control, one cannot succeed in regulation, and unless one regulates the mind, one cannot succeed in controlling it. Control without regulation never becomes lasting. Egocentric control does not stand the test of stress. On the other hand, regulation without control is dangerous. An uncontrolled mind is impure, and an impure mind, when roused through concentration, becomes destructive. A Sanskrit proverb says: "To feed a cobra with milk without first taking out its poison fangs is only to increase its venom." Again, control and regulation are to be practiced repeatedly, in thought, word, and deed, for a long time, without break, and with devotion. The psychology of repeated practice is to neutralize the deep-seated, distracting *samskaras* by developing counter-*samskaras*. Impure thought is countered by pure thought, impure imagination by pure imagination, uncontrolled speech by thoughtful speech, bad posture by good posture. A thought when repeated becomes a tendency, a tendency when repeated becomes a habit, and a habit when repeated becomes a character. So Swami Vivekananda says: "Never say any man is hopeless, because he only represents a character, a bundle of habits, which can be checked by new and better ones. Character is repeated habits, and repeated habits alone can reform character."[1]

MODERATION

The fourth aspect of facing the mind is moderation. The mind cannot be brought under control all of a sudden. Human nature cannot be hurried. Old habits die hard. They have deep roots and cannot be overcome all at once. The word *habit* has five letters. If the letter *h* is taken away, what remains is "a bit." If both the *h* and the *a* are taken away, "bit" remains. Even when *h, a,* and *b* are taken away, still "it" remains! A habit is formed bit by bit. So a counterhabit is to be developed bit by bit. If you drive a screw into a wall by a number of turns, you cannot simply pull it out. In order to remove it, you have to give the same number of turns in the opposite direction. The intensity of our effort to develop a counterhabit must be in keeping with the capacity of our mind to endure. Effort when too weak and casual fails to change the habits, but when it is too intense and accelerated, it can damage the mind itself.

No task is more urgent than gaining mastery over the mind by overcoming its restlessness. No sacrifice is too great to achieve this goal. No effort in this venture is ever lost or wasted. Success in self-mastery comes only to those who long for it, practice it, and persevere in their practice. Practice, however, is not talking, discussing, or debating but doing, and the secret of all doing is simply to do.

7

Self-Expression or Self-Control?

Self-control is the control of the mind and its desires, urges, emotions, and delusions. It is controlling the outgoing tendencies of the mind and the senses and bringing them back to our Self within. Self-control is the key to success in any field of life, and it is an indispensable necessity for Self-realization, the goal of spiritual quest. Self-control is the message of the sages and saints. It is the exhortation of the scriptures and traditions, the foundation of all yogas, and the very essence of all spiritual austerities and disciplines. Sri Shankaracharya says in his *Vivekachudamani:*

> The mental sheath is the (sacrificial) fire which, fed with the fuel of numerous desires by the five sense-organs which serve as priests, and set ablaze by the sense-objects which act as the stream of oblations, brings about this phenomenal universe.
>
> This is no ignorance (*Avidya*) outside the mind. The mind alone is *Avidya,* the cause of the bondage of transmigration. When that is destroyed, all else is destroyed, and when it is manifested, everything else is manifested.[1]

An unruly mind is our worst enemy. It is the root cause of all turmoil and mental darkness. Bringing the mind under control is the only way to inner peace and tranquillity. Control of this mind is the highest yoga and the most vital aspect of yoga practice. All spiritual practices, such as prayer, meditation, *japa*, and pilgrimage, lead to control of the mind. Sri Krishna says in his last message:

Charity, the performance of one's duty, the observance of vows, general and particular, the hearing of the scriptures, meritorious acts, and all other works—all these culminate in the control of the mind. The control of the mind is the highest Yoga.

Say, of what use are charity and the rest to one whose mind is controlled and pacified? Of what use, again, are this charity and the rest to one whose mind is restless or lapsing into dullness?[2]

There is a view upheld by a school of thought that says that any form of self-control is repressive, inhibitive, and reactive. It creates neurosis, depression, and fantasies that make a person experience so-called spiritual emotions and ecstasies. According to this view, a person's desire to renounce the world and worldly pleasures is often caused by the repression of sense urges. This view holds that self-control obstructs spontaneity, brings personality disorders, and forces a person to lead a false life. Cravings for sense enjoyment are natural and normal; when they are repressed, they go underground and create heightened desire for the objects craved, making such objects appear more real and alluring than they actually are. Self-control nurtures pessimism and is a practice of gradual suicide. Self-expression, not self-control, stands for freedom, authenticity, and spontaneity.

To the seers of Yoga and Vedanta, so-called self-expression is unhealthy and reckless. It is a philosophy of living that brings only dissipation, degradation, and disintegration. As Sri Shankaracharya so appropriately says:

In the forest tract of sense-pleasures there prowls a huge tiger called the mind. Let good people who have a longing for liberation never go there.[3]

Advocates of self-expression ask for free rein for all our thoughts, urges, and desires, with no restraint whatsoever. According to them, a human individual is driven by five basic urges: self-preservation, self-expression or power, sexual gratification, gregariousness, and knowledge of the world. They are of the opinion that the sexual urge is the master urge and that all other urges are overt or covert expressions of that master urge. The sexual urge, they say, is the desire for reproduction and is the most natural urge of life. When repressed, it creates an unhealthy mental condition and gives a person no rest or peace.

The seers and sages of Yoga and Vedanta maintain that the human individual has three basic urges: immortality, unbounded joy, and unrestricted awareness. Of these three, the master urge is unbounded joy. Life must have joy in some form or other for its nourishment. The Upanishads tell us that Self-knowledge brings the most intense and pure joy ever imaginable. Sense enjoyment and sense gratification are the most polluted and perverted forms of the pure joy of Self-knowledge. One who has not yet tasted this highest joy cannot think of any other joy except the pleasures of the senses, and so he or she lives on those pleasures that are like nectar at first but like poison in the end.

In fulfillment of this urge for unbounded joy, we look for a new body, new place, new possessions, new thrills of sense enjoyment, and a new environment, but nowhere in the universe, or in any sense enjoyment, is fulfillment found. Finally, we realize that appeasing the mind is not the way to peace and happiness, because sense desires are insatiable and sense enjoyments deplete the vigor of the mind. We then begin to control our thoughts and sense desires in search of our true Self, which is immortal, all pervading, and the one source of all joy. Success in this quest is possible only through self-control.

Emphasizing the need for self-control, the Bhagavad Gita says:

He who is able to withstand the force of lust and anger even before he quits the body—he is a yogi, he is a happy man.

Those who are free from lust and anger, who have subdued their minds and realized the Self—those *sannyasis,* both here and hereafter, attain freedom in Brahman.[4]

To Sri Ramakrishna, the main obstacles to yoga are two: lust and greed. Swami Vivekananda writes in his poem "Song of the Sannyasin":

Truth never comes where lust and fame and greed
Of gain reside. No man who thinks of woman
As his wife can ever perfect be;
Nor he who owns the least of things, nor he
Whom anger chains, can ever pass through maya's gates.

> So give these up, sannyasin bold! Say,
> "Om Tat Sat, Om!"[5]

Christ says:

> For there are eunuchs who have been so from birth, and there are
> eunuchs who have been made eunuchs by men, and there are
> eunuchs who have made themselves eunuchs for the sake of the
> kingdom of heaven. He who is able to receive this, let him receive
> it (Matt. 19:12).

Practice of self-control is most purifying because self-control transforms the quality of our mind. By controlling crude and raw impulses and emotions, we have developed reason, and by controlling reason, we have developed intuition, which is the purified form of reason. Self-control is the mark of a pure mind. It is this purity of mind that distinguishes a saint from a worldly person. While a worldly person is guided by instincts of self-love and self-preservation, a saint finds his or her connection with the entire universe and is guided by the spirit of self-sacrifice for the good of others. Self-control is asserting our higher Self over our lower self. Life is a rebellion against the laws of nature. Submission to them would leave us at the mercy of the whims of our mind. Such submission is natural for an animal but not for a human being.

The seers of Yoga and Vedanta speak of sublimation of urges and desires, not of their repression. Sublimation is spiritualizing all our urges and desires by channeling them toward the attainment of Self-knowledge, in which all desires and urges find their supreme fulfillment. Self-knowledge is not just cessation of suffering and attainment of peace but intense bliss. When a person advances toward this knowledge, he or she begins to taste the bliss of the Self and to find sense enjoyments increasingly tasteless and insipid.

True self-expression is the expression of our higher Self, and this calls for both freedom and control. In order to express our true Self in every phase of our life, we must recover it first by exercising self-control. Slaves of passion cannot express anything—they only follow the dictates of their urges and impulses. They do not enjoy sense pleasures but are addicted to them. Self-expression is always preceded by self-conquest. True self-expression is never a riotous living of license and whimsicality driven by endless sense desires. Those who uphold the view of "self-expression" equate promiscuity with affection and infatuation with love, and look upon violence, greed, and questionable morals as natural. Such living is the surest way to doom and destruction. In the words of Swami Vivekananda, those who uphold this view advocate living with the morals of a tomcat:

> He [Swami Vivekananda] held purity to be for the householder as well as for the monk, and laid great stress on that point. "The other day, a young Hindu came to see me," he said. "He has been living in this country for about two years, and suffering from ill-health for some time. In the course of our talk, he said that the theory of chastity must be all wrong because the doctors in this country had advised him against it. They told him that it was against the law of nature. I told him to go back to India, where he belonged, and to listen to the teachings of his ancestors, who had practised chastity for thousands of years." Then turning a face puckered into an expression of unutterable disgust, he thundered: "You doctors in this country, who hold that chastity is against the law of nature, don't know what you are talking about. You don't know the meaning of the word purity. You are beasts! beasts! I say, with the morals of a tomcat, if that is the best you have to say on that subject!" Here he glanced defiantly over the audience, challenging opposition by his very glance. No voice was raised, though there were several physicians present.[6]

TWO VIEWS ON SELF-CONTROL

While both Yoga and Vedanta regard self-control as the key to success in a spiritual quest, the two schools of thought have differing views on the subject.

THE YOGA VIEW

The Yoga methodology of self-control is based on the philosophy and psychology of Patanjali's Yoga way. The Yoga way says that all our pain and suffering are due to loss of contact with our true Self, our true identity. Because of this loss, the Self becomes entangled in the world of matter and is subjected to the laws of the material world, which is plagued by the pairs of opposites, such as pain and pleasure, birth and death. The goal of the Yoga way is to establish contact with our true Self. Only this contact can put an end to all the maladies of life. But this contact is not possible without controlling the mind. The first aphorism of Patanjali states, "Yoga is suppression of the thoughts of the mind." Suppression is different from repression. Suppression is positive; it is suppression of the mind's lower urges for the sake of the greater goal of Self-realization. In contrast, repression, having no greater goal, proves to be negative and reactive. According to the Yoga system, there is no yoga without self-control, and such self-control must be forcible.

The logic of the Yoga way says that the mind is material and its conditionings of impurities are mechanical. It is most difficult to know the nature, depth, and extent of these impurities. All we know is that the mind is restless and that restlessness is manifesting itself in our restless body movement, unevenness of breath, and changes in biochemistry. This restlessness is more than disturbing thought. Thoughts when repeated become ingrained and turn into deep-seated habits and tendencies. These do not go away by themselves. Passage of time and change of environment are of no help. Old age cannot lessen their fury, and distance cannot obliterate them. Habits and tendencies are to be overcome by cultivating counterthoughts and habits of tranquillity, and for that purpose we must hasten our steps. The reason for hastening is clear. Life is short and full of distractions; much of it is spent in sleep and daydreaming. Hence control of the mind must be effortful and forcible, and to that end the Yoga system prescribes an eightfold practice:

Yama. Five restraints: nonkilling, truthfulness, nonstealing, continence, and nonreceiving of gifts.

Niyama. Five observances: internal and external purification, contentment, mortification, study, and worship of God. (Internal purification is obtained through having friendship for all, being merciful toward those who are miserable, being happy with those who are happy, and being indifferent to the wicked.)

Asana. Posture that is firm and pleasant.

Pranayama. Control of the motion of exhalation and inhalation. (Controlling the breath is the easiest way of getting control of the *prana,* or the cosmic energy.)

Pratyahara. Drawing in of the organs. (Preventing the organs from taking the forms of external objects, and making them remain one with the mind-stuff.)

Dharana. Concentration, or holding the mind to some particular object.

Dhyana. Meditation, or an unbroken flow of knowledge about that object.

Samadhi. Complete absorption in meditation. (The state of meditation when the form is given up and only the internal sensations, or the meaning, is perceived.)

The first five are external practices, the last three internal ones.

The Yoga system asks a seeker to make relentless conscious efforts to overcome the mind, and to have unwavering determination and willpower to reach the goal of Self-realization. Reason, it says, is too weak to overcome the perverted mind. Devotion to God is most often passive; true prayer and worship call for strong faith in God, which many are not endowed with. Educating the mind to give up its old ways is a slow process. Auspicious desires are not always forthcoming. The goal is never attained unless we make an all-out effort for it. The Yoga system reminds us that the ocean of the mind is always turbulent. If you want to take a dip in this ocean, you cannot wait for the weather to improve and the ocean to become calm. You must plunge right into the ocean by learning how to handle the waves.

The Yoga system relies mainly on rigorous and willful self-control, as distinguished from persuading the mind to give up its old ways by cultivating dispassion. Patanjali refers to dispassion as a complementary means for controlling the mind. The main focus of the Yoga system is on the training and exercise of willpower for the development of reason and discrimination. The Yoga system seeks to modify our subconscious mind indirectly with the help of regulation of breath, posture, and diet. Modern psychology explains how our conscious thoughts and actions are heavily influenced by the deep-seated desires and urges of our subconscious mind. But the Yoga system further shows us how we can modify our subconscious mind by the efforts of our conscious mind, how repeated exercises of the will on the conscious level can influence the subconscious depths and modify them permanently. By controlling the manifested effects of impurities, the Yoga system seeks to eliminate the source of the impurities and regain contact with the true Self.

The Yoga system tells us that to achieve the goal of Self-realization the seeker must have full awakening of his or her mind, which is in deep slumber at the base of the spine. The mind must be made to rise to the upper centers of consciousness, and for that purpose the blockage of impurities in the *sushumna* canal, through which it has to travel upward, must be cleared. The Yoga system prefers "dredging of the canal" rather than "dissolving the blockage," which is the Vedanta method. Posture, diet, and *pranayama* (breath control) are the means to dredge. Conversion of physical energy into *ojas* (spiritual energy) through the practices of continence, concentration, and meditation provides the seeker the sustained strength to dredge. The manifestation of Yoga powers on the way generates confidence in the mind of the seeker regarding the infallibility of Yoga, and thus encourages him or her in the task of attaining the goal. The Yoga system is for those in whom reason has not yet established its natural supremacy.

THE VEDANTA VIEW

The second view of self-control is that of Vedanta. The goal of life, according to Vedanta, is Self-knowledge. Self-knowledge guarantees all fulfillment, whether material, mental, or spiritual, but Self-knowledge is never possible without self-control. Self-control is essentially the control of the libidinal urges for sense gratification, the withstanding of the impacts of lust and greed. Through self-control a seeker converts raw libidinal energy into spiritual energy. Without self-control, prayer, meditation, and the desire for Self-knowledge are empty dreams. Conversely, self-control is impossible and often dangerous without the desire for Self-knowledge. But the Vedanta system advises gradual control of mind, rather than forcible control of it.

Vedanta maintains that the impure mind cannot be made pure by posture, diet, and breath control. Thoughts and urges cannot be overcome by superficial, physical means. Vedanta seeks to control the gross, that is, the body and bodily habits and urges, by controlling the subtle, which is thought. Vedanta seeks to educate and discipline the intellect (the discriminating faculty of mind) in order to overcome the mind and the body, instead of disciplining the mind and the body for the purpose of educating the intellect. Vedanta relies mainly on the practice of dispassion and believes that the master urge in all of us is the need to move toward the Divine and experience unbounded joy. Spiritual longing, it says, cannot be generated by mechanical means. Withdrawal of the mind is not possible unless the mind cooperates in the process. Forcible control can rouse the mind untimely, before spiritual longing has matured and spiritual motivation has become sufficiently strong. A roused mind without much longing for the goal can be dangerous. Vedanta believes in gradual control so that the mind does not rebel and react violently. Its process is the way of least resistance. Maybe it is slow, but it is sure and tested.

Regarding control of the mind, *Jivan-Mukti-Viveka*, a Vedanta scripture, says:

> Study of the knowledge of the supreme Self, association with the good, total renunciation of desires, control of vital energy — these are, as is well known, the perfect means to conquer the mind.
>
> Those who apply *hathayoga* to control the mind while such effective means are available, resemble them who abandoning the lamp apply magic ointment to their eyes to dispel darkness.
>
> The deluded who attempt to control the mind by force, they, as it were, bind the large, frantic elephant by lotus-fibres (*Laghu Yogavasistha* 28.128–31).
>
> Control is of two kinds: violent control and gradual control. The first of them is done by blockading the knowledge-organs such as the eye, ear etc. and the action-organs such as the larynx, hands etc. at their respective seats by force. A deluded man, by this instance, wrongly thinks that in this manner he shall control the mind also. But the mind cannot be controlled in that way, since its centre—the lotus-like heart—is impossible to control. Therefore gradual control is justified.
>
> The means to gradual control are the study of the knowledge of the Self and others. The science of the Self gives rise to the

conviction of the unreality of all knowable things and of the Knower as the self-evident Reality. Having been convinced thus, the mind finds knowable things, that are within its purview, are useless, and realizes that the Knower, although a useful thing (Reality), is beyond its grasp, and dissolves of its own, like fire without fuel.[7]

Vedanta interprets the practices of Yoga differently. *Yama* (self-control) of Vedanta is restraint of all the senses by thinking "all this is Brahman," the Supreme Self. The continuous flow of this one kind of thought is called *yama*. Giving up of the illusory universe of multiplicity by knowing it as Brahman is true renunciation. Practice of silence is not a restraint of speech but dwelling on Brahman. Solitude is interior, not external. Real posture is that in which the mind flows toward Brahman spontaneously. The blessed vision is directing the mind to the knowledge of Brahman, not fixing the mind on the tip of the nose. *Rechaka* of *pranayama* is breathing out the thought that is not-Brahman; *puraka* is breathing in the thought of Brahman; and steadiness of thought thereafter is called *kumbhaka*. Those who do not know this only torture their nose.

Absorption of the mind in Brahman, knowing that it alone abides, is called true withdrawal. Steadiness in dwelling on Brahman is concentration. Constant awareness of the fact that "my true Self is verily Brahman" is called meditation. All obstacles on the way are overcome only by dissolving the mind in the ocean of infinite Brahman. By thinking of an object, the mind gets identified with it; by thinking of a void, it becomes blank. But by thinking of Brahman, it attains to perfection. Those who give up this supremely purifying thought of Brahman and put their minds on sense objects live in vain. Those who try to control the mind through posture, breath, diet, and other physical means are like those who hope to empty the ocean drop by drop with a blade of grass.

The goal of Self-knowledge in Vedanta is not just release from the world of matter but realization of the fact that all beings and things that are visible and perceptible are nothing but Brahman. To attain Self-knowledge, what is needed is to remove ignorance, the root cause, and not to fight against the habits, tendencies, and desires, all of which are numerous branches shooting forth from that root. Vedanta asks the aspirant to go to the very root of the matter and remove ignorance.

SELF-CONTROL IN PRACTICE

What is the preferred way to achieve self-control? The arguments in support of forcible control of the Yoga system and those in support of gradual control of the Vedanta system are equally strong. The two ways are equally time-honored and proven. However, spiritual seekers are not all of the same caliber and temperament. The way that is beneficial to one may not be beneficial to another. The fitness to pursue one way or the other depends upon the competence of the individual seeker.

8

Grasping the Essentials

THE ESSENTIAL AND THE NONESSENTIAL

The exhortation of Vedanta is: Grasp the essentials. Vedanta is neither a speculative philosophy that indulges in endless sophistries nor a teaching that promises miraculous solutions to the problems of life. It offers guidelines that are tested and verified. The spiritual guidelines of Vedanta are pragmatic, scientific, and universal. They are pragmatic because they are problem solving; scientific because they can be verified by personal experience; and universal in that they apply to all, regardless of place and time. Vedanta invites critical inquiry, encourages honest doubt, and provides realistic explanations of the mysteries of spiritual quest.

According to Vedanta, spiritual quest has four parts: direct perception, philosophy, mythology, and rituals. Direct perception is the essential part of spiritual quest. Swami Vivekananda describes this essential as follows:

> Each soul is potentially divine. The goal is to manifest this divinity by controlling nature: external and internal. Do this either by work, or worship, or psychic control, or philosophy—by one, or more, or all of these—and be free. This is the whole of religion. Doctrines, or dogmas, or rituals, or books, or temples, or forms, are but secondary details.[1]

Spiritual quest becomes meaningless when the essential part is forgotten or ignored.

The second part of spiritual quest, philosophy, is an attempt to give us an intellectual understanding of spiritual truth based on pure reason. But pure reason requires a pure mind, which is very rare. Too often philosophical reasoning lapses into rationalization. Reason is invoked to justify our preconceived notions, moves in a circle, creates doubt, and never arrives at finality. Some say that philosophy teaches us to feel unhappy intelligently. The so-called rationalistic analysis of life yields conclusions that are uncertain and tentative. The human mind is never sure of its own judgments and convictions. All we can trust about our own mind is that we cannot trust it.

The third part, mythology, seeks to describe the indescribable ultimate Truth through stories and anecdotes. The literal-minded overlook this fact and miss the real meaning of myths. In the Bible one reads that Jesus fed the multitude with five loaves and two fish. Some wonder how that was possible. To the follower of Vedanta, the explanation is that by coming near Jesus, all forgot about food and drink and were fully satisfied with whatever little food they received from Jesus. The essential message here is the infinite divine dimension of Jesus' personality, not the details of the number of loaves and fish.

The fourth part of spiritual quest consists of rituals. Rituals are symbolic observances to invoke concentration of mind. The offerings of fruits, flowers, candle, and incense; the practicing of certain postures and modes of breathing; bathing in sacred waters; making pilgrimages; and so forth are external expressions of the internal worship. Unthinking observance of rituals has no meaning unless the seeker is able to grasp their real purpose.

Philosophy, mythology, and rituals serve only to protect and preserve the kernel of spiritual truth. None of them can silence doubt and give certainty of faith, which calls for direct perception.

THE ESSENTIAL NATURE OF DIRECT PERCEPTION

Direct perception is more than blind belief, intellectual understanding, or emotional thrill. Blind belief lacks the support of either reason or experience and so cannot silence doubt. Intellectual understanding based solely on reason cannot withstand the stresses of circumstances that are always unpredictable. Emotion by itself supplies the seeker with feeling or passion but can make him or her wander into dark alleys or up dead ends. To protect the seeker from possible self-deception, Vedanta lays down three criteria of Truth: testimony of scripture, which serves as a working hypothesis; positive reasoning that seeks to separate the essential from the nonessential; and direct perception, which provides certainty of faith. When all three point to the same conclusion, the seeker may be assured that he or she has realized the whole truth. In order to free the mind from the pitfalls of rationalization and emotionalism, rigorous mental disciplines are prescribed so that the seeker may be well grounded in detachment, not only from the external world but also from blind loyalty to concepts and ideas.

Vedanta gives three tests of direct perception. First, it is never negated or superseded by any subsequent experience. Second, it does not contradict reason. The ultimate truth is never irrational. And third, it is always conducive to the welfare of all beings. Direct perception transforms the seeker forever. Moments of mystical intuition or ecstasies and trances, dreams and visions cannot be taken as meaningful until they transform the seeker's personality forever.

THE ESSENTIAL OF SCRIPTURES

Scriptures are various. Philosophers and theologians are not unanimous in their views. Spiritual truth remains hidden in the cave of the heart. Religious traditions claim that the scriptures contain the words of God—scriptures are infallible and are to be believed without question. Knowledge of history, however, tells us that all scriptures were written by human hands, and words of the scriptures reflect only the thoughts, beliefs and aspirations of their human authors. Scriptures, like all human documents, are subject to error. Many are not as ancient as they are thought to be and are of doubtful authenticity. Furthermore, because of their human authorship, scriptures of different traditions vary in their statements. While religious traditions ask for unquestioning loyalty to the words of the scriptures, the scientific-minded insist on verifiable facts. Vedanta maintains that those parts of the scriptures that contradict an evident truth of perception or inference should be discarded. The essential message of the scriptures is to be grasped by separating the embellishments from the facts, and the facts are to be verified by personal experience. Scriptures are like road maps. They are unnecessary for those who are adept in driving and useless for those who are not interested in it.

The study of scriptures is no substitute for direct perception of Truth. Shankaracharya in his *Vivekachudamani* says:

> The study of the scriptures is useless so long as the highest Truth is unknown, and it is equally useless when the highest Truth has already been known. The scriptures consisting of many words are a dense forest which merely causes the mind to ramble. Hence men of wisdom should earnestly set about knowing the true nature of the Self. For one who has been bitten by the serpent of ignorance, the only remedy is the knowledge of Brahman. Of what avail are the Vedas and (other) scriptures, mantras (sacred formulae) and medicines to such a one? A disease does not leave off if one simply utters the name of the medicine, without taking it; (similarly) without direct realization one cannot be liberated by the mere utterance of the word Brahman.[2]

Regarding the essential message of the scriptures, Sri Ramakrishna says:

> One should learn the essence of the scriptures from the guru and then practise sadhana. If one rightly follows spiritual discipline, then one directly sees God. The discipline is said to be rightly followed only when one plunges in. What will a man gain by merely reasoning about the words of the scriptures? Ah, the fools! They reason themselves to death over information about the path. They never take the plunge. What a pity!... I vowed to the Divine Mother that I would kill myself if I did not see God. I said to Her: "O Mother, I am a fool. Please teach me what is contained in the Vedas, the Puranas, the Tantras, and the other scriptures." The Mother said to me, "The essence of the Vedanta is that Brahman alone is real and the world illusory." The essence of the Gita is what you get by repeating the word ten times. It is reversed into "tagi," which refers to renunciation.[3]

Swami Vivekananda says:

> "Blessed are the pure in heart, for they shall see God" (Matt. 5:8). This sentence alone would save mankind if all the books

and prophets were lost. This purity of heart will bring the vision of God.[4]

The essential message of the Upanishads is "Know thyself." According to one interpretation, the story of the Bhagavad Gita is symbolic:

> Arjuna represents the individual soul, and Sri Krishna the Supreme Soul dwelling in every heart. Arjuna's chariot is the body. The blind King Dhritarashtra is the mind under the spell of ignorance, and his hundred sons are man's numerous evil tendencies. The battle, a perennial one, is between the power of good and the power of evil. The warrior who listens to the advice of the Lord speaking from within will triumph in this battle and attain the Highest Good.[5]

In *The Gospel of Sri Ramakrishna* the story of the pundit (philosopher) who could not swim describes the importance of direct perception:

> Once several men were crossing the Ganges in a boat. One of them, a pundit, was making a great display of his erudition, saying that he had studied various books—the Vedas, the Vedanta, and the six systems of philosophy. He asked a fellow passenger, "Do you know the Vedanta?" "No, revered sir." "The Samkhya and the Patanjala?" "No, revered sir." "Have you read no philosophy whatsoever?" "No, revered sir." The pundit was talking in this vain way and the passenger sitting in silence, when a great storm arose and the boat was about to sink. The passenger said to the pundit, "Sir, can you swim?" "No," replied the pundit. The passenger said, "I don't know the Samkhya or the Patanjala, but I can swim." What will a man gain by knowing many scriptures? The one thing needful is to know how to cross the river of the world. God alone is real, and all else illusory.[6]

THE ESSENTIAL WORSHIP

According to Vedanta, worship has various forms. The lowest form is worshiping the Divine in an image or a symbol; higher than this is *japa,* or repetition of a sacred word; higher still is meditation on the chosen form of the Divine; and the highest form of worship is communion with the Atman—maintaining a steady awareness of the fact that all we perceive is verily Brahman. Emphasizing the essential worship, the sacred texts of Vedanta say:

> In the lotus of my heart do I contemplate the divine Intelligence, the Brahman without distinction and difference, who is the object of realisation to even the creator, protector and destroyer of the universe; whom the Yogis attain through meditation; who destroys the fear of birth and death; and who is existence, intelligence, and the seed of all the worlds.[7]

And again:

> By virtue of even a moment's serenity, attained through knowledge of the identity of Atman and Brahman, the seeker attains the merit that one may obtain by bathing in the waters of all the holy rivers, by giving away the entire world in an act of charity, by performing a thousand sacrifices, by worshipping the three hundred and thirty millions of gods, and by rescuing, through after-death rites, one's ancestors from the suffering of the nether world.
>
> By the very birth of a man whose mind is absorbed in the Supreme Brahman—the immeasurable Ocean of Existence-Knowledge-Bliss Absolute—his family becomes sinless, his mother blessed, and the earth sacred.[8]

In this essential worship, the body is thought of as the abode of Brahman; the lotus of the heart is the seat where Brahman dwells as Atman. Prayer for illumination is the highest prayer. Self-mastery is the real austerity; giving up all desires is the highest renunciation; the virtues of discrimination, dispassion, purity, and kindness represent fragrant flowers. Real solitude is dwelling in Brahman, that alone exists. The true practice of *pranayama*, control of breath, is regarding all mental states as Brahman alone. The correct posture is that in which the meditation on Brahman flows spontaneously. Realizing Brahman in all objects is true withdrawal of the mind. True concentration is that steadiness in which the mind perceives everything as Brahman. Merging the mind completely in Brahman is the state of true illumination. Communion with Brahman as our true Self is the highest yoga.

In the words of Swami Vivekananda:

The fire of yoga burns the cage of sin which imprisons a man. Knowledge becomes purified and Nirvana is directly obtained. From yoga comes knowledge; knowledge, again, helps the yogi to obtain freedom. He who combines in himself both yoga and knowledge—with him the Lord is pleased. Those who practise maha-yoga either once a day, or twice, or thrice, or always—know them to be gods. Yoga is divided into two parts: one is called abhava-yoga, and the other, maha-yoga. That in which one's self is meditated upon as a void and without qualities is called abhava-yoga. That in which one sees one's self as blissful, bereft of all impurities, and as one with God is called maha-yoga. The yogi, by either of these, realizes the Self. The other yogas that we read and hear of do not deserve to be ranked with maha-yoga, in which the yogi finds himself and the whole universe to be God. This is the highest of all yogas.[9]

Those who forget the essential fact of the mystical nature of worship miss the goal.

THE ESSENTIAL OF PILGRIMAGE

A spiritual seeker makes pilgrimage to holy places and takes a dip in the holy waters of the rivers for self-purification. It is believed that the presiding spirit of God residing in those holy places and waters, out of compassion, removes the impurities of the visiting seeker. The holiness of a holy place, however, consists not of earth or stone but of the deposits of holy thoughts and vibrations which the worshipers leave behind in that place. Vedanta, however, tells us that the essential place of pilgrimage is the sacred shrine of the heart. According to Sri Shankaracharya:

He who, renouncing all activities, worships in the sacred and stainless shrine of Atman, which is independent of time, place, and distance; which is present everywhere; which is the destroyer of heat and cold, and the other opposites; and which is the giver of eternal happiness, becomes all-knowing and all-pervading and attains, hereafter, Immortality.[10]

And again:

> The word *shrine* in the text also means a holy place (*tirtha*). The
> allusion is to the pilgrimage of pious devotees to a holy place.
> There are certain disadvantages associated with holy places. As
> they may be situated at a great distance, pilgrimage may entail
> physical labour and suffering. The merit of a pilgrimage may be
> slight because of the inauspiciousness of the time. The comfort of
> the pilgrims may be disturbed by the weather. Robbers, thieves,
> or unscrupulous priests often give them trouble. Further, the merit
> accruing from a pilgrimage is not everlasting. But the worship in
> the sacred shrine of Atman is free from all these disadvantages
> and obstacles. Communion with Atman bestows upon the soul
> Immortality and Eternal Bliss.[11]

The *Mahabharata* describes Atman as the true sacred river, bathing in
which the soul becomes free from all impurities:

> The river of Atman is filled with the water of self-control; truth is
> its current, righteous conduct its banks, and compassion its
> waves. O son of Pandu, bathe in its sacred water; ordinary water
> does not purify the inmost soul.
>
> By worshipping a holy man who worships in the sacred shrine
> of Atman, the seeker obtains the results of pilgrimage:
>
> A visit to holy men bestows merit, because they may be
> regarded as moving holy places. The Lord, dwelling in their
> hearts, renders holy the place where they live.[12]

Describing the true significance of pilgrimage, Swami Vivekananda says:

> When the whole world is the Form Universal of the Eternal
> Atman, the Ishvara, what is there to wonder at in special influ-
> ences attaching to particular places? There are places where He
> manifests Himself specially, either spontaneously or through the
> earnest longing of pure souls, and the ordinary man, if he visits
> those places with eagerness attains his end easily. Therefore it
> may lead to the development of the Self in time to have recourse
> to holy places. But know it for certain that there is no greater
> *tirtha* (holy place) than the body of man. Nowhere else is the

Atman so manifest as here. That car of Jagannatha that you see is but a concrete symbol of this corporeal car. You have to behold the Atman in this car of the body. Haven't you read— "Know the Atman to be seated on the chariot" etc.,—"All the gods worship the Vamana (the Supreme Being in a diminutive form) seated in the interior of the body"? The sight of the Atman is the real vision of Jagannatha. And the statement—"Seeing the Vamana on the car one is no more subject to rebirth," means that if you can visualise the Atman which is within you, and disregarding which you are always identifying yourself with this curious mass of matter, this body of yours—if you can see that, then there is no more rebirth for you. If the sight of the Lord's image on a wooden framework confers liberation on people, then crores [tens of millions] of them would be liberated every year—specially with such facility of communication by rail nowadays.[13]

THE ESSENTIAL OF LIBERATION

What happens to a person after death? We live in an age of doubt, and any descriptions of the hereafter must be verifiable in order to be believable. In the absence of any objective, scientific proof, descriptions of heaven and hell seem like the wishful thinking of a few visionaries. Science has proved that humans are not the chosen people or chosen species but only one of the millions of biological systems. Scientific discoveries have made human beings responsible to themselves.

Vedanta takes a realistic view of the quest for liberation and says the following:

Liberation is freedom of the soul from the bondage of its body and mind.

Liberation is spiritual, not physical, and it is possible only through Self-knowledge, by which the soul realizes its true nature as immortal and incorporeal. Self-knowledge is neither an attainment nor a new production but a revelation that is dependent on self-purification.

Liberation is always personal and individual, because individually we are born, we suffer, and we die.

Liberation is the inescapable destiny of all souls and not, as some maintain, the prerogative of the elect, select, or chosen few.

Liberation is not merely absence of pain and suffering but a state of positive bliss.

Liberation, in order to be believable, must be achieved while living and not after death. One who dies in bondage will remain bound after death.

Heaven and hell are mere experiences of the mind. The state that exists between death and the next birth is that of dream.

Giving the essential of liberation, Shankaracharya says:

Neither by Yoga, nor by Sankhya, nor by work, nor by learning, but by the realization of one's identity with Brahman is liberation possible, and by no other means.[14]

THE ESSENTIAL OF BONDAGE

Truth is self-revealing and God is self-evident. Yet we are not able to see the truth and see God, because obstacles stand in the way. Vedanta identifies the real culprit as the ego, born of ignorance, living on illusion, and creating countless conceits of the body and mind. The main obstacles are what Sri Ramakrishna aptly points out, lust and greed. All desires, attachments, delusions, and fantasies are but the offshoots of these two. Wearing innumerable forms and disguises, lust and greed deceive the seeker in the spiritual path. Unable to perceive what is true, the seeker is forced to live in a world of false values and virtues. By striking root in our body and mind, lust and greed become malignant and destructive.

The obstacles that stand in the way are our own creations. They are the accumulated results of our past indulgent living and are to be overcome by our own effort. Swami Vivekananda points out the essential of bondage and says:

Vedanta says that the cause of all that is apparently evil is the limitation of the Unlimited. The love which gets limited into little channels and seems to be evil eventually comes out at the other end and manifests itself as God. Vedanta also says that the cause of all this apparent evil is in ourselves. Do not blame any supernatural being; neither be hopeless and despondent, nor think we are in a place from which we can never escape unless someone comes and lends us a helping hand. That cannot be, says Vedanta. We are like silk-worms. We make the thread out of our own substance, and spin the cocoon, and in the course of time are imprisoned inside. But this cannot be for ever. We shall develop spiritual realization in that cocoon and, like the butterfly, come out free. We have woven this network of karma around ourselves, and in our ignorance we feel as if we are bound, and weep and wail for help. But help does not come from without; it comes from within ourselves.

Cry to all the gods in the universe. I cried for years, and in the end I received help. But the help came from within myself; and I had to undo what I had done by mistake. That is the only way.[15]

THE ESSENTIAL OF THE WAY

The way to the goal is self-purification, and the essential of self-purification is the purification of the mind through the practice of self-control. The truth of the ever-shining divine Self is revealed in the mirror of the purified mind. All spiritual practices and austerities culminate in the control of the mind. Sri Krishna says in the *Uddhava Gita:*

Charity, the performance of one's duty, the observance of vows, general and particular, the hearing of the scriptures, meritorious acts, and all other works—all these culminate in the control of the mind. The control of the mind is the highest Yoga.[16]

The various spiritual practices and austerities do not give us anything new; they only take away the obstacles that are standing in the way.

Practice of purification has three parts: physical, verbal, and mental. Since the impurities are well entrenched in these three levels, they cannot be rooted out unless the practice includes all three parts. Further, such practice becomes effective only when it is continuous, conscious, and temperate. Practice, unless it is continuous, loses its transforming effect. It is required to be conscious because by controlling the conscious level of the mind, the subconscious level is brought under control. Practice is required to be temperate because human nature cannot be hurried. Habits cannot be altered overnight. A hard-line practice can provoke reactions of the mind, while a lukewarm and intermittent practice can make the seeds of impurities resistant to change. The essential fact is that the mind never becomes controlled unless controlled, never becomes purified unless purified. Control of the mind is never possible without the control of the senses, and the essential of self-control is control over lust and greed. When these two are controlled, the mind is automatically controlled. Without self-control the practice of meditation, prayer, and repetition of a holy name becomes fruitless. So Shankaracharya says:

> He who is free from the terrible snare of the hankering after sense-objects, so very difficult to get rid of, is alone fit for liberation, and none else—even though he be versed in all the six Sastras [six systems of orthodox Hindu philosophy].
>
> The shark of hankering catches by the throat those seekers after liberation who have got only an apparent dispassion [*vairagya*] and are trying to cross the ocean of Samsara [relative existence], and violently snatching them away, drowns them halfway.... Whoever seeks to realise the Self by devoting himself to the nourishment of the body, proceeds to cross a river by catching hold of a crocodile, mistaking it for a log.[17]

Vedanta asserts that one who wants gold must dig for it. Affirming this view, Shankaracharya says:

> As a treasure hidden underground requires (for its excavation) competent instruction, excavation, the removal of stones and other such things lying above it, and (finally) grasping, but never comes out by being (merely) called out by name, so the transparent Truth of the Self, which is hidden by Maya and its effects, is to be attained through the instructions of a knower of Brahman, followed by reflection, meditation and so forth, but not through perverted arguments.[18]

Control of the mind has positive and negative aspects. The positive aspect is observance of purity by dwelling on the Divine; the negative aspect is restraint from sense gratification. The restraint aspect teaches the seeker to withstand the impacts of the surging waves of lust and greed, while the observance aspect teaches to persist in dwelling on the Divine. Mere restraint without observance is never possible, while mere observance without restraint will have no transforming effect.

THE ESSENTIAL MESSAGE

The essential message is that a human individual is basically divine. Our true Self, the focus of the infinite, all-pervading Self of the universe, is our real identity. The manifestation of this identity is the goal of all spiritual quest. All living creatures, consciously or unconsciously, are proceeding toward this goal. The divine Self, when neglected or forgotten, confronts us at every step of our life in the form of the inexorable laws of pain and pleasure, birth and death. Denial of the divine Self is the surest way to doom. When acknowledged and worshiped with eyes open as well as with eyes closed, the Self endows us with everlasting life, eternal fulfillment, and endless bliss. Outlining this essential message, Swami Vivekananda says:

> Perception is our only knowledge, our real religion. Talking about our soul for ages will never make us know it. There is no difference between theories and atheism. In fact, the atheist is the truer man. Every step I take in the light is mine for ever. When you go to a country and see it, then it is yours. We have each to see for ourselves. Teachers can only bring the food; we must eat it to be nourished. Arguments can never prove God's existence save as a logical conclusion.
>
> It is impossible to find God outside ourselves. Our own souls contribute all the divinity that is outside us. We are the greatest temple. The objectification is only a faint imitation of what we see within ourselves.
>
> Concentration of the powers of the mind is our only instrument to help us see God. If you know one soul—your own—you know all souls, past, present, and to come. The will concentrates the

mind; certain things excite and control this will, such as reason, love, devotion, and breathing. The concentrated mind is a lamp that shows us every corner of the soul.[19]

Vedanta says that the root cause of all human problems is spiritual and offers spiritual solutions. It seeks to discover the spiritual truth often lost in the wilderness of superstitions, dogmas, and myths. It maintains that there will be nothing new if all the people of the world convert to Hinduism, Christianity, Islam, Buddhism, or any other religion. But certainly the world will be a different place if some rise above the walls of the nonessentials of religion and realize the essential truth.

9

Four Steps toward the Goal

THE GOAL: DIRECT EXPERIENCE

Direct experience of the Ultimate Reality is the goal of spiritual quest. It is knowing Reality by being one with it and is the result of the total response of the whole mind. Knowing is more than believing. We believe in something that we do not really know. Reasoning, too, is not knowing. Reasoning begins with doubt and also ends in doubt. Reasoning may indicate possibility or probability but can never arrive at certainty. Most often we rationalize and do not reason. Our so-called rational conviction is the result of a mental process that follows the herd instinct. Tradition and convention influence us heavily and determine what we call rational. The reality of God can be neither proved nor disproved by reason. Emotional experiences, too, do not constitute knowing. They come and go, are often the result of mere sentimentalism, and have no lasting value because they do not transform us. Direct experience is perceiving things and beings as they really are and not as we think of them. What we generally think of as direct experience is not really direct, because we perceive everything through the prism of our mind with its in-built predispositions. Direct experience is intuitive and immediate. It is corroborated by scripture, verified by reason, and felt within as deep and transforming knowledge. Such experience alone can silence all our doubts and give certainty to our conviction. Direct experience carries its own irrefutable testimony. It transforms us permanently.

But direct experience is not a sudden revelation or a spiritual windfall.

It cannot be attained miraculously or vicariously, and there is no shortcut to it. There are four vital steps that a seeker takes to attain this direct experience. These steps are scripture, teacher, practice, and time factor.

THE FIRST STEP: SCRIPTURE

The first step toward direct experience is the study of the scriptures. This provides the seeker with a spiritual hypothesis, or road map, for the journey. Scriptures are called *aptavakyas,* or words of the saints and sages. Among the indirect proofs of the reality of God and God-realization, scriptural testimony is more reliable than others, such as inference, analogy, and reasoning. Yet, just as reading about a country, no matter how well described, cannot take the place of seeing it with one's own eyes, so study of scripture alone cannot be a substitute for direct experience. Again, scriptures vary in their views, and the saints and sages are not always unanimous in their conclusions.

Study of the scriptures is nothing more than gathering information about the spiritual journey. But this information is useless unless one is ready to undertake the journey.

The scriptures of Vedanta describe four paths to reach the goal: (1) the direct way of knowledge, or *jnana-yoga;* (2) the natural way of devotion, or *bhakti-yoga;* (3) the scientific way of concentration and meditation, or *raja-yoga;* and (4) the practical way of selfless action, or *karma-yoga.* After reading about the different paths, the seeker must choose one specific path and forge ahead. At this point the seeker is bound to face the question: "Which path is for me?" The path must be right, in keeping with the seeker's inner disposition and physical and mental fitness. How should he or she make the right choice? Thus arises the necessity for a competent teacher.

THE SECOND STEP: TEACHER

THE NECESSITY OF A TEACHER

The role of the teacher is indispensable in any spiritual path. The sacred texts of Vedanta maintain that no direct experience of the Real is possible without a teacher. We cannot have faith in our spiritual destiny merely from study of scriptures. Precepts are not enough to inspire us spiritually—we need examples. We need to meet someone whose life demonstrates the reality of God and the validity of scriptures and thus inspires us toward God-realization. It is true that God alone is the ultimate guide and teacher, and those who can approach God directly with utmost sincerity, deep longing, and absolute self-surrender may not always need a human teacher. But earnestness, longing, and surrender are very rare. Hence, there is the need of a teacher.

The Divine Incarnations and the prophets set examples in this regard. Even though they were born with knowledge of their oneness with God, they accepted teachers. Sri Krishna, Buddha, Christ, Shankaracharya, Ramanuja, Sri Chaitanya, and Sri Ramakrishna—all had spiritual teachers to guide them. The need of a spiritual teacher is not anything peculiar or special to the paths of Yoga and Vedanta. Other sacred traditions also emphasize this need for those who long for spiritual enlightenment. The name may differ from one tradition to another. For example, in Yoga and Vedanta the teacher is called guru, or dispeller of ignorance; in some traditions of Christianity the teacher is called spiritual director; in Judaism, tzaddik; in Russian Orthodox Christianity, starets; and in Sufism, *murshid*. The task each performs is the same, that is, leading the seekers in his or her care to spiritual enlightenment, or illumination.

The teacher is a specialist, or expert, who has traveled the path and reached the goal. He or she knows the path, its peaks and valleys, dangers and difficulties. It is extremely hazardous to undertake any spiritual journey without the guidance and direction of such an expert. Furthermore, if the advice of specialists is necessary for us in many areas of our everyday life, the advice of a teacher is all the more necessary in spiritual matters, which are so subtle and vital. As one cannot be one's own doctor, so also one cannot be one's own teacher. Swami Brahmananda, the eminent disciple of Sri Ramakrishna, says: "One requires a teacher even when one wants to learn stealing."[1]

THE TEACHER AS AWAKENER OF INNER-CONSCIOUSNESS

Without inner awakening no direct experience of Reality is ever possible. No amount of intellectual reasoning or study of scripture can bring about this awakening. Regarding awakening, Sri Ramakrishna says:

> Can one attain knowledge of God by merely repeating the word "God"? There are two indications of such knowledge. First, longing,

that is to say, love for God. You may indulge in reasoning or dis-
cussion, but if you feel no longing or love, it is all futile. Second,
the awakening of the Kundalini [inner-consciousness]. As long as
the Kundalini remains asleep, you have not attained knowledge
of God. You may be spending hours poring over books or discussing philosophy, but if you have no inner restlessness for God,
you have no knowledge of Him.[2]

Awakening of inner consciousness comes when the whole soul feels
intensely restless for the Divine. But self-effort by itself cannot achieve the
goal. There is the need of divine grace, and this grace comes in the form of the
caring guidance of an illumined teacher. Only an awakened person can wake
someone who is sleeping. Emphasizing the need of a teacher, Swami
Vivekananda says:

Religion, which is the highest knowledge and the highest wisdom, cannot be bought, nor can it be acquired from books. You
may thrust your head into all the corners of the world, you may
explore the Himalayas, the Alps, and the Caucasus, you may
sound the bottom of the sea and pry into every nook of Tibet and
the desert of Gobi, but you will not find it anywhere until your
heart is ready to receive it and your teacher has come. And when
that divinely appointed teacher comes, serve him with childlike
confidence and simplicity, freely open your heart to his influence, and see in him God manifested. Those who come to seek
the truth with such a spirit of love and veneration—to them the
Lord of truth reveals the most wonderful things regarding truth,
goodness, and beauty.[3]

THE TEACHER AS TRANSMITTER OF SPIRITUAL POWER

The teacher not only selects the path but also transmits spiritual power to the
seeker. After assessing the seeker's temperament, fitness, liabilities, and
depth of spiritual longing, the teacher prescribes a path, which may be one
of the four paths of yoga or some combination of them. The teacher also
points out a specific aspect of the Divine as the seeker's Chosen Ideal. This
is a unique feature of Vedanta. While each of the other systems presents only

one Ideal to its followers, Vedanta offers an infinite variety of paths and Ideals. After selecting the path and the Ideal, the teacher then transmits spiritual power to the seeker. Mere instruction on how to proceed is not enough for the seeker. He or she must also have the inspiration and strength to persevere until the goal is reached. The power that disciples receive from their teachers guides and inspires them on the way. The transmission of spiritual power is done through a process called initiation, when the teacher passes the power to the seeker through a spiritually charged sacred word. As Swami Vivekananda observes:

> The guru passes the thought-power, the mantra, that he has received from those before him; and nothing can be done without a guru—in fact, great danger ensues. Usually without a guru these yoga practices lead to lust; but with one this seldom happens. Each Ishta [Chosen Ideal] has a mantra. The Ishta is the Ideal peculiar to the particular worshipper; the mantra is the external word to express it.[4]

Initiation has several different forms. The first form is called *anavi,* or mantra initiation. Using this form, the teacher initiates a seeker by uttering a sacred word in the seeker's ear or by writing it on the tongue. Sri Ramakrishna in a few cases wrote mantras on the tongues of some of the seekers. Another form of initiation is called *shakti,* by which the teacher transmits spiritual power to the seeker in silence, or by touch or by look. A third form of initiation is called *shambhavi,* where the power of the teacher is transmitted to the seeker without the knowledge of either of them. The most widely practiced form of initiation, however, is *anavi,* mantra initiation.

The spiritual power of a teacher depends primarily on the depth of his or her God-realization. The deeper the realization, the greater is the power. The Divine Incarnations are the greatest of all teachers. They can impart illumination to anyone at any time. Next to them are the companions or direct disciples of the Incarnations. They are ever-free souls, who, when in an exalted mood, can also impart illumination to anyone. Then there are illumined souls who are capable of teaching and guiding seekers along the path to God-realization. The power of an illumined teacher acquires an extraordinary dimension if his or her spiritual ancestry originates from a giant soul, such as a Divine Incarnation. This is because the spiritual power of the Divine

Incarnation flows from one generation of disciples to the next. Regarding this flow of power, Swami Vivekananda says:

> These great ones, whom you call Incarnations of God, are mighty spiritual giants. They come and set in motion a tremendous spiritual current by transmitting their power to their immediate disciples, and through them to generation after generation of disciples.[5]

Loyalty to Teacher and Chosen Ideal

Vedanta makes a distinction between the primary teacher and secondary teachers. A seeker can learn from other teachers, but the primary teacher, or guru, is the one from whom he or she receives initiation and spiritual power. One-pointed loyalty to the guru and to the Chosen Ideal is absolutely necessary. As Swami Vivekananda says:

> Without faith, humility, submission, and veneration in our hearts towards our religious teacher, there cannot be any growth of religion in us. It is a significant fact that where this kind of relation between the teacher and the taught prevails, there alone do gigantic spiritual men grow, while in those countries which have neglected to keep up this kind of relation, the religious teacher has become a mere lecturer—the teacher expecting his five dollars and the person taught expecting his brain to be filled with the teacher's words, and each going his own way after this much has been done. Under such circumstances spirituality becomes almost an unknown quantity.[6]

In choosing a teacher, seekers may reason, waver, and take time. But once they select a teacher, they must trust and depend upon the teacher completely. This is very necessary because seekers in their inward journey to the goal are solitary travelers. They are alone with their mind and cannot trust it. It is because the unregenerate human mind is restless and changeable. It is unpredictable by nature and assumes unthinkable forms. Furthermore, a true teacher is worthy of our trust because he or she is our greatest well-wisher. As Swami Vivekananda says:

> The relationship with the teacher is the greatest in life. My guru is my nearest and dearest relative in life; next, my mother; then my father. My first reverence is to my guru. If my father says,

"Do this," and my guru says, "Do not do this," I do not do it. The guru frees my soul. The father and mother give me this body, but the guru gives me rebirth in the Spirit.[7]

Loyalty to the teacher and to the Chosen Ideal provides the seeker with the much-needed spiritual roots for spiritual growth and development. There is a humorous saying that for the seeker, "One guru leads to illumination, two gurus to confusion, and three gurus to cremation!" So Vedanta advises the seeker to follow one teacher and faithfully adhere to his or her instructions. The seeker may appreciate all, honor all, but should follow one. He or she may draw inspiration from all but should practice the teachings of only one. When seekers develop strong and deep spiritual roots, they realize that their Chosen Ideal is worshiped in all other ideals, by all sects, under all names, and through all forms. The injunction of Vedanta is that a teacher, once accepted, is the teacher forever. As one does not give up one's father or mother, so one does not give up one's teacher. Sri Ramakrishna says:

A man should have faith in the words of his guru. He doesn't have to look into his guru's character. "Though my guru visits the grog-shop, still he is the Embodiment of Eternal Bliss."[8]

Tradition has it that the sins of the disciple affect the teacher. If a teacher gives initiation to many without examining their moral nature, some mortal illness may afflict the teacher and shorten his or her life. Nevertheless, true teachers, out of boundless compassion, give no thought to their own body and willingly lay down their life for the welfare of their disciples. Sri Ramakrishna used to say that he had all of his physical ailments (cancer in the throat, etc.) because he had taken upon himself the sins of others. In this regard Swami Vivekananda says:

A [true teacher] is one on whom the spiritual power has descended by Guru-parampara, or an unbroken chain of discipleship. To play the role of a spiritual teacher is a very difficult thing. One has to take on oneself the sins of others. There is every chance of a fall in less advanced men. If merely physical pain ensues, then he should consider himself fortunate.[9]

The blessing and grace of the teacher are absolutely necessary for success in the spiritual path. In the *Vivekachudamani*, Shankaracharya says:

"There are three things which are rare indeed and are due to the grace of God—namely, a human birth, the longing for liberation, and the protecting care of a perfected sage."[10] The Bhagavad Gita points out that the grace of the teacher must be sought by rendering personal service to him or her: "Learn it [knowledge] by prostration, by inquiry, and by service. The wise, who have seen the Truth, will teach you that Knowledge."[11] Ideal loyalty to the guru and to the Ishtam (Chosen Ideal) has been compared to that of a pet dog to its master. Even when a pet dog is ignored, ill-treated, or forgotten by the master, it remains steadfast in its devotion and faithfulness. Only such steadfast loyalty to the guru and to the Ishtam under all circumstances makes the seeker worthy of their grace. It is said in the sacred traditions of Vedanta that both the teacher and the Chosen Ideal follow the seeker from birth to birth until he or she attains to final liberation through direct experience.

MARKS OF A TRUE TEACHER

According to Vedanta, a true teacher has the following marks. First, a true teacher is well versed in the scriptures and knows that the essential message of all sacred texts is: God alone is real, all else is illusory, and God-realization is the goal of life. Second, a teacher is a knower of God and not merely a scholar, ritualist, or philosopher. Only a direct knower of truth can impart true enlightenment. Third, the teacher is stainless and pure—a person of renunciation and dispassion, free from all attraction of lust and gold. Fourth, a true teacher is free from all selfish motive. The only medium through which spiritual power can be transmitted is unselfish love and service. The fifth mark, which is a corollary to the fourth, is that a true teacher is compassionate, caring, and patient and understands the needs of the seeker, knowing that change does not come overnight.

MARKS OF A TRUE SEEKER

Often we are concerned with the quality and character of a teacher and discover that a true teacher is very rare. But then, a true seeker is also very rare. Both the teacher and the taught must be authentic; otherwise the seed of spirituality cannot sprout. One has to be truly thirsty to appreciate a cool drink.

One has to be truly hungry to enjoy a sumptuous dinner. In the Bible, Jesus says:

> A sower went forth to sow. And when he sowed, some seeds fell by the wayside, and the fowls came and devoured them up. Some fell upon stony places, where they had not much earth, and forthwith they sprung up, because they had no deepness of earth. And when the sun was up, they were scorched; and because they had no root, they withered away. And some fell among thorns; and the thorns sprung up and choked them. But others fell into good ground and brought forth fruit, some a hundredfold, some sixtyfold, some thirtyfold. He who has ears to hear, let him hear (Matt. 13:3–9).

The marks of a true seeker, according to Swami Vivekananda, are four. First, the seeker sincerely longs to know the truth, and for this quest is ready to give up all desires for gain in this world or hereafter. Second, the seeker has control over body, mind, and senses. Third, the true seeker has faith in the teacher, in the words of the sacred texts, and most of all in him- or herself. Fourth, the seeker has the ability to discriminate the Real from the unreal, that is, the fact that God alone is true and everything else is illusory. So Swami Vivekananda says:

> These are the four conditions which one who wants to be a disciple must fulfill. Without fulfilling them he will not be able to come in contact with a true guru. And even if he is fortunate enough to find one, he will not be quickened by the power that the guru may transmit. There cannot be any compromising of these conditions. With the fulfillment of these conditions—with all these preparations—the lotus of the disciple's heart will open and the bee will come. Then the disciple knows that the real guru was within the body, within himself. He unfolds. He realizes the Spirit. He crosses the ocean of life, goes beyond.[12]

FINDING A TRUE TEACHER

There are, indeed, difficulties in finding a true teacher. First, realized souls are very rare and do not wear any outward mark. They avoid the gaze of the merely curious. Second, a seeker, because of preconceived notions and fanciful expectations, may fail to recognize a worthy spiritual guide even when coming into contact with one. There is a third difficulty. The average seeker is susceptible to credulity, too ready to respond to sensationalism or follow mass opinion. Many consider occult power a mark of spirituality. A fourth difficulty that sometimes stands in the way of finding a teacher is social prejudice, such as that associated with caste, class, or dogmatic family tradition. It is not always easy for a spiritual seeker to rise above conventional ideas and follow what is spiritually beneficial. A fifth difficulty is that a teacher, though illumined, may be one-sided. The teacher may believe only in a personal God, or only in God without form. All these difficulties limit the seeker's choice of a spiritual teacher. Under such circumstances, it would be wise for a seeker to select a teacher who has the authority of a well-recognized spiritual community or who traces his or her spiritual ancestry to a Divine Incarnation or a God-realized personality. There is an element of divine intervention in the meeting of the teacher and the disciple. Finding a true teacher has a connection with finding God. God as the indwelling Self is the ultimate teacher. As Sri Ramakrishna says: "Satchidananda alone is the Guru. If a man in the form of a guru awakens spiritual consciousness in you, then know for certain that it is God the Absolute who has assumed that human form for your sake."[13] When our soul sincerely longs for God and becomes restless for him, the Lord as the Divine Teacher, wearing the disguise of a human form, comes to show the way. It is he who chooses us as his disciples. We cannot be drawn to him unless he draws us by his grace. So Sri Ramakrishna says:

> Pray to God with a longing heart. He will surely listen to your prayer if it is sincere. Perhaps He will direct you to holy men with whom you can keep company; and that will help you on your spiritual path. Perhaps someone will tell you, "Do this and you will attain God."[14]

It is said that the seed and the field attract each other. When the field is ready, the seed comes. When we become ready, the true teacher appears. Perhaps the best way to find the true teacher is to make ourselves ready for his or her coming.

THE THIRD STEP: PRACTICE

After the teacher initiates the seeker into the sacred mysteries of the spiritual path, the latter begins the third step—spiritual practice. Spiritual practice in any path of yoga has two aspects: foundational and structural. Foundational practice is for control of mind and structural practice for its regulation.

FOUNDATIONAL PRACTICE

Foundational practice calls for mastery of moral and ethical virtues. The essence of foundational practice is self-control—that is, gaining control over body, mind, and senses, which are accustomed to submitting to the demands of every impulse and passion. Carried along by the waves of impulses, darkened by imaginations, unstable, fickle, and full of desires, the mind is constant prey to delusions and fancies. It is either dull or excited or scattered, and never concentrated. It never comes under control unless conscious effort is made to control it. Again, the mind cannot be controlled unless the senses are brought under control, and the senses cannot be controlled unless the body and bodily habits are controlled.

The practice of foundational virtues provides the seeker with a solid moral foundation, which is vital for spiritual success. Many obstacles beset the spiritual path until the goal is reached. There are the distractions of desires, storms of passions, upheavals of emotions, and agitations of the subconscious. Only a seeker with a purified mind and moral stamina can overcome them and persevere in the path. Morality is the steel-frame foundation of spiritual life. Without it, spiritual practice can bring harmful results.

STRUCTURAL PRACTICE

Structural practice of the different paths consists of prayer, ceremonial worship, meditation, and self-enquiry. Structural practice is meant for directing the mind for concentration on the Chosen Ideal. Concentration culminates in meditation, and meditation in absorption. Concentration is holding the mind on a single thought without interruption for a certain length of time.

Concentration, when it becomes spontaneous and continuous, takes the form of meditation, and meditation culminates in the absorption of *samadhi,* when Truth reveals itself, shining in full glory.

While foundational practice collects the mind from its worldly preoccupations, structural practice enables the seeker to devote the collected mind to spiritual concentration. The two practices are interdependent and must be carried on simultaneously. Unless one practices self-control, one cannot succeed in concentration and meditation. Again, unless one practices concentration and meditation, one can never succeed in self-control. Control without regulation proves repressive and provokes reaction from the mind. A repressed desire creates heightened awareness of the desired object. As the Bhagavad Gita points out: "The objects of the senses fall away from a man practicing abstinence, but not the taste for them. But even the taste falls away when the Supreme is seen."[15] Hence the need for regulation of the mind, by which the mind is led to concentrate on the Chosen Ideal within. Spiritual practice ceases to be effective when not followed in both aspects—foundational and structural.

THE NEED OF SPIRITUAL PRACTICE

Spiritual practice is an absolute necessity for the attainment of the spiritual goal, and the reasons are compelling.

First, practice is necessary for spiritual assimilation of the teaching. Receiving the teaching and grasping it by the mind do not assure its assimilation and absorption into our soul. Assimilation and absorption require repeated practice of reflection and meditation on the teaching. Spiritual practice converts our intellectual conviction into spiritual inspiration. That which was initially considered a possibility is later felt as a certainty.

Second, practice is required for developing concentration of mind. As mentioned above, concentration leads to meditation, and meditation to the absorption of *samadhi*. But concentration does not develop by itself. Absence of mental agitation does not automatically bring spiritual concentration. Concentration calls for repeated practice over a long period with undaunted enthusiasm. The basic idea is to cultivate one single thought-wave reminiscent of the Ultimate and strengthen it through regular, systematic, and conscious repetition with devotion, over a long time. Then the whole mind takes the form of a huge thought-wave, which is the state of meditation. As meditation culminates in *samadhi*, the mind with all its thoughts gets dissolved in the ocean of the all-pervading Ultimate Reality.

Third, by practice we align our thought, word, and deed to the goal. Direct experience of the Reality calls for the unified response of all the faculties of our mind—willing, feeling, and thinking. This unified response does not come automatically. It, too, requires long and repeated practice.

Fourth, practice is needed for purifying our heart and cleansing our vision. We are not able to perceive Reality because of the impurities of our mind, which are the accumulated results of past self-indulgent living. These impurities create a veil that either distorts or blocks our perception of Reality. Impurities are impure thoughts that, when repeated, strike roots in our psyche and body chemistry, creating habits and conditionings and becoming the determinants of our behavior and mental predispositions, or *samskaras*. *Samskaras* die hard. Time cannot erase them. Intellectual reasoning cannot obliterate them. The only way to deal with them is to neutralize them by developing counter-*samskaras*, or conditionings, and this is the goal of spiritual practice. Spiritual conditioning, developed through spiritual practice, first neutralizes the unspiritual conditionings and then dissolves by itself. So Swami Vivekananda says:

> The infinite future is before you, and you must always remember
> that each word, thought, and deed lays up a store for you, and that
> as the bad thoughts and bad works are ready to spring upon you
> like tigers, so also there is the inspiring hope that the good
> thoughts and good deeds are ready with the power of a hundred
> thousand angels to defend you always and for ever.[16]

The direct perception of Reality is a revelation and not a production of spiritual practices. Such practices do not give us anything new. They only help us to purify our mind. In the mirror of the pure heart the revelation of the Ultimate is perceived.

Fifth, practice prepares our psychophysical system for the impact of direct spiritual experience, which can be likened to both fire and light. As fire, it burns all that is false, unauthentic, and fanciful in us. As light, it reveals that which is true in us. This experience can be shattering for our body, mind, and nerves if they are not rebuilt and made strong beforehand.

This rebuilding is accomplished through spiritual practice. Through spiritual practice we voluntarily evolve and undergo transformation. In one life we go through many lives with intense speed.

Sixth, practice enables us to discover the limits of our ego and to make possible the descent of divine grace. Both self-effort and divine grace are necessary for the realization of the spiritual goal. Self-effort removes the obstacles in the path and then divine grace follows as a matter of course. If the descent of divine grace depends upon self-surrender, then self-effort in spiritual practice is really making effort for self-surrender. So the Bible says, "Seek, and ye shall find; knock, and it shall be opened unto you" (Matt. 8:7). One must do something in order to get something. Nothings happens by chance. Only active effort can bring tangible results, not mere idle wishes.

Seventh, practice is necessary not only for spiritual attainment but also for spiritual enjoyment. The spiritual quest is a conscious journey to the Ultimate, with many wonderful experiences at different stages. There is relish in the name of God, serenity in meditation, ecstasy of divine inebriation, bliss of total absorption in God-consciousness, and the joy of self-dedication to the welfare of all beings. The seeker is rewarded with these incomparable transforming experiences as he advances along the way.

THE FOURTH STEP: TIME FACTOR

The fourth step is the time factor. Direct experience of Ultimate Reality or God-vision cannot be programmed or scheduled. Human nature cannot be hurried. Spiritual urgency and hunger cannot be generated by artificial means. As a child cannot be made to grow into an adult all of a sudden, so also our spiritual growth cannot be attained suddenly. Our mind takes time to assimilate spiritual instruction and attain the desired spiritual growth.

The reason for the practice of moderation is that our ingrained habits and deep-rooted tendencies cannot be overcome all at once. A counterhabit is to be developed by intense effort. The intensity of effort must be in keeping with the capacity of the mind. Again, direct experience of Reality is a gift of the Divine and not the result of mere effort. Grace descends only when we keep ourselves ready and wait patiently for it. This patient waiting intensifies our longing, tests our determination, and prepares our mind to recognize the moment of final revelation when it comes. The story of the ten virgins in the Bible illustrates this point:

> Then shall the kingdom of heaven be likened unto ten virgins, which took their lamps and went forth to meet the bridegroom. And five of them were wise, and five were foolish. They that were foolish took their lamps, and took no oil with them. But the wise took oil in the vessels with their lamps. While the bridegroom tarried, they all slumbered and slept. And at midnight there was a cry made, Behold, the bridegroom cometh; go ye out to meet him. Then all those virgins arose and trimmed their lamps. And the foolish said unto the wise, Give us of your oil; for our lamps are gone out. But the wise answered, saying, Not so: lest there be not enough for us and you: but go ye rather to them that sell and buy for yourselves. And while they went to buy, the bridegroom came; and they that were ready went in with him to the marriage: and the door was shut. Afterward came also the other virgins, saying, Lord, Lord, open to us. But he answered and said, Verily I say unto you, I know you not. Watch therefore, for ye know neither the day nor the hour wherein the Son of man cometh" (Matt. 25:1–13).

The seeker must be ever ready, ever alert, so that he or she may not miss the auspicious moment. Revelation comes in a flash, but it takes a lifetime of preparation to make us ready for that light.

The growth of our spiritual life can be compared to that of a tree. Like a tree it grows naturally and spontaneously. Its growth is organic and cannot be measured from day to day. The nourishment of this tree does not come like dew from the sky but rises from the roots to spread throughout the tree. The seed of a tree is planted in the soil, where it sprouts as a delicate plant. The plant in its early stages is hedged around for protection. When nurtured and fertilized, the plant develops into a sapling and then into a full-grown tree, bringing forth first flowers and then fruit. In the same way, the seed of spiritual life, provided by the teacher, is planted in the soil of the seeker's mind, where it sprouts as a delicate plant. In the early stages, the seeker protects the plant by hedging it around and nurturing it with orthodox observances and one-pointed loyalty to the Ideal. The plant gradually grows into a sapling as it is nourished by the seeker's austerities, self-control, prayer, *japa,* and meditation. In the fullness of time, the sapling develops into a full-grown tree, bringing forth first flowers of virtues, such as purity, devotion, knowledge, and compassion for all beings. Finally, the flowers are followed by the fruit of spiritual illumination. Those who long for the spiritual fruit must take good care of the spiritual tree. They must protect it, nurture it, and wait patiently for its ultimate growth and fulfillment.

10

The Mood for Meditation

Meditation is a state of inner absorption in which the mind of the meditator flows continuously and spontaneously toward the object of meditation. The Bhagavad Gita compares this inner absorption to the steady flame of a lamp sheltered in a windless place. Patanjali describes this state as the unbroken flow of the whole mind toward the object of concentration. According to the *Shrimad Bhagavatam,* this is a state in which the meditator becomes one with the object meditated upon. Ramanuja considers this state to be a spontaneous and loving remembrance of the most beloved.

The state of meditation is reached by a process of gradual devolution, or folding oneself back. The speech is folded back into the mind, the mind into the intellect, and the intellect into the indwelling Self. Meditation culminates in the state of *samadhi,* in which the individualized consciousness, or microcosm, becomes completely merged in the infinite expanse of absolute and all-pervading Pure Consciousness, the macrocosm. It is like a piece of ice slowly getting dissolved in the water of the ocean. The *Mandukya Upanishad* speaks of the three states of our existence—waking, dream, and dreamless sleep. Beyond these three there is another state, which the same Upanishad describes as Turiya, or the fourth. The state of *samadhi* is the state of Turiya and the state of Turiya is reached by transcending the three states of waking, dream, and dreamless sleep. The goal of meditation is to achieve this transcendence consciously and voluntarily.

Meditation, as a spiritual discipline, has three aspects: the object of meditation, the act of meditation, and the meditator. As absorption in meditation deepens, the three aspects begin to merge into one. Meditation is not just one of the many spiritual practices; it is the culmination and consummation of all spiritual practices, irrespective of the meditator's philosophy and creed. In the words of Sri Ramakrishna: "The *sandhya* merges in the *gayatri,* the *gayatri* in Om, and Om in *samadhi.*"[1] That is to say, ritualistic worship and prayer merge in the *gayatri,* which is the highest and most concentrated prayer of the Vedas. The *gayatri* then becomes further concentrated into the sacred word *Om,* from which all words emanate; and finally, Om merges in the profound silence of *samadhi.* It is not that the meditator attains to the state of meditation. It is, rather, the other way: the meditator is taken over by that state. As a weary person is taken over by the state of deep sleep in spite of efforts to remain awake, even so, the aspirant weary of the unsubstantiality of the world is taken over by the state of *samadhi,* the boundless and fathomless ocean of silence.

The depth of inner absorption is measured by the intensity of each of the following three kinds of spontaneous transcendence: First, meditators, as they lose themselves in the state of inner absorption, transcend the idea of time and, therefore, become oblivious of the lapse of time. Second, they transcend the idea of place and are not aware of the surrounding environment. And third, they completely transcend their I-consciousness and, therefore, everything about themselves. This inner absorption cannot be attained in a single day; it cannot be programmed, hastened, or scheduled. It is not dependent on specific posture, diet, duration of sitting, or any other factor accessory to the practice of meditation. That which is most vital is the meditative mood. The aspirant must feel the mood for meditation. Sri Ramakrishna describes this spiritual mood as a kind of divine inebriation. No meditation is possible without this inebriation.

THE FAVORABLE AND UNFAVORABLE MOODS

An ordinary person experiences many moods and is at the mercy of them. Our moods are diverse and variable, and we have no control over them. All our thoughts and perceptions, cognitions and volitions, are greatly and variously charged by these moods. The Bhagavad Gita broadly classifies the different moods into three categories: *sattvika, rajasika,* and *tamasika.* The *tamasika* and *rajasika* moods are not favorable for meditation. The first one, the *tamasika* mood, darkens the mind and forces it to lapse into the state of inertia, which is the opposite of contemplative alertness. The second one, the *rajasika* mood, brings in its wake turbulence and restlessness, which make the mind unfit for any meditative endeavor. The third variety of mood, *sattvika,* is a mood of tranquillity and detachment and is therefore the only favorable mood for the practice of meditation.

Different aspirants experience different degrees of the contemplative mood, depending upon their respective inner disposition and self-control. Therefore aspirants have been classified into four categories: the beginners, the striving, the adept, and the perfect. Those who are perfect in meditation always remain absorbed in a contemplative mood, irrespective of time, place, and circumstances. The adept aspirants can call forth this mood without much difficulty. The striving ones are able to experience this mood only under favorable circumstances and conditions; meditators who are beginners are very much dependent upon the favorable disposition of their mind. The practice of meditation for beginners is not always inspired by any contemplative mood, and therefore their practices frequently prove to be dry, monotonous, and mechanical. Even when they are in a favorable mood, that too proves to be very short-lived and unsteady. Lacking stability in the proper mood, beginners fail to participate emotionally in their practices and very often are filled with a sense of frustration. Therefore beginners, until they have developed an inner mood that is strong enough to overcome external distractions, must depend upon circumstances favorable to their practices.

THE CULTIVATION OF THE RIGHT MOOD

The conditions that contribute to the cultivation and development of the meditative mood are said to be the following: right living place, congenial environment, propitious time, favorable physical condition, holy company, right speech, purity of food, right method, one-pointed loyalty to the Ideal, acts of service, right motive, practice of discrimination, devotional music, chanting of the sacred texts, ritualistic practices, *pranayama, japa*—practice of the repetition of a holy name, and regularity and balance of practice.

Right living place. Place plays a vital role in the development of the meditative mood. It is easy for a beginner to feel the mood for meditation in a solitary place, away from the distractions of the world. Meditation, according to the traditions of Yoga, is to be practiced in solitude. A beginner, especially, is required to withdraw from the preoccupations of everyday life and retire into solitude from time to time. Physical withdrawal from objects of distraction eventually leads to the withdrawal of the mind from such things. It is extremely difficult to devote one's mind to meditation by living in proximity of things that are disturbing and distracting, and therefore inner solitude must be sought in the solitude of nature.

Accustomed to living in the midst of the bustle of everyday life, many, however, find it difficult to live in solitude, enjoy its silence, and derive spiritual benefit thereby. For them external solitude often proves to be suffocating and oppressive. Therefore a beginner is advised to go into solitude occasionally for short periods, for example one or two days at a time, and then to extend this period gradually. Solitude, as Holy Mother, Sri Sarada Devi, points out, deepens one's spiritual mood: "If you practice spiritual disciplines for some time in a solitary place, you will find that your mind has become strong, and then you can live in any place or society without being in the least affected by it. When the plant is tender it should be hedged around. But when it has grown big not even cows and goats can injure it."[2]

In the words of Sri Ramakrishna: "To meditate, you should withdraw within yourself or retire to a secluded corner or to the forest."[3] Meditation is to be practiced in secret and in solitude, and Sri Ramakrishna indicates three solitary places that are appropriate for this purpose: the inner recess of one's own mind, some secluded corner of one's own house, and the solitude of the forest. Beginners are advised to select for their practice any or all of these places, according to the opportunities available. Under any circumstances they must seek solitude for their practice until they have developed inner solitude. Living in solitude calms the mind. It has been said that distracting things and situations that are out of sight also tend to drop from the mind. The practice of withdrawal into solitude, however, must be supported by a spirit of dispassion and prayerfulness, in the absence of which a beginner is likely to be taken over by a holiday mood instead of a meditative one.

Congenial environment. A congenial environment is a powerful aid in creating the mood for meditation. The environment, in order to be congenial, must be tranquil, far from the haunts of the worldly minded, pure, and pleasant to the sight. According to the Hindu scriptures, the following places are favorable for the practice of meditation: a mountain, a riverbank, a temple, a place where the practice of meditation has been successfully carried out by many spiritual seekers, and a solitary place free from distractions. The yogi should always live alone. As stated in the *Shrimad Bhagavatam,* where many dwell in one place there is the possibility of noise and quarreling. Even where there are only two people, there is the possibility of harmful gossip. Therefore the yogi should live in solitude and be alone. By living in solitude and being alone, the yogi gradually overcomes the tumult of the external world, and by the repeated practice of meditation, eventually rises above the distracting vibrations of the mind. The state of meditation is achieved when the heart becomes tranquil. When one is no longer stirred by desires, one attains tranquillity of heart, which has been likened to the stillness of a fire that is no more being fed by any fuel.

The environment selected for the practice of meditation must not be merely solitary; it must also be pure. An environment that is not clean, and where holy persons are not honored and adored, is not to be considered pure and is, therefore, not conducive to the practice of meditation. The purity of an environment depends upon the purity of its spiritual vibrations. The sacred traditions of Yoga mention that every person is constantly emitting, as it were, some subtle essence of personality, known as *tanmatra,* which remains present in the environment where he or she lives or spends much time. The environment of a temple, or a place of worship or pilgrimage, is naturally pure because of the accumulated deposits of spiritual vibrations and is, therefore, most congenial for the practice of meditation.

Swami Vivekananda emphasizes the need of a congenial environment and observes the following:

> Those of you who can afford it should have a room where you can practice alone. Do not sleep in that room; it must be kept holy. You must not enter the room until you have bathed and are perfectly clean in body and mind. Place flowers in that room always—they are the best surroundings for a yogi—and pictures that are pleasing. Burn incense morning and evening. Have no quarrel or anger or unholy thought in that room. Only allow those persons to enter it who are of the same thought as you. Then gradually there will be an atmosphere of holiness in the room, so that when you are miserable, sorrowful, or doubtful, or when your

mind is disturbed, if you then enter the room you will feel inner peace. This was the real idea behind the temple and the church; and in some temples and churches you will find it even now; but in the majority of them this idea has been lost. The fact is that by preserving spiritual vibrations in a place you make it holy.[4]

It is traditionally believed that meditation should always be practiced in a lonely spot, in dim light or in darkness. The ideal environment, however, is never given. Yogis must build their own inner environment by their own effort, so that they may remain unaffected by the distractions of the external world.

Propitious time. The meditative mood depends to a certain extent on the temper of the time selected for practice. The traditions of Yoga consider the following times most propitious for the practice of meditation: (a) the conjunction of day and night—that is to say, at dawn, when night disappears and day arrives, and at dusk, when day disappears and night arrives; (b) the moment of Brahman, which is an hour before sunrise; (c) midday—that is to say, the conjunction of the two halves of the day, and (d) midnight, the conjunction of the two halves of the night. The mind is said to remain collected and pure at those periods because the spiritual current of the spinal column generally remains active and breathing is done through both nostrils, which is the indication of inner tranquillity. At other times one or the other of the two nerves *ida* and *pingala,* located on either side of the *sushumna* nerve, becomes active, quite in keeping with the heightened vibrations of nature, and breathing is done through either the right or the left nostril, indicating unsteadiness of mind. Yogis are often advised to observe carefully the *sushumna* nerve by monitoring their breathing to determine when they are breathing evenly through both nostrils, and at that point to throw everything aside and sit for meditation as soon as possible. The yogi's mind, like a tidal river, has its ebb and flow, particularly in the early stages of the practice of meditation. But such ebb and flow are overcome when practice becomes regular and steady.

It is also said that in every place of pilgrimage there are special times each day when the spiritual current flows throughout the surroundings, and practice of meditation at those times helps the aspirant to attain absorption in the Divine. According to the orthodox Hindu view, there are particular days that are especially auspicious for the practice of meditation: new moon day, full moon day, the eighth day after the new or full moon, and days of special religious celebrations.

Favorable physical condition. The mood for meditation does not come if the physical condition of an aspirant is not favorable. Body and mind are closely related to each other, and so when the body is not as ease, the mind too becomes distracted. Meticulous care is very necessary to maintain the proper health of the body through regulated diet, exercise, and rest. Even a little overeating or overfasting or lack of sleep or any imbalance of the elements of the body makes the physical condition unfavorable for meditation. No effective practice of meditation is possible when the body is tired through overwork, or tense or charged owing to mental distractions. The body must be healthy, rested, and free from tension. Steadiness of posture is also an important prerequisite for the practice of meditation. An aspirant is advised not to overdo this practice when his or her physical condition is not favorable. The brain becomes overheated as the result of forced practice and on account of constantly sitting on the meditation seat.

A favorable physical condition, however, is dependent not just on proper diet, exercise, and rest but also on purity of habits. The aspirant is required to be endowed with three gifts: purity of character, tenacity of purpose, and strength of body. Without having the first, one cannot have the other two. One aspiring after the meditative mood must be careful not to overtax the body by overeating or overfasting or any form of overindulgence. One who eats indiscriminately, lives a disordered existence, or is a slave to passions and whims is never capable of any tenacity of purpose. A person who regularly overeats wastes half of his or her energy in digesting food, and even eight to ten hours of sleep is not enough to provide rest. Whatever energy is left may be frittered away in idle gossip and aimless pursuits, leaving no energy whatsoever for the practice of meditation. Small wonder then that such persons feel no real mood to meditate, and even should they force themselves to sit for meditation, they only yawn and doze.

Holy company. There is nothing more powerful than holy company to uplift the depressed mind of a spiritual aspirant and infuse it with the fervor of the spiritual mood. There are times when an aspirant feels no enthusiasm or inspiration for spiritual practices. For no apparent reason the mind suddenly comes up against an impenetrable wall, as it were, and everything seems dry, monotonous, and dull. No amount of study or chanting of the holy name or repeated attempts to concentrate the mind is of any avail. All attempts to keep the mind from falling into the mire of low thoughts and tendencies prove futile, and as a consequence, the aspirant is overcome by frustration, despair, and feelings of defeat. Under these circumstances, the only remedy is the company of the holy. As a piece of red-hot iron radiates heat, so also a holy personality who remains charged with an intense spiritual mood emits great spiritual fervor, and an aspirant coming into association with such a personality is able to imbibe some of that mood. As evil company is contagious and stirs up the dormant evil tendencies in a mind, so also holy company easily awakens all the divine propensities in it.

The effectiveness of holy company, however, depends on the right attitude of an aspirant, and the factors that make for the right attitude are the following: First, an aspirant is required to have *shraddha,* which is faith in oneself and in holy company. The opposite of *shraddha* is skepticism and cynicism, a general negative attitude about everything. The second factor is humility. As Sri Ramakrishna says: "The water of God's grace cannot collect on the high mound of egotism. It runs down."[5] Similarly, the spiritual mood builds up only in a humble heart. The third factor is the spirit of service. An aspirant may seek the company of the holy, but the holy personality must be pleased with the sincerity of the aspirant. Holy company is more mental than physical. Mahendranath Gupta, the chronicler of *The Gospel of Sri Ramakrishna,* beautifully highlights this idea and says that to see a holy man is itself holy company, and a holy man is to be seen when he is absorbed in meditation.

Right speech. The growth of the mood for meditation is intimately related to the control of speech, which has been spoken of by Shankaracharya as the first doorway to yoga. Too much talking or indulgence in fruitless controversy dissipates the energy of the mind, distracts it from its purpose, and is inimical to the development of the meditative mood. Such control is necessary also for the preservation of the meditative mood. The average person cannot remain without talking even for a single moment. If there is no one to talk to, we talk to ourselves, that is, engage in a continuous inner monologue. Control of speech, however, is not forced silence; nor would such forced silence be desirable or possible. It has been found that if a beginner takes a vow of silence for a day or two, he or she often indulges in too much talking after this observance of silence has ended and thereby makes the vow counterproductive. Control of speech means making the speech right by saying that which is true, pleasing, and beneficial to all.

Meditation is the practice of silence and a person who has no control over speech cannot practice this silence all of a sudden. Therefore a beginner is advised to develop the habit of practicing *japa,* or repetition of a holy name. Such repetition keeps the mind preoccupied with one single thought and creates a mood for meditative silence. *Japa,* practiced mentally, matures into contemplation; contemplation further strengthened takes the form of meditation; and meditation when it is effortless becomes the first stage of *samadhi. Vrittis,* or various thought-waves, cannot be stopped by suppressing them. They are to be first neutralized and then overcome by the deliberate cultivation of one single thought, which is accomplished by the practice of *japa.* The continuous repetition of a single thought makes its wave grow bigger and stronger and thus subdues the countless smaller thought-ripples on the surface of the mind.

Purity of food. The influence of food over the mind cannot be exaggerated. The mood for meditation is greatly affected by the purity or impurity of food. Any food that is not consecrated or is contaminated by the touch of impure vibrations is considered impure and, therefore, not conducive to a spiritual mood. Pure food purifies the blood and the mind. The Bhagavad Gita describes pure food as that which increases the *sattva guna.* The meditative mood comes only in the wake of the *sattva guna.* Contrary moods are of two types. They are either *rajasic,* exciting desire for worldly objects and enjoyments, or *tamasic,* adding to the dullness and darkness of the mind. According to the *Uddhava Gita,* the rise of the *sattva guna* is possible only when an aspirant is able to ensure the *sattvika* quality of ten factors: scripture, water, people, place, time, work, birth (meaning spiritual rebirth), meditation, mantra, and purification (of mind).

Commenting on this, Swami Madhavananda says:

Only those scriptures are to be followed which teach Nivritti or the march back to the oneness of Brahman, not those that teach Pravritti or continuing the multiplicity (*rajasika*) or those that teach downright injurious tenets (*tamasika*); similarly, holy water only is to be used, not scented water or wine etc.; one should mix only with spiritual people, not with worldly-minded or wicked

people; a solitary place is to be preferred, not a public thorough-
fare or a gaming house; early morning or some such time is to be
selected for meditation in preference to hours likely to cause distraction or dullness; the obligatory and unselfish works only
should be done, not selfish or dreadful ones; initiation into pure
and non-injurious forms of religion is needed, not those that
require much ado or those that are impure and harmful; meditation should be on the Lord, not on sense-objects or on enemies
with a view to revenge; mantras such as Om are to be preferred,
not those bringing worldly prosperity or causing injury to others;
purification of the mind is what we should care for, not trimming
of the body merely...[6]

Right method. The meditative mood has been designated by some texts
as *bhava*, or an emotional relationship with the Ideal of meditation. The
state of *bhava* is the intensified form of *bhakti,* or sincere devotion. The
aspirant must have love for his or her Ideal of meditation, and love comes
only as a result of the commitment of the heart to the object of meditation.
The aspirant's Chosen Ideal of meditation must be compatible with his or
her inner disposition and temperament. There are instances where an aspirant who, when asked to meditate on an impersonal Ideal, felt no enthusiasm for such meditation but felt great emotional fervor for practice when
advised to meditate on a personal form of the Godhead. Also, a beginner
who does not feel any mood for the practice of meditation when asked to fix
the mind on a concept or image or idea may find great interest in ritualistic
and devotional worship. The method of meditation must be appropriate for
an individual and in keeping with his or her heredity, temperament, and spiritual background.

One-pointed loyalty. One-pointed loyalty to the object of meditation is
the most important condition for the cultivation of the meditative mood. This
one-pointed loyalty has been indicated by various scriptures as *nishtha,* which
alone can give rise to *bhakti,* or love. *Bhakti* when it matures becomes *bhava,*
or fervor, and *bhava* when it deepens becomes *bhavana,* which is a spontaneous loving remembrance. Ramanuja designates this *bhavana* state as meditation. *Nishtha* is a conservative, one-pointed loyalty that fosters and intensifies
one's spiritual growth. Those who are liberal from the very beginning never

grow. *Nishtha* is not a dogma or a narrowness of vision. It is not love for one's own Ideal and hatred toward other Ideals. An aspirant with true *nishtha* has love for all Ideals but keeps a special love and adoration for his or her own Ideal. A worshiper of Krishna, when he or she goes to a temple of Shiva, for example, tries to visualize Krishna in the form of Shiva.

One-pointed loyalty helps the aspirant to develop a strong emotional relationship with the object of meditation and this emotional commitment alone can make the Ideal of meditation living. No meditative mood is possible unless the aspirant is able to have some definite knowledge that his or her object of meditation, whether personal or impersonal, is not just a picture or a form or a concept but a living presence of the Divine within. According to Patanjali, the state of meditation is reached when practiced continuously over a long period and with great love. Only an aspirant with an inborn gift may have this great love from the beginning; others have to cultivate love, and the way to cultivate it is to develop *nishtha,* or one-pointed loyalty. Adherence to repeated practice, even though it appears to be mechanical in the beginning, in course of time gives rise to love for the Ideal, and one-pointed loyalty alone can make an aspirant adhere to practice.

Acts of service. The practice of meditation has its counterpart in the practice of service. The practice of seeing God with eyes closed must be supported by the effort to see God also with eyes open. What is realized in the depths of meditation must find its application in everyday life. Meditation and action always go together. Service to all beings by looking upon them as a reflecting medium of one's spiritual Ideal makes the practice of meditation spiritually positive and creative and heightens the meditative mood in an aspirant. The practice of service is to do everything with an attitude of worshipfulness. Each act that the aspirant performs is required to be an offering to God. The two sides of the practice of meditation must be properly aligned for the cultivation and development of the meditative mood.

Right motive. The mood for meditation is a manifestation of the spiritual emotions. Emotions are inspired and guided by the intellect, which determines the motive behind all actions and emotions. As is one's motive, so is one's mood; and as is one's mood, so is one's meditation. The motive is, therefore, a significant factor in arousing the mood for performing any action. In order to feel the mood for meditation, a spiritual motivation is necessary, because a spiritual motive alone can evoke spiritual fervor. The opposite of a spiritual motive is the worldly motive that always seeks to acquire or avoid something, and meditation practiced with worldly desire is usually burdened with anxiety about the results. Spiritual motivation ensues from a spiritually inspired intellect that is firmly convinced about the spiritual goal to be pursued and about the transitoriness of all worldly objects and enjoyments, here and hereafter. Practice of meditation, as the Bhagavad Gita points out, must be supported by the practice of dispassion. The aspirant is required to cultivate dispassion by repeatedly focusing attention on the impermanence of all worldly enjoyments and the bitter disappointments that inevitably come in their wake. No real mood for meditation is possible unless one is imbued with the spirit of dispassion.

Practice of discrimination. Aspirants desiring the mood for meditation must be very discriminating in every respect. They are required to discriminate the Real from the unreal, love of God from self-love, spiritual conversation from idle gossip, and whims and emotions from true, spiritual aspirations. The aspirant has to evaluate all things from a spiritual point of view. Anything that is spiritually inspiring is desirable, and anything that is not is to be considered undesirable. The guideline of evaluation for the aspirant is: "Does it help me spiritually?" The contemplative mood can neither be developed nor maintained as long as the spiritual goal and everyday conduct are not aligned properly. Moreover, aspirants of meditation often manifest two types of behavior: either they isolate themselves completely from the external world or they try to be too liberal and universal from the very beginning. Both are extreme behavior and both bring remorse or reaction in the end. Discrimination is therefore very necessary at every step.

Devotional music. Devotional music is considered very effective in rousing the dormant spiritual emotions in us. It soothes the mind and serves as a spiritual diversion, by which spiritual aspirants detach themselves from the depressive thoughts to which they often cling unconsciously. Singing devotional songs or listening to them is regarded as one of the supporting practices of meditation.

Chanting of the sacred texts. Chanting of the sacred scriptures with proper intonation is regarded by the traditions of Yoga as a potent practice for the cultivation of the spiritual mood. Rhythmic chanting of sacred texts creates spiritual thought-waves within the mind and builds up the necessary mood for meditation. The sound of rhythmic chanting also creates thought-waves within the mind reminiscent of the spiritual goal. As the chanting continues, such thought-waves gradually prevail over all other contrary thought-waves and evoke the mood for meditation.

Ritualistic practices. Practice of meditation varies from one individual to another, depending upon the method a particular individual has chosen or that has been prescribed by a competent teacher. Each method of meditation is related to certain specific ritualistic observances that often form part of the practice of meditation. The development of the mood for meditation is intimately associated with the performance of these ritualistic practices. Anything that an aspirant does regularly and repeatedly eventually becomes a ritual, and rituals greatly help the aspirant to summon the spiritual mood. For example, one aspirant may sprinkle holy water before sitting for meditation, and by that may feel the necessary mood for meditation, while another aspirant may find it easy to summon the spiritual mood by burning incense; and still others may like to chant a holy text in a rhythmic way for the same purpose. Aspirants, therefore, must develop their own ritualistic ways that are best suited for them, according to their inner conviction and disposition, and adhere to their practices scrupulously for the cultivation of the spiritual mood. In the absence of any ritualistic observances, the practice of meditation becomes an altogether casual vocation, the effects of which often prove to be short-lived and even negative.

Pranayama. Pranayama, or control of breath, is considered one of the means for evoking the mood for meditation. The flow of breath is an indicator of the mood of the mind. While evenness of the flow signifies a spiritual mood, its uneven nature indicates a contrary mood. According to the advocates of the Yoga system of thought, the mood for meditation can be summoned by deliberately making the breath flow evenly. They contend that there is no use trying to convince a perverted mind about the efficacy of the spiritual goal, for the habits of the mind that are chronically perverted cannot be changed by reasoning and discrimination. Therefore an aspirant is required to adopt means that are external to concentrate the mind, such as the practice of *pranayama.* But the practice of *pranayama,* when not supported by intense dispassion and purity of character, proves to be ineffective and mechanical, and positively harmful for the aspirant. According to the *Yogavasishtha Sara,* one of the authoritative scriptures on Yoga and Vedanta, of the four methods of evoking the meditative mood—holy company, practice

of discrimination, eradication of desires, and *pranayama—pranayama* is
regarded as the most drastic method, and its practice can be justified only
when the other three methods have failed.

Japa. Japa is the practice of the repetition of a holy name, a mystic syllable or word, chosen by the aspirant or prescribed by a competent teacher.
Such a word or syllable, when repeated with devotion and for a long time,
becomes charged with spiritual consciousness and is a most powerful aid for
the evocation of the mood for meditation. Repetition may be audible, semi-
audible, or silent, and an aspirant is instructed to concentrate on the meaning
of the word or syllable along with the repetition. When the practice of *japa*
becomes continuous, it takes the form of meditation. The state of meditation
is attained when concentration becomes effortless. Each *japa,* or repetition,
is like the droplet of a new thought-wave deposited in the depths of mind, and
as these thought-waves increase in number, they bubble up to the surface of
the mind as spontaneous remembrance, which is itself meditation. The practice of *japa* is therefore not only an aid for the cultivation of the meditative
mood, but also a means to prolong and maintain the mood all the time.

Regularity and balance of practice. In order to develop the spiritual
mood, one must subscribe to a particular method of meditation and be regular
in one's practice. Practice becomes firmly grounded when it is followed for a
long time, unremittingly and with devotion. Steadfast adherence to practice
without any lapse is itself considered very significant, because even a lapse of
one day can very well take the aspirant back to the position where he or she
had been several days before. For a spiritual aspirant journeying toward the
spiritual goal, there is no such thing as status quo. He or she must either proceed or recede. "Balance of practice" means harmonious exertion and practice
of moderation in every respect; it also indicates balance between meditation
as a principal practice and other disciplines, such as worship, spiritual study,
and service, which are its adjunct and supporting practices. The cultivation of
the spiritual mood requires the participation of all four faculties of the mind—
willing, feeling, thinking, and acting—and therefore the aspirant's spiritual
living must allow the four faculties to develop harmoniously.

Ramprasad, the poet-saint of India, describes the spiritual mood as
divine inebriation in one of his songs:

> I drink no ordinary wine, but Wine of Everlasting Bliss,
> As I repeat my Mother Kali's name;

It so intoxicates my mind that people take me to be drunk!
First my guru gives molasses for the making of the Wine;
My longing is the ferment to transform it.
Knowledge, the maker of the Wine, prepares it for me then;
And when it is done, my mind imbibes it from the bottle of the
    mantra,
Taking the Mother's name to make it pure.
Drink of this Wine, says Ramprasad, and the four fruits of life
    are yours.[7]

Thus an aspirant experiences a genuine spiritual mood only when he or she has tasted genuine spiritual bliss, which Ramprasad compares to the Wine of Everlasting Bliss. No one can drink this Wine of Everlasting Bliss unless one has prepared it for oneself.

11

The Quest for Peace and Happiness

Happiness is the eternal and universal quest that has engaged the human mind since the beginning of creation. People may differ in their religious and political views, philosophies of life, psychological profiles, culture, and race, but all without exception want to be happy. Happiness is the quest of the poor and the rich, the learned and the ignorant, the saint and the sinner, the atheist and the believer, the ascetic and the indulgent. It is for the sake of happiness that spiritual seekers pray, cheaters cheat, hoarders hoard, the charitable give in charity, drunkards drink, robbers rob, and the penitent repent. Desiring happiness, some marry, some divorce, some commit suicide, and some become homicidal. Yet the pursuit of happiness remains a wild-goose chase.

No one is sure how to attain it. No branch of study has given us any knowledge regarding the secret of happiness. Religion emphasizes salvation, and philosophy the quest for truth. Moralists talk about duty, and psychologists ask us to cope with unhappiness. Scientists do not care about our feelings, and economists care only about wealth and prosperity. None of them addresses the issue of happiness.

In search of happiness, people often behave strangely. Some are happy when others are happy, some are happy when others are unhappy, and some are even happy when they themselves are unhappy. Some hope to buy happiness, while others try to borrow it from others. Some seek to achieve happiness by domination, others by clinging. So we are constantly in pursuit of happiness instead of being happy.

The usual responses to the question of how to achieve happiness are generally three: "giving in," "giving up," and "escape." Some, who call themselves pragmatists, uphold "giving in," maintaining that there is no use in looking for the secret of how to be happy. This is the only world we have, and so make the best of it. "Make hay while the sun shines." Life is like an orange, so squeeze the orange hard and get the most juice out of it. The upholders of this view forget that the sun does not always shine for making hay and that squeezing the orange too hard makes the juice bitter. Their philosophy of "giving in" to endless desires and whims is a death wish. Our life is short and our desires are numerous. We are unhappy as long as our desires go unfulfilled. When our desires are fulfilled, we are also unhappy, because we are afraid of losing the object acquired, and when fresh desires appear, we continue to be unhappy.

Desires create fantasy and distort the perception of reality. Because of the upsurge of desires, the control mechanisms of the conscious mind give way to exaggerations and fabrications, and the seeker's grasp of reality becomes shattered by the impact of emotions. Neurosis is an unreality created by a person's own desire-intoxicated mind.

The second response to achieving happiness proposes "giving up"—the philosophy of self-denial and elimination of all desires, advocated by the hard-line ascetics. But forced self-denial is unnatural, unrealistic, and impossible. Desires are the very stuff of life; when repressed or suppressed, they go underground and cause disorders in our psyche, disturbing our well-being in all levels of life. Such repressed desires prompt even monks and ascetics to unconsciously seek compensation in different ways.

If desires create self-deception, then a reasonable amount of self-deception makes life possible. When the intensity of self-deception crosses a critical threshold, trouble and a breakdown become inevitable. Below this threshold, self-deception is an enjoyable sport. Desires, no doubt, create stress, but then, there is no life without stress. Doctors advise stress management, not stress elimination. It is said that when there is no stress, we are in distress.

The third response seeks to "escape" the cause of unhappiness. Happiness, according to this view, consists of fleeting moments and is unreliable and impermanent. Earthly life is a vale of tears, and the process of nature is sinful and corrupt. Nothing endures until tomorrow. Why hope for something you can never get? Why run after a mirage to quench your thirst? Happiness lies in withdrawal to our transcendental spiritual self and in renunciation of all hope of being happy here on earth. However, the happiness of the transcendental self does not suit the lives of average men and women. Their material needs and fulfillment cannot be brushed aside as unimportant. Humans are not disembodied souls or disenchanted angels. The followers of this view may escape some of the tribulations and tragedies of life but will also miss the joys, fulfillments, and thrills of living in the world. To hold that we are *only* the Self is utter delusion.

HAPPINESS DEPENDS UPON PEACE OF MIND

Happiness, Vedanta maintains, lies not in giving in, nor in giving up nor in escape. Happiness is not an object but the state of contentment of a mind at peace. Without peace of mind, all our possessions, acquisitions, and pursuit of happiness become a hideous torment and an intolerable burden. Peace of mind is not a pleasure-fearing withdrawal or lapsing into a state of passivity or inertia. Nor is it a temporary response one feels in hearing serene music or seeing beautiful, natural scenery. It is the peace of a mind made tranquil through education, training, and discipline. This peace results from its inherent strength, and this strength is characterized by integration, stability, temperate nature, and freedom from all forms of dependency. The tranquil mind is like a compass holding to the true north of maturity and self-understanding that enables us to accept life as a whole. Only through our tranquil mind can we discover that when we are unhappy and depressed, it is probably due not to the cosmos in general but to our thyroid in particular, and that often the cause of our pessimism and hopelessness is our bad liver or zero bank balance. We are able to see how our attachment wears the disguise of love, our possessiveness of duty, and our self-concern of concern for the welfare of others. To have a tranquil mind is to be one's true self and to remain whole in the midst of the storms and stresses of life.

The dilemma of the modern seekers of happiness is that while we feel free to behave as a subhuman, our moral nature revolts and produces a sense of guilt about our own unbridled pursuit of pleasure. Happiness is possible within limits. Where there are limits, there is the law of relativity. If a person wants to enjoy eating, he or she knows that enjoyment is possible only within limits. So also with happiness and all other enjoyments. No happiness comes to a slave of passion, obsession, and addiction.

PEACE OF MIND CALLS FOR SELF-MASTERY

Peace of mind does not come by itself, nor is it ever achieved miraculously. It results from the conscious practice of self-mastery. Self-mastery is asserting control over our subconscious urges, desires, habits, and tendencies that increase the level of our fantasies and paralyze our will power, actions, and communications. The essential aspects of self-mastery are control of the senses, reduction of dependence, and bringing desires to their economic limit. Self-mastery is not letting things happen but making them happen.

There are those who maintain that any form of control inhibits our self-expression and makes us inauthentic in our behavior. They seek happiness in chaotic self-indulgence, catering to the tumultuous demands of their impulses. They regard impulses as sacred and cloak their irrationality in sanctimony. They forget that desire is unappeasable and is fated never to be satisfied. To look upon life as an uninterrupted pursuit of enjoyment is a mark of credulity. Self-expression is not synonymous with sensuality. The cure for neurosis is not more neurosis. Self-expression is not involuntary and subconscious but voluntary and conscious. True self-expression presupposes self-mastery. Our march toward maturity is willed and not given.

There is no alternative to self-mastery. True, those who practice self-mastery and uphold the need for moral values may not be considered normal in present-day society, but surely they are not neurotic in any sense.

SELF-MASTERY IS DEPENDENT ON SELF-AWARENESS

Self-mastery, according to Vedanta, is dependent on self-awareness— connecting ourselves to our true Self, the focus of the Universal Self, the witness consciousness in all living beings. Unity in multiplicity is the law of the universe. We are different from one another in our physical and mental aspects but one and united with regard to our Self. To deny this Self is the surest and most certain way to doom and self-destruction.

The Vedanta view of life is integral, and its approach to the question of happiness is realistic. The human individual is not just the soul but the body-mind-soul. Happiness depends upon the fulfillment of the needs and urges of all the three aspects of our being—physical, mental, and spiritual. When our spiritual fulfillment is denied or ignored, we court spiritual disintegration and death, and the soul takes revenge upon us.

Self-awareness is an impossible task without the practice of self-control. Emphasizing the need for self-control, the Bhagavad Gita tells us:

> The man of self-control, moving among objects with his senses under restraint, and free from attachment and hate, attains serenity of mind. In that serenity there is an end of all sorrow; for the intelligence of the man of serene mind soon becomes steady. The man whose mind is not under his control has no Self-knowledge and no contemplation either. Without contemplation he can have no peace; and without peace, how can he have happiness?[1]

Modern secular culture ignores the need for self-mastery and self-awareness. Any form of self-control is branded as repressive. Individuals talk like heaven but feel like hell. For them, material success is the only source of virtue; promiscuity is no longer a moral violation but a mark of normal behavior; and marriage is no longer a sacrament but a contract. They are ever ready to sell their souls in order to gain the world.

Many attempt to acquire tranquillity of mind through drugs and herbs, and mechanical means, or simply by abstaining from sense enjoyments. But none of these can remove our mental restlessness, which is the root cause of all unhappiness. The furies of sense desires, attachments, and urges, which rob a person first of all peace and then of all happiness, cannot be brought under control without self-awareness. True self-awareness is not just casual thinking about our true Self; it is deepening our spiritual consciousness and being our true Self, the source of all peace and happiness.

12

Liberation of the Soul

Liberation is the goal of all the goals of life. It is the motive force behind all morality and unselfishness. Prayer and meditation, charity and austerity, performance of sacraments and doing good to others, all culminate in liberation—the infinite expansion of the soul.

Liberation of the soul is the promise and central teaching of every religion. It is this promise that distinguishes the religious quest from all other quests of life. Prophets and saints, mystics and philosophers, theologians and the scriptures all assure us of ultimate liberation from the pain and suffering of life. All seekers—whether Jewish, Christian, Buddhist, Hindu, Muslim, dualist, qualified nondualist, or nondualist—strive for liberation. All believe that through liberation they will attain immortality. The desire for immortality is inherent in human nature. Desiring immortality, people beget children, create works of art, erect monuments, sacrifice their self-interest, and practice charity, contemplation, and prayer. What is the meaning of liberation? What happens to one who becomes liberated?

THE DIFFERING VIEWS

The view of most religions is that liberation is eternal life in heaven and is possible only after death, as the reward for the virtuous and the believers. The nonbelievers and the sinners go to hell to expiate their wrongful actions on earth. Enjoyment in heaven and suffering in hell are described in vivid terms in the scriptures of different traditions. But the religions vary in their views of the nature of liberation and how to attain and verify it. Some claim that liberation is reserved only for their own followers and ask for unquestioning faith in their dogma. Others assert that liberation is only for the elected and chosen ones and is not universal. Immortality for some is physical; for others it is spiritual. Some insist that liberation is dependent on effort, while for others it is solely a matter of divine grace. Some traditions declare that the soul is created at birth, that life on earth is only for one term, and therefore there is only one opportunity to strive for liberation. Others speak of the soul's potential divine nature, its transmigration, and its many terms of life.

The scientific minded often raise the following questions:

1. If liberation is possible only after death, how can its reality be verified? The dead do not return to testify about the validity of liberation. Scriptural assurances are not enough to silence our doubt, since, having been written by human hands, they are subject to human error. Could the ideas of liberation be merely the result of pious imagination? Such doubt persists. There is the story of a mountain climber who was scaling a five-thousand-foot peak. At one point he lost his balance and began to fall. Desperately grabbing hold of the stump of a tree, he found himself hanging in midair. An avowed atheist, the man did not believe in prayer or liberation. But facing this harrowing situation, he looked toward the sky and called out, "Is there anyone to save me?" To his utter surprise, a deep voice resounded from the sky, saying, "My son, let go thy hold. I shall bear thee up." There was a pause, and then the man again looked toward the sky and asked, "Is there anyone else?"

2. Are the descriptions of the hereafter true? If so, why do the accounts differ? Immortality in heaven is said to be of infinite duration, that is, not bound by time. But how can everlasting life be described in terms of time? Heavenly life has been described as enjoyment without suffering, youth without old age, pleasure without pain—an untenable claim from the point of view of reason. How can an embodied person be immortal? The gross, subtle, or spiritual body through which one experiences heavenly happiness cannot last forever. One wonders whether our individual desires create our ideas of heaven and whether our definition of heaven changes with the change of our desires. As Swami Vivekananda says: "Everyone's idea of pleasure is different. I have seen a man who is not happy unless he swallows a lump of

opium every day. He may dream of a heaven where the land is made of opium. That would be a very bad heaven for me."[1]

3. The claim that the soul is created at birth and has only one term of life is arbitrary and unjust. It is arbitrary because it fails to explain the inequalities between one person and another in the physical, mental, moral, and spiritual spheres. To say that inequalities are all due to environment and heredity is not an adequate explanation. To attribute inequalities to the will of God only makes God cruel and whimsical. The claim is unjust because most people die with imperfections; therefore if there is only one term of life, it must follow that most are destined to suffer eternally in hell. How can the soul, God's own creation, be punished forever? Eternal punishment of the soul for the mistakes of a few years on earth goes against all sense of justice.

4. Can all religious traditions be equally true? Some traditions claim that theirs is the only way. This is possible only in a nonmoral universe created by an unjust God. Claims of exclusiveness create suspicion. Spirituality is a universal phenomenon, not the exclusive possession of any particular faith. No religious tradition has a monopoly on Truth. Moral and ethical virtues of purity, compassion, truthfulness, and self-sacrifice—the means to liberation—are common to all traditions. All are children of one and the same God, to whom all return at the time of liberation.

MANY PATHS TO ONE GOD

Prophets and saints of different religions are the messengers of that one God. Different religions are only the different paths to reach God. Those who deny these facts only deny God. Individuals brought up today with a scientific outlook insist on the rule of law. In the classroom and the workplace they are encouraged to raise honest doubt and make critical enquiry about everything; thus they feel puzzled when asked to accept as infallible the teachings of a scripture or the tenets of a particular tradition. Two reasons are generally invoked in support of scriptural infallibility: the teachings and tenets have been handed down from ancient times, and our ancestors believed in them. However, mere dogmatic assertion of the infallibility of a teaching about liberation cannot silence the doubts of the modern mind. Until Galileo stated otherwise, the world believed that the sun moved around the earth. If the laws of science work everywhere and at all times, should not the same laws apply to religion? Science has thrown open a window on the cosmos. Our sun is a speck on the edge of a vast galaxy—one of innumerable galaxies—and the earth is a mere particle of dust circling that speck. The creation did not begin at a certain time on a particular day but evolved over billions of years. The view of a universe with God at the top, the devil below, and the world of humans in between can be accepted only by the most naive.

Science demands deduction from facts, not from beliefs. In religion there is a tendency to create facts based upon preconceived conclusions. Scientific methods require us to accept a proposition only when it can be proven. Skeptics believe that the notion of liberation is nothing but wishful thinking on the part of visionaries who hope to fulfill their heart's desire for eternal life in defiance of the laws of science and reason.

THE VEDANTA VIEW OF LIBERATION

Liberation is called *jivanmukti,* or freedom while living in the body. It is not going to another realm or attaining something new. It is realizing our true nature that is ever pure and divine. Liberation is not freedom from anything but freedom in the midst of everything. Liberation as happiness in heaven is only a halfway house. Vedanta asserts that liberation, in order to be believable, must be attained before death. One who dies in bondage will remain bound after death. Life's bondage created while living cannot be overcome by any readjustment after death. Vedanta views after-death experiences, whether of enjoyment or suffering, as dreams, and like all dreams they are heavily influenced by the actions and thoughts of the waking state. The *Katha Upanishad* says: "What is here, the same is there; and what is there the same is here. He goes from death to death who sees any difference here."[2] Further, if it were accepted that liberation is possible only after death, then there would be none to teach the truth of liberation and demonstrate its reality.

Vedanta's liberation is spiritual and depends upon Self-knowledge. Self-knowledge is direct perception of one all-pervading Self, dwelling as the individual self in all beings. It is seeing the Self with eyes closed in meditation as well as with eyes open in action. Self-knowledge carries its own credentials: it transforms our consciousness forever, silences all doubt, is not antagonistic to reason and common sense, and is conducive to the welfare of all beings.

Liberation is universal and is the inevitable destiny of all living beings.

Vedanta speaks of the three basic desires of all living beings: eternal life, limitless knowledge, and unbounded joy. We first seek to fulfill our basic desires through change of form and place. But nothing limited can give us the fulfillment of all three desires. At last we begin to change our thoughts and practice spiritual disciplines for self-purification. Eventually our true Self, which is the Self of the universe, becomes revealed in the mirror of our pure heart and we discover our real identity. In Biblical terms, liberation is the return of the prodigal son to his all-loving father. Consciously or unconsciously, all beings are striving for liberation. When the striving is unconscious, we call it evolution of nature; when it is conscious, we call it spiritual quest.

Self-knowledge alone can confer true liberation. It is the liberation of not only the soul but also the mind. By raising the blaze of spiritual consciousness, Self-knowledge frees us from the bondage of highly personalized life and separative existence. Swami Vivekananda beautifully describes this liberation through Self-knowledge:

> One day a drop of water fell into the vast ocean. When it found itself there, it began to weep and complain just as you are doing. The great ocean laughed at the drop of water. "Why do you weep?" it asked. "I do not understand. When you join me, you join all your brothers and sisters, the other drops of water of which I am made. You become the ocean itself. If you wish to leave me, you have only to rise up on a sunbeam into the clouds. From there you can descend again, a little drop of water, a blessing and a benediction to the thirsty earth."[3]

Liberation through Self-knowledge is not only cessation of sorrow and suffering but also bliss. Cessation of sorrow is not in itself happiness; happiness is something positive. Tasting the overpowering bliss of the Self, the liberated soul goes beyond all sorrow and suffering.

Liberation through Self-knowledge requires both human effort and divine grace. Making effort is necessary in order to recognize its limits. Ultimately we discover that even effort was possible because of grace. We strive for the Divine only when the Divine draws us toward it.

One who is liberated while living is called a free soul. Only free souls demonstrate the reality of God, the validity of the sacred texts, the divinity of the human soul, and the oneness of existence. They are also known as awakened ones or illumined ones. Ever aware of their identity with all beings, they feel through all hearts, walk with all feet, eat through all mouths, and think with all minds. They regard the pain and pleasure of others as their own pain and pleasure and their hearts overflow with compassion for all.

In modern times, Sri Ramakrishna's life is a perfect example in this context. In April 1885, Sri Ramakrishna felt a soreness in his throat. Prolonged conversation and absorption in God-consciousness aggravated the pain. As simple treatment brought him no relief, a specialist was called for, and the illness was diagnosed as cancer. Although the doctor cautioned him, he could neither control his *samadhi* (ecstasy) nor turn away any sincere spiritual seeker. Despite his excruciating pain and emaciated physical condition, Sri Ramakrishna continued to minister to the spiritual needs of his disciples and devotees. As we read in *The Gospel of Sri Ramakrishna:*

> Pandit Shashadhar [a renowned religious leader of the time] one day suggested to Sri Ramakrishna that the latter could remove the illness by concentrating his mind on the throat, the scriptures having declared that yogis had power to cure themselves in that way. The Master rebuked the pundit. "For a scholar like you to make such a proposal!" he said. "How can I withdraw the mind from the Lotus Feet of God and turn it to this worthless cage of flesh and blood?"
>
> "For our sake at least," begged Narendra [Swami Vivekananda] and the other disciples.
>
> "But," replied Sri Ramakrishna, "do you think I enjoy this suffering? I wish to recover, but that depends on the Mother."
>
> Narendra: "Then please pray to Her. She must listen to you."
>
> Master: "But I cannot pray for my body."
>
> Narendra: "You must do it, for our sake at least."
>
> Master: "Very well, I shall try."
>
> A few hours later the Master said to Narendra: "I said to Her: 'Mother, I cannot swallow food because of my pain. Make it possible for me to eat a little.' She pointed you all out to me and said: 'What? You are eating through all these mouths. Isn't that so?' I was ashamed and could not utter another word."[4]

This is the liberation in life that Vedanta believes in.

Notes

CHAPTER 1: THE RELEVANCE OF VEDANTA TO THE WORLD TODAY

1. Quoted in R. C. Majumdar, ed., *Swami Vivekananda Centenary Memorial Volume* (Calcutta: Swami Vivekananda Centenary Committee, 1963), p. 245.

CHAPTER 2: LIFE AND ITS MEANING: THE VEDANTA VIEW

1. *Svetasvatara Upanishad* 3.16, in *The Upanishads*, vol. 2, trans. Swami Nikhilananda (New York: Ramakrishna-Vivekananda Center, 1990), p. 103.
2. *Mundaka Upanishad* 2.1.4, in *The Upanishads*, vol. 1, trans. Swami Nikhilananda (New York: Ramakrishna-Vivekananda Center, 2003), p. 282.
3. Swami Nikhilananda, trans., *The Bhagavad Gita* 4.7–8 (New York: Ramakrishna-Vivekananda Center, 1992), p. 126.
4. From Shankaracharya's invocation to the *Mandukya Upanishad*, in *Upanishads*, vol. 2, Swami Nikhilananda, p. 218.
5. *Katha Upanishad* 1.3.15, in *Upanishads,* vol. 1, Swami Nikhilananda, p. 156.
6. *Brihadaranyaka Upanishad* 3.8.10, in *The Upanishads*, vol. 3, trans. Swami Nikhilananda, (New York: Ramakrishna-Vivekananda Center, 1990), p. 232.

7. *Katha Upanishad* 2.3.4, in *Upanishads*, vol. 1, Swami Nikhilananda, p. 182.

CHAPTER 3: THE HUMAN CONDITION

1. Swami Nikhilananda, trans., *Self-Knowledge* (New York: Ramakrishna-Vivekananda Center, 1989), p. 1.
2. Henry Wadsworth Longfellow, "A Psalm of Life," in *English Poetry III: From Tennyson to Whitman*. vol. 42 of *The Harvard Classics,* ed. Charles W. Eliot (New York: P. F. Collier & Son Company, 1937), p. 1264.
3. William Shakespeare, *Macbeth* 5.5. (New York: Oxford University Press, 1990), p. 204.
4. Pratap Chandra Roy, trans., *The Mahabharata,* vol. 2, "Vana Parva" (Calcutta: Datta Bose, n.d.), p. 668.
5. Commentary to *Katha Upanishad* 2.3.1, in *Upanishads,* vol. 1, Swami Nikhilananda, p. 180.
6. Swami Nikhilananda, trans., *The Gospel of Sri Ramakrishna* (New York: Ramakrishna-Vivekananda Center, 2000), p. 793.
7. Swami Nikhilananda, *Vivekananda: The Yogas and Other Works* (New York: Ramakrishna-Vivekananda Center, 1996), p. 870.
8. W. Macneile Dixon, *The Human Situation* (New York: Longmans, Green, 1937), p. 297.
9. From W. Macneile Dixon, *The Human Situation,* quoted in Swami Nikhilananda, *Man in Search of Immortality* (New York: Ramakrishna-Vivekananda Center, 1992), p. 26.
10. S. Radhakrishnan, *The Hindu View of Life* (New York: Macmillan, n.d.), pp. 49–50.
11. Swami Nikhilananda, *Vivekananda: The Yogas and Other Works,* p. 803.
12. Ibid., p. 806.
13. Heraclitus frag. 3, in *Ancient Philosophy*. vol. 1 of *Philosophic Classics,* eds. Forrest E. Baird and Walter Kaufmann (Englewood Cliffs, N.J.: Prentice Hall, 2000), p. 16.

14. *Katha Upanishad* 1.3.14, in *Upanishads,* vol. 1, Swami Nikhilananda, p. 156.

15. Swami Nikhilananda, *Self-Knowledge,* p. 28.

16. Swami Nikhilananda, *Vivekananda: The Yogas and Other Works,* pp. 498–99.

17. Swami Madhavananda, trans., *Uddhava Gita or The Last Message of Sri Krishna* 20.3 (Calcutta: Advaita Ashrama, 1971), pp. 300–301.

18. Ibid. 20.4, p. 301.

19. Swami Nikhilananda, *Vivekananda: The Yogas and Other Works,* p. 803.

20. Ibid., pp. 805–6.

21. M. Srinivasa Rau and K. A. Krishnaswamy Aiyar, trans., *Panchadasi of Vidyaranya* 12.10–12, 15–17 (Srirangam, India: Sri Vani Vilas Press, 1912), pp. 526–28.

22. Swami Madhavananda, trans., *Vivekachudamani of Sri Sankaracarya,* vv. 104–5, 305–9 (Calcutta: Advaita Ashrama, 1970), pp. 37–38, 116–18.

23. Swami Nikhilananda, *Gospel of Sri Ramakrishna,* p. 168–69.

24. Swami Nikhilananda, *Vivekananda: The Yogas and Other Works,* pp. 375–76.

25. Swami Nikhilananda, trans., *The Bhagavad Gita* 6.17–18, 24–25 (New York: Ramakrishna-Vivekananda Center, 1992), pp. 166–67, 168–69.

26. Paul Carus, *The Gospel of Buddha* (Chicago: Open Court Publishing, 1910), p. 173.

27. *Katha Upanishad* 1.1.22 in *Upanishads,* vol. 1, Swami Nikhilananda, p. 143.

28. J. M. Kennedy, trans., *The Satakas or Wise Sayings of Bhartrihari,* vv. 9, 14 (London: T. Werner Laurie, n.d.), pp. 93, 95.

29. Jere Daniel, "Society Fears Aging," in *An Aging Population: Opposing Viewpoints,* ed. Charles P. Cozic (San Diego: Greenhaven Press, 1996), pp. 167–68.

30. Charles F. Longino Jr., "An Aging Population May Not Be Harmful to America," in *An Aging Population,* pp. 26–27.

31. Nat Hentoff, "A Duty to Die," *Liberal Opinion Week* 8, no. 24 (June 16, 1997), p. 5.

32. From Carl Jung, *Modern Man in Search of a Soul,* p. 126, quoted in Swami Akhilananda, *Mental Health and Hindu Psychology* (Boston: Branden Press, n.d.), p. 104.

33. From a reminiscence of Swami Saradananda by Swami Nikhilananda in *Glimpses of a Great Soul,* Swami Aseshananda (Hollywood, CA: Vedanta Press, 1982), p. 243.

34. *Teachings of Swami Vivekananda* (Calcutta: Advaita Ashrama, 1971), p. 259.

35. Swami Nikhilananda, *Bhagavad Gita* 2.40, 1992, p. 84.

36. Ibid. 6.32, p. 171.

37. Ibid. 6.40, p. 174.

38. Thomas Gray, "Elegy Written in a Country Churchyard," stanza 9, in *English Poetry I: From Chaucer to Gray.* vol. 40 of *The Harvard Classics,* ed. Charles W. Eliot (New York: P. F. Collier & Son Company, 1937), p. 444.

39. C. Rajagopalachari, trans., *Mahabharata* (Bombay: Bharatiya Vidya Bhavan, 1990), p. 142.

40. Swami Nikhilananda, *Bhagavad Gita* 2.13, 1992, p. 72.

41. Ibid., pp. 210–11.

42. Ibid., pp. 211–13.

43. Ibid., p. 211.

44. From the Bhagavad Gita, quoted in Swami Nikhilananda, *Hinduism: Its Meaning for the Liberation of the Spirit* (New York: Ramakrishna-Vivekananda Center, 1992), p. 50.

45. Swami Nikhilananda, *Bhagavad Gita* 8.6, 1992, p. 199.

46. *Brihadaranyaka Upanishad* 4.4.14, in *The Upanishads,* vol. 3, trans. Swami Nikhilananda (New York: Ramakrishna-Vivekananda Center, 1990), p. 299.

47. Ibid. 4.4.7, p. 295.

48. Swami Nikhilananda, *Bhagavad Gita* 4.5, 1992, p. 124.

49. Ibid. 2.27, p. 79.

50. *Svetasvatara Upanishad* 2.8, in *Upanishads,* vol. 2, Swami Nikhilananda, p. 91.

51. *Mahabharata,* quoted in Swami Nikhilananda, *Self-Knowledge,* p. 172.

CHAPTER 4: AWAKENING OF SPIRITUAL CONSCIOUSNESS

1. St. John of the Cross, Plotinus, and Whitman quoted in Swami Yatiswarananda, *Adventures in Religious Life* (Madras: Sri Ramakrishna Math, 1969), pp. 238, 240, 290; William James, *The Varieties of Religious Experience* (London: Longmans, Green, 1908), p. 419.
2. Swami Nikhilananda, trans., *The Gospel of Sri Ramakrishna,* abridged ed. (New York: Ramakrishna-Vivekananda Center, 1996), p. 344.
3. Ibid., p. 580.
4. Swami Nikhilananda, *Vivekananda: The Yogas and Other Works,* pp. 614–15.
5. Swami Saradananda, *Sri Ramakrishna, the Great Master,* trans. Swami Jagadananda (Madras: Sri Ramakrishna Math, 1970), pp. 457, 458–59.
6. *Complete Works of Swami Vivekananda,* vol. 7 (Calcutta: Advaita Ashrama, 1972, pp. 254–55.
7. Swami Nikhilananda, *Self-Knowledge,* p. 2.
8. Swami Madhavananda, *Vivekachudamani,* vv. 419–20, p. 159.
9. Swami Nikhilananda, *Bhagavad Gita* 2.69, 1992, p. 99.
10. Quoted in Swami Yatiswarananda, *Adventures in Religious Life,* p. 251.

CHAPTER 5: FAITH OR REASON?

1. *Kena Upanishad* 1.2, in *Upanishads,* vol. 1, Swami Nikhilananda, p. 229.
2. Ibid. 2.3, p. 238.
3. Quoted in Swami Nikhilananda, *Hinduism,* p. 116.
4. Swami Nikhilananda, *Gospel of Sri Ramakrishna,* 2000, pp. 475–76.
5. See *Gaudapada Karika* 3.23, in *Upanishads,* vol. 2, Swami Nikhilananda, pp. 295–96.

6. Swami Nikhilananda, *Vivekananda: The Yogas and Other Works*, p. 888.

7. Ibid., p. 316.

8. Quoted in Swami Nikhilananda, *Hinduism*, p.174.

9. Swami Nikhilananda, *Vivekananda: The Yogas and Other Works*, pp. 380–81.

10. Ibid., p. 546.

11. *Katha Upanishad* 1.2.8, in *Upanishads,* vol. 1, Swami Nikhilananda, p. 133.

12. Swami Nikhilananda, *Vivekananda: The Yogas and Other Works*, p. 622.

13. Swami Madhavananda, *Vivekachudamani,* v. 62, p.22.

14. Swami Nikhilananda, *Vivekananda: The Yogas and Other Works*, p. 881.

15. Swami Saradananda, *Sri Ramakrishna, the Great Master,* trans. Swami Jagadananda (Madras: Sri Ramakrishna Math, 1970), p. 520.

16. *Katha Upanishad* 2.2.12, in *Upanishads,* vol. 1, Swami Nikhilananda, p. 175.

17. *Katha Upanishad* 1.2.20, in *Upanishads,* vol. 1, Swami Nikhilananda, p. 141.

CHAPTER 6: MASTERING THE RESTLESS MIND

1. Swami Nikhilananda, *Vivekananda: The Yogas and Other Works*, pp. 629–30.

CHAPTER 7: SELF-EXPRESSION OR SELF-CONTROL?

1. Swami Madhavananda, *Vivekachudamani,* vv. 168–69, p. 65.

2. Swami Madhavananda, *Uddhava Gita,* vv. 18.46–47, p. 282.

3. Swami Madhavananda, *Vivekachudamani,* v. 176, p. 68.

4. Swami Nikhilananda, *Bhagavad Gita* 5.23, 5.26, 1992, pp. 157–58.

5. Swami Nikhilananda, *Vivekananda: The Yogas and Other Works*, p. 864.

6. Eastern and Western Disciples, *The Life of Swami Vivekananda,* vol. 2 (Calcutta: Advaita Ashrama, 2001), p. 518.

7. Swami Moksadananda, trans., *Jivan-Mukti-Viveka of Swami Vidyarana* (Calcutta: Advaita Ashrama, 1996), pp. 186–87.

CHAPTER 8: GRASPING THE ESSENTIALS

1. Swami Nikhilananda, *Vivekananda: The Yogas and Other Works,* p. 575.

2. Swami Madhavananda, *Vivekachudamani,* vv. 59–62, pp. 21–22.

3. Swami Nikhilananda, trans., *The Gospel of Sri Ramakrishna,* abridged ed., pp. 332–33.

4. Swami Nikhilananda, *Vivekananda: The Yogas and Other Works,* p. 572.

5. Swami Nikhilananda, *Bhagavad Gita,* 1992, p. 2.

6. Swami Nikhilananda, trans., *The Gospel of Sri Ramakrishna,* pp. 392.

7. *Mahanirvanatantra* 3.50, in *Universal Prayers,* trans. Swami Yatiswarananda (Madras: Sri Ramakrishna Math, 1977), p. 147.

8. Swami Nikhilananda, *Self-Knowledge,* p. 172.

9. Swami Nikhilananda, *Vivekananda: The Yogas and Other Works,* p. 618.

10. Swami Nikhilananda, *Self-Knowledge,* v. 68, p. 171.

11. Ibid., pp. 171–72.

12. Ibid., p. 172.

13. *Talks with Swami Vivekananda* (Calcutta: Advaita Ashrama, 1939), pp. 107–8.

14. Swami Madhavananda, *Vivekachudamani,* v. 56, p. 20.

15. Swami Nikhilananda, *Vivekananda: The Yogas and Other Works,* p. 375.

16. Swami Madhavananda, *Uddhava Gita* 18.46, p. 282.

17. Swami Madhavananda, *Vivekachudamani,* vv. 78–79, 84, pp. 29, 31.

18. Ibid., v. 65, p. 23.

19. Swami Nikhilananda, *Vivekananda: The Yogas and Other Works,* pp. 545–46.

CHAPTER 9: FOUR STEPS TOWARD THE GOAL

1. First Disciples of Sri Ramakrishna, *Spiritual Talks* (Calcutta: Advaita Ashrama, 1968), p. 43.
2. Swami Nikhilananda, *Gospel of Sri Ramakrishna*, 2000, pp. 610–11.
3. Swami Nikhilananda, *Vivekananda: The Yogas and Other Works*, pp. 418–19.
4. Ibid., pp. 547–548.
5. Ibid., p. 797.
6. Ibid., p. 418.
7. Ibid., p. 796.
8. Swami Nikhilananda, *Gospel of Sri Ramakrishna*, 2000, p. 658.
9. *The Complete Works of Swami Vivekananda*, vol. 5 (Calcutta: Advaita Ashrama, 1970), p. 322.
10. Swami Madhavananda, *Vivekachudamani*, v. 3, p. 2.
11. Swami Nikhilananda, *Bhagavad Gita* 4.34, 1992, p. 141.
12. Swami Nikhilananda, *Vivekananda: The Yogas and Other Works*, p. 801.
13. Swami Nikhilananda, *Gospel of Sri Ramakrishna*, p. 217.
14. Ibid., p. 672.
15. Swami Nikhilananda, *Bhagavad Gita* 2.59, 1992, p. 95.
16. Swami Nikhilananda, *Vivekananda: The Yogas and Other Works*, p. 301.

CHAPTER 10: THE MOOD FOR MEDITATION

1. Swami Nikhilananda, *Gospel of Sri Ramakrishna*, 2000, p. 465.
2. Swami Nikhilananda, *Holy Mother* (New York: Ramakrishna-Vivekananda Center, 1997), p. 223.
3. Swami Nikhilananda, *Gospel of Sri Ramakrishna*, 2000, p. 81.
4. Swami Nikhilananda, *Vivekananda: The Yogas and Other Works*, p. 591.
5. Swami Nikhilananda, *Gospel of Sri Ramakrishna*, 2000, p. 111.
6. Swami Madhavananda, trans., *Uddhava Gita*, 8.4–6, pp. 111–12.
7. Swami Nikhilananda, *Gospel of Sri Ramakrishna*, 2000, p. 111.

CHAPTER 11: THE QUEST FOR PEACE AND HAPPINESS

1. Swami Nikhilananda, *Bhagavad Gita* 2.64–66, 1992, pp. 97–98.

CHAPTER 12: LIBERATION OF THE SOUL

1. Swami Nikhilananda, *Vivekananda: The Yogas and Other Works*, p. 265.
2. *Katha Upanishad* 2.1.10, in *Upanishads*, vol. 1, Swami Nikhilananda, p. 165.
3. Eastern and Western Admirers, *Reminiscences of Swami Vivekananda* (Calcutta: Advaita Ashrama, 1964), pp. 265–66.
4. Swami Nikhilananda, *Gospel of Sri Ramakrishna*, 2000, pp. 69–70.

Glossary

adharma Unrighteousness; the opposite of *dharma*.

advaita Nonduality; also a school of Vedanta philosophy declaring the oneness of God, soul, and universe.

advaitins Those who subscribe to nondual philosophy (*Advaita*).

agami **(karma)** The action that will be performed by an individual in the future.

ajna The sixth center of consciousness in the *sushumna*, at the space between the eyebrows.

akasha Space; the first and subtlest of the five elements that constitute the universe. The other four are fire, air, water, and earth.

anahata The fourth center of consciousness in the *sushumna*, at the level of the heart.

anandakanda Literally, root of bliss; refers to the lotus in the heart.

anandamaya-kosha Sheath of bliss through which the human individual experiences varying degrees of happiness.

annamaya-kosha The gross physical sheath.

aptavakyas Scriptures or words of saints and sages.

artha Attainment of worldly prosperity; one of the four values of life.

asana Yogic posture for meditation.

Atman Self. It denotes also the Supreme Soul, which, according to Advaita Vedanta, is one with the individual soul.

avidya Ignorance, cosmic or individual, which is responsible for the nonperception of Reality.

Bhagavad Gita An important Hindu scripture, part of the *Mahabharata* epic, containing the teachings of Sri Krishna.

bhakti Love of God; single-minded devotion to one's Chosen Ideal.

bhakti-yoga The path of devotion followed by dualistic worshipers.

bhava Feeling; emotion; ecstasy; *samadhi*.

bhavana Spontaneous loving remembrance of God; mature form of *bhava*.

Brahma The creator god; the first of the Hindu Trinity, the other two being Vishnu and Shiva.

Brahmaloka The highest heaven.

Brahman The Absolute; the Supreme Reality.

buddhi The intelligence or discrimination faculty; the seat of wisdom.

chakra Any one of the six energy centers, or lotuses, in the *sushumna*, through which the kundalini rises.

chitta The "mind-stuff"; one of four functions of the mind (along with *buddhi, ahamkara,* and *manas*); that part of the inner organ which is the storehouse of memory.

dharana Concentration.

dharma Righteousness; religion; duty; one of the four values of life.

dhyana Meditation, in which the mind flows continuously toward its object.

Durga A name of the Divine Mother.

dvaitins Those who subscribe to dual philosophy (Dvaita).

gayatri (1) The *gayatri* mantra, a sacred verse of the Vedas, repeated by brahmins as part of their devotions. (2) The *gayatri* meter, an important meter in Vedic verses, containing twenty-four syllables.

guna One of the basic modifications of nature. According to the Samkhya philosophy, Prakriti (Nature), in contrast with Purusha (Spirit), consists of three *gunas* (qualities or strands), known as *sattva, rajas,* and *tamas.*

Hari God; a name of Vishnu.

hatha-yoga A school of yoga that aims chiefly at physical health and well-being.

Hiranyagarbha Literally, the golden egg or womb. The first manifestation of Saguna Brahman, or Brahman with attributes, in the relative universe. The Cosmic Mind.

Holy Mother, Sri Sarada Devi (1853–1920) Wife and spiritual companion of Sri Ramakrishna.

ida One of three important *nadis* or nerves, in the nervous system. *See sushumna.*

Ishtam Chosen Ideal.

Ishvara The personal God.

japa Repetition of the Lord's name or of a sacred formula taught to the disciple by a spiritual teacher.

jiva The individual soul; a living being; an ordinary person.

jivanmukta One who has attained liberation from maya while living in the body.

jivanmukti Liberation from maya while living in the body.

jivatman The embodied soul; individual consciousness.

jnana-yoga Spiritual discipline mainly based upon philosophical discrimination between the Real and the unreal, and renunciation of the unreal.

Kali An epithet of the Divine Mother, the Primal Energy.

kama Enjoyment of legitimate pleasures; one of the four values of life.

karma (1) Action in general; duty. (2) The law of cause and effect.

karma-yoga Spiritual discipline based upon the unselfish performance of duty without attachment to the fruits of action.

kosha Literally, sheath or covering. One of five layerings or bodies that cover the soul, which is unaffected by any of them. They are the gross sheath, or physical body (*annamaya-kosha*), the vital sheath (*pranamaya-kosha*), the mental sheath (*manomaya-kosha*), the sheath of intelligence or intellect (*vijnanamaya-kosha*), and the sheath of bliss (*anandamaya-kosha*).

kundalini Literally, the serpent power. The spiritual energy lying coiled up, or dormant, at the base of the spine in all individuals. When awakened through spiritual practice, it rises through the spinal column, passes through various centers—chakras—and at last reaches the brain, whereupon the yogi experiences *samadhi*.

lila Divine sport or play. Creation is often explained by the Vaishnavas as the spontaneous *lila* of God.

Mahabharata A celebrated Hindu epic.

manana Reflection on what has been heard or read; one of the three processes for reasoning.

manipura The third center of consciousness in the *sushumna,* in the region of the navel.

manomaya-kosha The mental sheath.

mantra A sacred word or mystic syllable in Sanskrit, used in *japa*.

maya Ignorance obscuring the vision of God; the Cosmic Illusion that causes the One to appear as many, the Absolute as the relative.

moksha Liberation; one of the four values of life.

muladhara The first and lowest center of consciousness in the *sushumna,* at the base of the spine.

muni A holy man given to solitude and contemplation.

nadi One of the innumerable nerves in the nervous system. *See sushumna.*

Nirguna Brahman Brahman without qualities or attributes.

nirvikalpa samadhi The highest state of *samadhi;* the realization of one's total oneness with Brahman.

nishtha Single-minded devotion or love.

niyama Discipline, one of the aspects of yoga. It consists of observances such as cleanliness, contentment, austerity, study of the scriptures, and surrendering the fruits of all action to the Divine.

ojas The highest form of energy in the human body. That part of human energy expressed through sexual action and sexual thought, when checked and controlled, easily becomes changed into *ojas* and is stored in the brain.

Om The most sacred word of the Vedas; a symbol of God and of Brahman.

Paramatman The Supreme Soul.

Patanjali The author of the Yoga system, one of the six systems of orthodox Hindu philosophy, dealing with concentration and its methods, control of the mind, and similar matters.

pingala One of three important *nadis,* or nerves, in the nervous system. *See sushumna.*

Prakriti Primordial Nature, which, in association with Purusha, creates the universe, according to Yoga philosophy.

prana (1) The vital energy or life force. (2) The breath. (3) One of five functions of the vital force; the names of these five *pranas* are *prana, apana, vyana, udana,* and *samana.* (4) A name of the Cosmic Soul as endowed with activity.

pranamaya-kosha The vital sheath, consisting of the five *pranas.*

pranayama Control of the breath; one of the disciplines of yoga.

prarabdha (**karma**) The action that has begun to fructify, the fruit of which is being reaped in this life.

pratyahara Restraining the sense organs; one of the disciplines of yoga.

Puranas Books of Hindu mythology.

Purusha Literally, a person. The eternal principle of Pure Consciousness; the Self; the Absolute.

raja-yoga A system of yoga ascribed to Patanjali, dealing with concentration and its methods, control of the mind, *samadhi,* and similar matters.

rajas Activity or restlessness; one of the three *gunas.*

rajasika Pertaining to, or possessed of, *rajas.*

Ramakrishna, Sri (1836–1886) A great saint of Bengal, regarded as a Divine Incarnation, whose life inspired the modern renaissance of Vedanta.

Ramanuja (1017–1137) A great philosopher-saint of southern India, the foremost interpreter of the school of Qualified Nondualistic Vedanta.

sadhana Spiritual discipline.

Saguna Brahman Brahman with attributes and qualities; the Absolute conceived as the creator, preserver, or destroyer of the universe; the personal God, according to Vedanta.

sahasrara The thousand-petaled lotus, or highest plane of realization, beyond the sixth center of consciousness, at the crown of the head.

samadhi Total absorption in the object of meditation or in the Godhead; ecstasy.

Samkhya (also Sankhya) One of the six systems of orthodox Hindu philosophy.

samskara A tendency, habit, predisposition, or mental impression created by thoughts and actions.

sanchita **(karma)** The vast storehouse of accumulated actions done in the past, the fruits of which have not yet been reaped.

sandhya Devotions or ritualistic worship.

sannyasin A monk who has renounced the world in order to realize God (pl. *sannyasis*).

Saradananda, Swami (1865–1927) A monastic disciple of Sri Ramakrishna.

Satchidananda Literally, Existence-Knowledge-Bliss. A name of Brahman, the Ultimate Reality.

sattva Balance or wisdom; one of the three *gunas.*

sattvika Pertaining to, or possessed of, *sattva.*

savikalpa samadhi In Vedanta, the first of two stages of *samadhi,* in which the seeker remains conscious of the realization of the unity of his or her inmost Self with the Supreme Self.

Shakti The creative power of Brahman; a name of the Divine Mother; *shakti* also pertains to initiation.

Shankaracharya (c. 788–820) One of India's greatest philosopher-saints and the chief exponent of Advaita Vedanta. Also known as Sri Shankara.

Shiva The destroyer god; the third of the Hindu Trinity, the other two being Brahma and Vishnu.

shraddha Faith.

Shrimad Bhagavatam One of the Puranas, a well-known scripture dealing with the life of Sri Krishna. Also known as the *Bhagavata Purana*.

Siva *See* Shiva.

Sri (also Shri) Literally, "blessed" or "holy." A prefix used with names or the titles of certain scriptures. It serves as an honorific title before the name of a deity or holy man.

sushumna The central *nadi,* or nerve, situated within the spinal column from the base of the spine to the brain. It is the point of harmony between the *ida* to the left of the spinal column and the *pingala* to the right. The *sushumna,* through which the awakened spiritual energy (kundalini) rises, is described as the pathway to Brahman.

svadhisthana The second center of consciousness in the *sushumna,* at the base of the organ of generation.

tamas Inertia or dullness; one of the three *gunas.*

tamasika Pertaining to, or possessed of, *tamas.*

tanmatra One of the subtle elements of matter.

Tantra A system of religious philosophy in which the Divine Mother, or Power, is the Ultimate Reality; also the scriptures dealing with this philosophy.

Turiya Literally, the "fourth." The state of the transcendental self, beyond the three states of waking, dream, and dreamless sleep.

Uddhava Gita A text that forms part of the *Shrimad Bhagavatam.* It is the parting instructions of Sri Krishna to his beloved devotee and follower Uddhava.

Upanishads The sacred Hindu scriptures containing the philosophy of the Vedas.

upasana Intense mental worship.

vairagya Renunciation.

Vaishnava Literally, a follower of Vishnu. A member of the dualistic sect of that name, generally followers of Chaitanya in Bengal and Ramanuja and Madhva in southern India.

Vedanta One of the six systems of orthodox Hindu philosophy.

Vedas The revealed scriptures of the Hindus, consisting of the *Rig Veda, Sama Veda, Yajur Veda,* and *Atharva Veda.*

vichara Reasoning.

videha Detached from the body; without body-consciousness.

vidya Knowledge leading to liberation (i.e., to the Ultimate Reality).

vijnanamaya-kosha The sheath of intelligence.

Virat The Cosmic Person or Primordial Man; the Cosmic Body.

Vishnu The preserver god; the second of the Hindu Trinity, the other two being Brahma and Shiva.

visishtadvaitins Those who subscribe to qualified nondualism.

visuddha The fifth center of consciousness in the *sushumna,* at the lower end of the throat.

Vivekachudamani Crest jewel of discrimination; a treatise on Vedanta philosophy by Shankaracharya.

Vivekananda, Swami (1863–1902) Narendranath Datta, monastic disciple and chief apostle of Sri Ramakrishna.

vritti A "thought-wave" in the mind. Restricting these mental fluctuations is the aim of yoga, according to Patanjali.

yama Self-restraint, one of the disciplines of yoga. It consists of the moral virtues of nonviolence, truthfulness, noncovetousness, continence, and nonreceiving of gifts.

Yoga (1) One of the six systems of orthodox Hindu philosophy. The Yoga system of Patanjali. (2) Union of the individual soul with the Universal Soul. (3) The method by which to realize union through control of mind and concentration.

yogi (also yogin; fem. yogini) One who practices yoga.

Credits

Grateful acknowledgment is given for permission to use material from the following sources:

From *Vivekachudamani of Sri Sankaracarya* translated by Swami Madhavananda, 1970; *Uddhava Gita or The Last Message of Sri Krishna* translated by Swami Madhavananda, 1971; *Teachings of Swami Vivekananda,* 1971; *The Life of Swami Vivekananda,* vol. 2 by His Eastern and Western Disciples, 2001; *Jivan-Mukti Viveka of Swami Vidyarana* translated by Swami Moksadananda, 1996; *Talks with Swami Vivekananda,* 1939; *Spiritual Talks* by the First Disciples of Sri Ramakrishna, 1968; *The Complete Works of Swami Vivekananda,* vol. 5, 1970; *Reminiscences of Swami Vivekananda* by His Eastern and Western Admirers, 1964; "The Problem of Suffering," "Self-Expression or Self-Control?" "Grasping the Essentials," "The Mood for Meditation," and "The Meaningful Liberation" from *Prabuddha Bharata.* 1994, 1994, 1999, 1980, 1997 by Swami Adiswarananda, used by permission of the publisher, Advaita Ashrama, Calcutta, West Bengal, India.

"Hinduism" from *How Different Religions View Death and Afterlife,* First Edition, edited by Christopher Johnson and Marsha McGee, © 1991, used by permission of the publisher, The Charles Press, Philadelphia, Pennsylvania.

From *Adventures in Religious Life* by Swami Yatiswarananda, 1969; *Sri Ramakrishna, the Great Master* by Swami Saradananda, translated by Swami Jagadananda, 1970; *Universal Prayers* translated by Swami Yatiswarananda, 1977; "Relevance of Vedanta to the World Today," "Fear of Old Age," "Fear of Death," "Four Steps Toward the Goal" from *Vedanta*

Index

Inspiration

The Golden Rule and the Games People Play
The Ultimate Strategy for a Meaning-Filled Life
By Rami Shapiro
A guidebook for living a meaning-filled life—using the strategies of game theory and the wisdom of the Golden Rule.
6 x 9, 176 pp, Quality PB, 978-1-59473-598-1 **$16.99**

Deepening Engagement
Essential Wisdom for Listening and Leading with Purpose, Meaning and Joy
By Diane M. Millis, PhD; Foreword by Rob Lehman
A toolkit for community building as well as a resource for personal growth and small group enrichment.
5 x 7¼, 176 pp, Quality PB, 978-1-59473-584-4 **$14.99**

The Rebirthing of God
Christianity's Struggle for New Beginnings
By John Philip Newell
Drawing on modern prophets from East and West, and using the holy island of Iona as an icon of new beginnings, Newell dares us to imagine a new birth from deep within Christianity, a fresh stirring of the Spirit.
6 x 9, 160 pp, HC, 978-1-59473-542-4 **$19.99**

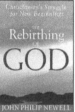

Finding God Beyond Religion: A Guide for Skeptics, Agnostics & Unorthodox Believers Inside & Outside the Church
By Tom Stella; Foreword by The Rev. Canon Marianne Wells Borg
Reinterprets traditional religious teachings central to the Christian faith for people who have outgrown the beliefs and devotional practices that once made sense to them. 6 x 9, 160 pp, Quality PB, 978-1-59473-485-4 **$16.99**

Fully Awake and Truly Alive: Spiritual Practices to Nurture Your Soul
By Rev. Jane E. Vennard; Foreword by Rami Shapiro
Illustrates the joys and frustrations of spiritual practice across religious traditions; provides exercises and meditations to help you become more fully alive.
6 x 9, 208 pp, Quality PB, 978-1-59473-473-1 **$16.99**

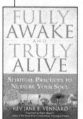

Perennial Wisdom for the Spiritually Independent
Sacred Teachings—Annotated & Explained
Annotation by Rami Shapiro; Foreword by Richard Rohr
Weaves sacred texts and teachings from the world's major religions into a coherent exploration of the five core questions at the heart of every religion's search.
5½ x 8½, 336 pp, Quality PB, 978-1-59473-515-8 **$16.99**

Journeys of Simplicity: Traveling Light with Thomas Merton, Bashō, Edward Abbey, Annie Dillard & Others By Philip Harnden
5 x 7¼, 144 pp, Quality PB, 978-1-59473-181-5 **$12.99**

Saving Civility: 52 Ways to Tame Rude, Crude & Attitude for a Polite Planet
By Sara Hacala 6 x 9, 240 pp, Quality PB, 978-1-59473-314-7 **$16.99**

Spiritually Healthy Divorce: Navigating Disruption with Insight & Hope
By Carolyne Call 6 x 9, 224 pp, Quality PB, 978-1-59473-288-1 **$16.99**

Or phone, fax, mail or email to: SKYLIGHT PATHS Publishing
Sunset Farm Offices, Route 4 • P.O. Box 237 • Woodstock, Vermont 05091
Tel: (802) 457-4000 • Fax: (802) 457-4004 • www.skylightpaths.com
Credit card orders: (800) 962-4544 (8:30AM–5:30PM EST Monday–Friday)
Generous discounts on quantity orders. SATISFACTION GUARANTEED. Prices subject to change.

Bible Stories / Folktales

Abraham's Bind & Other Bible Tales of Trickery, Folly, Mercy and Love By Michael J. Caduto
New retellings of episodes in the lives of familiar biblical characters explore relevant life lessons. 6 x 9, 224 pp, HC, 978-1-59473-186-0 **$19.99**

Daughters of the Desert: Stories of Remarkable Women from Christian, Jewish and Muslim Traditions By Claire Rudolf Murphy,
Meghan Nuttall Sayres, Mary Cronk Farrell, Sarah Conover and Betsy Wharton
Breathes new life into the old tales of our female ancestors in faith. Uses traditional scriptural passages as starting points, then with vivid detail fills in historical context and place. Chapters reveal the voices of Sarah, Hagar, Huldah, Esther, Salome, Mary Magdalene, Lydia, Khadija, Fatima and many more. Historical fiction ideal for readers of all ages.
5½ x 8½, 192 pp, Quality PB, 978-1-59473-106-8 **$18.99** Inc. reader's discussion guide

The Triumph of Eve & Other Subversive Bible Tales
By Matt Biers-Ariel These engaging retellings of familiar Bible stories are witty, often hilarious and always profound. They invite you to grapple with questions and issues that are often hidden in the original texts.
5½ x 8½, 192 pp, Quality PB, 978-1-59473-176-1 **$14.99**

Also available: **The Triumph of Eve Teacher's Guide**
8½ x 11, 44 pp, PB, 978-1-59473-152-5 **$8.99**

Religious Etiquette / Reference

How to Be a Perfect Stranger, 6th Edition: The Essential Religious Etiquette Handbook Edited by Stuart M. Matlins and Arthur J. Magida
The indispensable guidebook to help the well-meaning guest when visiting other people's religious ceremonies. A straightforward guide to the rituals and celebrations of the major religions and denominations in the United States and Canada from the perspective of an interested guest of any other faith, based on information obtained from authorities of each religion. Belongs in every living room, library and office. Covers:

African American Methodist Churches • Assemblies of God • Bahá'í Faith • Baptist • Buddhist • Christian Church (Disciples of Christ) • Christian Science (Church of Christ, Scientist) • Churches of Christ • Episcopalian and Anglican • Hindu • Islam • Jehovah's Witnesses • Jewish • Lutheran • Mennonite/Amish • Methodist • Mormon (Church of Jesus Christ of Latter-day Saints) • Native American/First Nations • Orthodox Churches • Pentecostal Church of God • Presbyterian • Quaker (Religious Society of Friends) • Reformed Church in America/Canada • Roman Catholic • Seventh-day Adventist • Sikh • Unitarian Universalist • United Church of Canada • United Church of Christ

"The things Miss Manners forgot to tell us about religion."
—*Los Angeles Times*

"Finally, for those inclined to undertake their own spiritual journeys ... tells visitors what to expect." —*New York Times*

6 x 9, 416 pp, Quality PB, 978-1-59473-593-6 **$19.99**

Struggling in Good Faith: LGBTQI Inclusion from 13 American Religious Perspectives Edited by Mychal Copeland and D'vorah Rose; Foreword by Bishop Gene Robinson; Afterword by Ani Zonneveld
A multifaceted sourcebook telling the story of reconciliation, celebration and struggle for LGBTQI inclusion across the religious landscape in America.
6 x 9, 240 pp, Quality PB, 978-1-59473-602-5 **$19.99**

The Perfect Stranger's Guide to Funerals and Grieving Practices
A Guide to Etiquette in Other People's Religious Ceremonies
Edited by Stuart M. Matlins 6 x 9, 240 pp, Quality PB, 978-1-893361-20-1 **$16.95**

The Perfect Stranger's Guide to Wedding Ceremonies
A Guide to Etiquette in Other People's Religious Ceremonies
Edited by Stuart M. Matlins 6 x 9, 208 pp, Quality PB, 978-1-893361-19-5 **$16.95**

Children's Spiritual Biography

MULTICULTURAL, NONDENOMINATIONAL, NONSECTARIAN

Ten Amazing People
And How They Changed the World
By Maura D. Shaw; Foreword by Dr. Robert Coles
Full-color illus. by Stephen Marchesi

For ages 7 & up

Shows kids that spiritual people can have an exciting impact on the world around them. Kids will delight in reading about these amazing people and what they accomplished through their words and actions.

Black Elk • Dorothy Day • Malcolm X • Mahatma Gandhi • Martin Luther King, Jr. • Mother Teresa • Janusz Korczak • Desmond Tutu • Thich Nhat Hanh • Albert Schweitzer

"Best Juvenile/Young Adult Non-Fiction Book of the Year."
—*Independent Publisher*

"Will inspire adults and children alike."
—*Globe and Mail* (Toronto)

8½ x 11, 48 pp, Full-color illus., HC, 978-1-893361-47-8 **$18.99** For ages 7 & up

Spiritual Biographies for Young People
For Ages 7 & Up

By Maura D. Shaw; Illus. by Stephen Marchesi
6¾ x 8¾, 32 pp, Full-color and b/w illus., HC

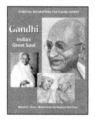
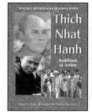

Black Elk: Native American Man of Spirit
Through historically accurate illustrations and photos, inspiring age-appropriate activities and Black Elk's own words, this colorful biography introduces children to a remarkable person who ensured that the traditions and beliefs of his people would not be forgotten.
978-1-59473-043-6 **$12.99**

Dorothy Day: A Catholic Life of Action
Introduces children to one of the most inspiring women of the twentieth century, a down-to-earth spiritual leader who saw the presence of God in every person she met. Includes practical activities, a timeline and a list of important words to know.
978-1-59473-011-5 **$12.99**

Gandhi: India's Great Soul
The only biography of Gandhi that balances a simple text with illustrations, photos and activities that encourage children and adults to talk about how to make changes happen without violence. Introduces children to important concepts of freedom, equality and justice among people of all backgrounds and religions.
978-1-893361-91-1 **$12.95**

Thich Nhat Hanh: Buddhism in Action
Warm illustrations, photos, age-appropriate activities and Thich Nhat Hanh's own poems introduce a great man to children in a way they can understand and enjoy. Includes a list of important Buddhist words to know.
978-1-893361-87-4 **$12.95**